FAR FROM LORD'S

England's Cricketers and Correspondents on Tour

RICHARD KNOTT

pitch

First published by Pitch Publishing, 2026
1

Pitch Publishing
9 Donnington Park, 85 Birdham Road
Chichester, West Sussex, PO20 7AJ
www.pitchpublishing.co.uk
info@pitchpublishing.co.uk

Set in Adobe Caslon 11.9/16.5pt

Typeset by Pitch Publishing

Cover design by Olner Design

Printed and bound in India by Thomson Press India Private Limited

The authorised representative in the EEA is
Easy Access System Europe OÜ, Mustamäe tee 50, 10621 Tallinn, Estonia gpsr.requests@easproject.com

A CIP catalogue record for this book is available from the British Library

ISBN 978 1 83680 472 7

Papers used by Pitch Publishing are from well-managed forests and other responsible sources

FSC
www.fsc.org
MIX
Paper | Supporting responsible forestry
FSC® C010615

Contents

Part One: The Fifties 5

1. Opening With Hutton 7
2. 'This Unhappy Tour' 18
3. The SS *Orsova* 37
4. 'The Experience of Australia' 46
5. Best Laid Plans 58
6. A Tale of Three Cities 72
7. The Accession of May 83
8. Start of a Cricket War 95
9. 'This Most Disappointing of Cricket Teams' 109

Part Two: The Sixties 129

10. Bottle-Throwing in Trinidad 131
11. Towards the End of May 142
12. On the Road 154
13. Watching Benaud Bowl 171
14. A Short Tour in India 194
15. The Long Goodbye 207
16. Under Smith Down Under 219
17. A Close Call 230
18. Riot and Heat 248
19. Corridors of Uncertainty 257
20. 'And That, Gentlemen, Is Over' 264

Afterword 272

Appendix A 276

Bibliography 279

Index 283

Part One

The Fifties

Kingston, Jamaica to Melbourne, Australia 1954–59

1

Opening With Hutton

Summer, 1953

THE CRICKET writer Alan Ross in his poem *Remembering Hutton* describes the England captain pensively standing on the deck of an ocean liner. Both men, it would seem, are Australia-bound, an Ashes tour soon to begin. It is the autumn of 1953, and the ship is the SS *Orsova*. Hutton is the England captain, Ross the cricket correspondent of *The Observer*. They come from very different backgrounds: Haileybury and Oxford (Ross) plays Littlemoor Council School in Pudsey, Yorkshire (Hutton). Cricket has elevated the Yorkshireman to a high pedestal, one that is both short-lived and vulnerable.

Leonard, I see you as by Rodin, head in hand,
Leaning on a rail. The chipped blue ocean
Repeats the colour of your eyes.

Looking out over the sea, the Yorkshireman is on his own. The writer reflects on the batter's 'ethereal presence', admires the range and glory of his batting 'repertoire'. As well as admiration for Hutton's skill, Ross hints at a real understanding between cricketer and member of the press. Given the length of tours – almost half a year on occasions – the lives of players and the press are woven tightly together, although the pressures on both are quite different. For the latter the time is one of deadlines and placating those sitting at the London desk; for the players there are the pressures of the game itself – the need to repeat sporting excellence day after day.

John Arlott – whose tour with Hutton's men in 1953/54 was his second and final tour – believed that 'the pressmen on the tour were more closely incorporated in terms of feeling than they seem to be nowadays'.[1] He was sufficiently close, as we shall see, to put a consoling arm around the England captain after the latter's gamble at Brisbane failed lamentably. Press and players socialised and played golf, shared hotels, while late-afternoon cricket nets might see old Test players – now scribes on the game – turn an arm to bowl at a current England star.

Between 1953 and 1969, the years covered by this book, England made 13 tours, playing 69 Test matches and winning only 18 of them. Cricket became slower, draws more frequent (38 over 16 years) and towards the end of the period was more troubled by politics and concerns about the way the game was played. This book charts that journey and the individual cricketers and writers who travelled some of the way, troubled by the discomforts, tensions and uncertainty of being so far from home for long periods of time. It is salutary to reflect on the fact that Colin Cowdrey, one of the five men who captained England in that time, went on nine tours in those 16 years. No wonder his epitaph at Poling church near Arundel – and written by John

---

1 *Basingstoke Boy* by John Arlott, page 240. Arlott's book came out in 1990.

Woodcock of *The Times* – reads 'Some journey, some life, some cover drive, some friend.'

The game of cricket was very different in the 1950s: the counties played 28 three-day games in the 1952 Championship season; batters completed far more innings (Surrey's Peter May batted 59 times all told in 1953, scoring 2,554 runs at an average of 51.08). Bowlers regularly bowled well over 25 overs in a day. The medium-pacer Trevor Bailey, for example, playing at Hull for Essex against Yorkshire on 9 May 1953, bowled 31 overs in the day, taking 3-96, and then bowled another 17 in the Yorkshire second innings. Matches were played at venues long since lost to the county game. In 1952, for example, there was Championship cricket played at Burton-on-Trent, Romford, Ebbw Vale, Dover, Hinckley, Glastonbury, Dudley and Hull. In a world of very different travel arrangements – no motorways in the UK and railway journeys usually steam-driven – travelling from game to game was often demandingly slow and lengthy. In the summer of 1953 Trevor Bailey progressed from Southampton to Ilford via Westcliff-on-Sea and Worcester in May; Llanelli, Nottingham, London and Kettering (June); Lord's, Manchester, Leeds and Chelmsford (July); Chelmsford, Weston-super-Mare, Southend-on-Sea, the Oval and Clacton-on-Sea (August).

Crowds for the extended form of the game were bigger; there was no cricket on Sundays; batters' heads were unprotected except for caps; equipment was more basic; newspaper coverage was more detailed and with bigger headlines; and the age profile of players was older, while many still playing had experienced the last war at first hand. Significantly too there were concerns about technicalities in the game, some of which rumbled on into the next decade, including the legitimacy of some bowlers' actions. In 1952, for example, both CN McCarthy (for Cambridge University against Worcestershire) and Surrey's Test bowler Tony Lock (against the Indian tourists) were no-balled for 'throwing'.

***

Of the 13 England cricket tours between 1953 and 1969, four were to Australia, three to the West Indies, and two to each of South Africa, India and Pakistan. The first (West Indies) and last (Pakistan) were marked by predictably steamy weather conditions and were made notorious through the riotous behaviour of the crowds, culminating in the abandonment of a Test and the remainder of the series against Pakistan. The latter took place in an atmosphere of serious political unrest which culminated in the war of 1971, as a result of which Bangladesh achieved its independence. The touring parties over that decade and a half – both cricketers and the correspondents who shadowed their games – were led by five different captains: Len Hutton, Peter May, Ted Dexter, Mike Smith and Colin Cowdrey. Some of the players were almost ever-present during those 16 years. Colin Cowdrey, for example, wintered overseas nine times; Ken Barrington of Surrey, eight times; while others were frequent tourists like Brian Statham (six tours), Tom Graveney (five) and Fred Trueman (four).

Unsurprisingly, the winter tour became a regular feature for the cricket correspondents too, some more enthusiastically than others – EW (Jim) Swanton of the *Daily Telegraph* being more assiduous than John Arlott, for example. When Swanton flew into Jamaica in time for the first Test he was embarking on his seventh tour abroad. Arlott, on the other hand, only went to

Australia once and never watched a Test in India or Pakistan. Just as the cricketers became accustomed to those who played the game on the cricket fields of the world, so too did those charged with reporting on their progress and prowess. In telling the story of these 13 tours this book follows not just the players, but also the men – and one woman – who travelled, if not with them, then in close and critical conjunction.

* * *

Before the tour of the West Indies got underway there was the question of who would captain the side: would it be an amateur cricketer, or would the selectors opt to see a professional – Len Hutton – continue in the role? The divide between amateur and professional was much discussed.

For example, when Maurice Tremlett, tall and blond and 'a former office boy at Taunton', was appointed captain of Somerset in 1956 it represented another tentative step by the West Country club into the modern world. He became the county's first professional captain. Hitherto the role had been the preserve of the gifted amateur, probably a public school-educated batter and someone with a definite air of entitlement. It was taking a long time for the game to resolve the issue. For example, the county's second professional captain, Harold Stephenson, would find himself involved in a 'corrosive exchange' with Bunty Longrigg, Somerset's chairman and erstwhile captain (and an amateur, naturally). Stephenson captained the side for five years in the sixties during which time Longrigg asked him who in the present side might be omitted to 'make way for an amateur or two'. The plain-speaking Stephenson indicated that if he wanted to see such changes then 'he had better skipper the county himself'. It did not go down well: later, at the annual dinner, Longrigg, a Bath solicitor, made his disapproval abundantly clear.[2] Interestingly, the former Somerset medium-pacer Bill Andrews firmly believed that the amateurs tended to avoid the harder games if they could.

Two years after Tremlett's appointment – and three after the first of the England tours which are the subject of this book – Marylebone Cricket Club (MCC) established a committee to review the continuing distinction between 'Gentlemen' and 'Players', while suggesting that 'the distinctive nature of the amateur cricketer is not obsolete, is of great value to the game and should be preserved'. It is significant that Len Hutton, who captained England on the 1953/54 series in the West Indies, was his country's first professional captain. It would be nearly a decade before the final 'Gentlemen versus Players' fixture, appropriately played in the autumn of 1962 and far from Lord's, at Scarborough. The fixture was duly abolished in 1963, ending a tradition that stretched back to 1806. Over the immediate post-war years (1946–53) the Gentlemen were almost always on the losing side and the tour party selected for the West Indies in 1953 included only two 'Gentlemen' cricketers almost certain to start the Test series – Peter May (Surrey) and Trevor Bailey (Essex). The game was changing, but the process was slow, and the first post-war victory for the Gentlemen over the Players – at Lord's in July – was perhaps enough for the diehards to feel that the status quo was fixed.

There were some at the heart of the Lord's establishment who would have been much happier not to appoint a professional cricketer as captain for the tour to the West Indies in 1953/54,

2 See the obituary for David Foot in *The Guardian*, 29 April 2008.

despite Len Hutton's success in the coronation summer of 1953. The home series against Australia had been closely fought with four successive drawn Tests before England won the final encounter at the Oval by eight wickets. The series was unusual in that Hutton lost the toss on every occasion and was also marked by relatively low scores. Only five times did either side make in excess of 300 runs. In the end England's success in the final game was down to the bowlers – Jim Laker and Tony Lock taking nine wickets between them in the Australian second innings. It was, however, the captain's 82 in the home side's first innings of 306 that helped create the opportunity for the two spin bowlers to win the match.

Despite that win it was not a foregone conclusion that Hutton should be given the captaincy for the forthcoming tour of the West Indies. Jim Swanton, as one would expect from the *Telegraph*'s cricket correspondent, was a man of conservative tastes, an advocate of the tried and tested. Predictably he would have much preferred an amateur player to lead the touring party, while recognising Hutton's stature as a batter. He would watch the forthcoming series in the West Indies with a jaundiced eye. A photograph in his biography reveals the familiar image to those who watched cricket on television in the fifties and sixties. Swanton has a patrician look with his oiled hair sleeked back from a bullish head. He is wearing tinted glasses, a sober tie over a white shirt and a lightweight, pale jacket. His lips are open as if either to pass a weighty opinion or to take a slurp from the wine glass in his left hand – perhaps both. He has the look of a man who wears cufflinks and chooses a set from his extensive collection to match the striped club tie.

His urbane appearance belied his background. Born just off Catford Hill in south London, he was denied the opportunity to go to university because of the cost. Instead, he became a 'general dogsbody' at Amalgamated Press, 'expected to make the tea, teach himself to type and do the odd jobs around the office'.[3] By the age of 20, however, he had become a rugby correspondent with the *Evening Standard* and in the summer of 1928 began reporting on cricket.

Swanton greatly admired Hutton as a batter but believed that England on tour should be led by someone with amateur credentials and diplomatic skills honed and perfected in the corridors of privilege. The Yorkshireman, he believed, lacked the necessary warmth and empathy to encourage and develop younger cricketers trying to make their way in the game. Added to that was an evident reluctance to put his trust in the use of spin bowling as an option when on the attack. The MCC committee charged with the selection of the squad was anything but radical: they shared similar backgrounds with a strong emphasis on the amateur – gentlemen, not players. Both Bob Wyatt and Freddie Brown had captained England, while the remaining three – Pelham Warner, Gubby Allen and Walter Robins – had all been captains of Middlesex. Warner, at 80, was the senior man, while the rest were in their forties and fifties. Oddly, three were born abroad, Brown in Peru, Warner in Trinidad and Allen in Australia. Gubby Allen had led the England tour to Australia in 1936 – and had the misfortune to win the first two Tests but go on to lose the series. Both then and 30 years later he saw himself as a preserver of the status quo: 'I have to play every match as I know the MCC do not want a professional to captain,' he wrote in a letter home in 1936.[4]

---

3 *Jim – the Life of EW Swanton* by David Rayvern Allen, page 19.

4 See *Gubby Under Pressure* ed. Rendell, ACS Publication: letter of 26 October 1936.

Very much a man of strong, forceful opinions, Allen had described England's pace attack at that time (Harold Larwood and Bill Voce) as 'swollen-headed, gutless, uneducated miners'. Arguably this was a view of the professional cricketer held by some in the 'inner circle' at Lord's of which Hutton was so understandably wary. That inner circle did not think it right for a professional to lead MCC abroad. Significantly it was only after the Manchester Test against Australia (concluded in mid-July) that Hutton was proposed for the tour captaincy. The crucial selection meeting was not held until Monday, 17 August, at the end of the second day of the final Australian Test; in fact, just at the most tense and pivotal moment of the game. Despite that, Hutton was required to attend the crucial evening meeting where the touring party was to be decided. The meeting was held then to accommodate Pelham Warner, who could not otherwise attend.

What particularly focused selectors' minds was that three years previously the West Indies had won the series in England 3-1, with their two spinners Ramadhin and Valentine proving decisive. Where once it might have been acceptable to send a less than full strength MCC party to the Caribbean, circumstances had changed, with the West Indies now likely to be very competitive in a home series. Coincidentally, the England captain in the Oval Test in August 1950 had been Freddie Brown (by then in the twilight of his career). He had scored 0 and 15, while Hutton made an unbeaten 202 in the first innings.

The chosen squad was a strong one, although the most experienced pace bowler, Surrey's Alec Bedser, was not included, the decision determined by his age (36) and the importance of having him fit to manage the workload on the forthcoming tour to Australia in 1954/55. Bill Edrich of Middlesex, an experienced and combative batter with 34 appearances for his country going back to 1938, was also omitted, a victim of his perceived uncertainty against spin and an ill-advised escapade during the first Test against West Indies at Old Trafford in 1950 when, after a night of celebration, he had needed to be put to bed by the hotel porter with the Test due to resume the following morning. The batting was strong on paper, although it lacked depth and an obvious opening partner for Hutton. The spine of the Test batting would probably comprise Hutton, Denis Compton, Tom Graveney and Peter May. The pace attack was Trueman and Brian Statham (Lancashire), supported by Alan Moss (Middlesex) and Trevor Bailey. Three spinners were selected: Tony Lock and Jim Laker (both of Surrey) and Yorkshire's Johnny Wardle. Godfrey Evans was the first-choice wicketkeeper. The squad numbered only 15, which may have caused some early anxiety about whether injury or illness might put the captain and his players under undue pressure. Yorkshire provided four players, Surrey three and Middlesex two, with the remainder drawn from six counties.

A further potential problem was the choice of tour manager. The selectors surprisingly opted for Leicestershire's captain Charles Palmer. Palmer was a popular cricketer but as an amateur it must have crossed Hutton's mind that if things on tour did not go well he could be summarily consigned to the ranks. That thought will not have been helped by the fact that Robins's daughter would go on the tour to provide Palmer with secretarial support. In the event she was more occupied with darning players' socks and helping Jim Swanton with his typing than acting as the selectors' spy on the tour's progress. For his part, Swanton was scathing about the appointment, although his opinions would have been viewed with some cynicism by the players: he was thought to be unduly pompous – so snobbish it was said that he would object to being seen in the same motor car as his chauffeur. Certainly, the players, some of them at least, were uneasy about matters, noting the absence of a vice-captain and a player-manager almost three years younger than his captain and who had never been to the West Indies, or indeed 'managed'.

Before departure there was the traditional pre-tour dinner held at Lord's where the players were addressed by Sir Walter Monckton, a Minister in Churchill's Conservative government. His cricket experience included playing for Harrow against Eton. Yorkshire's Fred Trueman took exception to the minister's political advice, taking the view that he should have been paid more as a cricketing tourist if he was additionally required to act as a member of Her Majesty's Diplomatic Service. For his part Palmer thought the overall briefing for the tour was less than thorough and regretted the fact that the tourists were set to fly to the Caribbean, believing that the squad benefited from the 'valuable breathing space' weeks at sea provided. As for Jim Swanton's view of the tour's selection committee, it is interesting that 30 years later he would write a biography of Gubby Allen and make no mention of the West Indies tour in 1953/54, the issues surrounding its contentious nature nor the attitude of the selectors towards their chosen captain.

2

'This Unhappy Tour'

West Indies, 1953/54

IF CRICKET was different in the 1950s so too was the world in which cricketers lived. That world was volatile, divided between east and west, awash with Cold War currents and living under the permanent threat of the hydrogen bomb. A week before the MCC party set off on their West Indian tour the American president, Dwight Eisenhower, had given his 'Atoms for Peace' speech to the UN General Assembly in New York. In it he talked of speaking a 'new' language, that of atomic warfare. Europe was firmly divided between communist and non-communist ideologies, both hunkered down on either side of the 'iron curtain'. Nor was the Caribbean seen as on the fringes of such a divide. Britain's Conservative government was sufficiently troubled by the communist leanings of those in power in British Guiana that it despatched a battalion of the Argyll and Sutherland Highlanders as a precaution against what might transpire.

It would not be communism on the minds of England's cricketers when they returned to Britain in the spring of 1954 but rather issues to do with race and empire. From the start of the West Indian tour, the players had been aware of the racial tensions on the islands, not least the fears and resentment felt by the white section of the population. It became, according to the manager, Charles Palmer, 'a big millstone around our necks … and after a while it ate into our souls.'[5]

Before the series against West Indies even began there were two unsettling events. First, MCC touring parties had never previously set out on tour by air; hitherto they would arrive having been at sea for weeks. This time they flew from London Airport on 14 December 1953 in a BOAC Stratocruiser. Some members of the party were uncertain, all too conscious that they had never flown before. The decision to divert mid-flight to Gander in Newfoundland because of 'electrical problems' over the Atlantic was distinctly worrying, particularly for those who remembered all too well that there had been a fatal accident involving another Stratocruiser earlier in the year. In Gander there was a bitter frost and deep-lying snow, while the engine trouble needed time for it to be fixed and so the players retired in pairs to share log cabins, still wearing their lightweight, hot-weather suits. With the engine fixed and a blizzard expected, the players were awoken in the early hours, and the flight was resumed and arrived just one day late.

They landed in Bermuda (over 1,200 miles from the venue for the first Test in Jamaica) because of MCC's wish both to spread the influence of the game and to benefit from the offer of the Bermuda Cricket Board to help with the costs of air travel. The outcome was anything but successful – the cricket played (on matting wickets) was mundane and Hutton was out first ball to the opening delivery of the tour; the tourists were away from

5 *Charles Palmer – More Than Just a Gentleman* by Douglas Miller, page 85.

home over the Christmas period although the serious cricket would not begin for more than two weeks; the accommodation they occupied was in single rooms but they were obliged to share; and there was the unsettling first glimpse of the prevailing attitudes to the issue of colour and race. By law – the Hotel Keepers' Act (1930) – black people were not permitted to enter hotels. The issue had surfaced at the airport where Palmer had been discussing arrangements before being warned that 'black and white were not allowed to fraternise at the hotel'.[6]

Jim Swanton arrived in the West Indies just in time for the first Test which was to begin in mid-January in Jamaica, a month after the players had left England. There were already signs that all was not well: there was a distinct tension both within the group, unhappy about those preparatory fixtures on matting wickets and unease amongst some about the captain's evident wish not to fraternise with the opposition, while, more widely, there was talk of the series being promoted as an unofficial contest for the world championship. The former player and cricket correspondent, Alex Bannister, would later comment on the levels of prejudice and bitter acrimony that characterised the West Indies tour of 1953/54, suggesting that only the infamous 'Bodyline' tour to Australia two decades before was more unpleasant. As for the players, 'the dominant memory of this unhappy tour' was the intensity of feeling held by the white West Indians.

The first Test began on Friday, 15 January 1954 at Sabina Park, Kingston. For England there were difficult decisions to take about which members of the squad should be omitted for the game – inevitably there would be four disappointed players – and

6 *The Way it Was* by Stephen Chalke, page 100.

the selection would reveal something of Hutton's overall plans for the series. The two warm-up games had seen the potential pace attack enjoying more success than the spinners, while of the batters Dick Spooner would have been expecting not to make the Test XI having made just one run in his two innings. Predictably he missed out, along with Ken Suttle and both Jim Laker and Johnny Wardle; the player-manager Palmer was also not included. So it was that England went into the game with what looked like a strong set of fast and medium-pace bowlers, with Alan Moss perhaps the most fortunate to make the cut.

It would seem that the selection had been influenced by a Test strip judged to favour the quick men. For some 'the preponderance of pace and the absence of Laker was clearly a gamble'.[7] More widely, Hutton's approach to the series was evident from the outset: he made clear that 'fraternisation' between the teams was inappropriate and there should be a sustained intensity about the visitors' approach to the contest. Evidently the skipper thought that quick bowlers personified aggression, while spin was a more defensive option. Significantly Hutton spurned a suggestion by the West Indian captain, Jeff Stollmeyer, that bouncers should be limited to two per over. Even at this early stage it was clear that the Yorkshireman's gritty approach was not designed to win many friends, either on the field or in the stands. Tours can all too easily acquire a 'siege mentality' and there were signs of such a mood already: mutterings about the low standard of umpiring with England's wicketkeeper, Godfrey Evans, believing that England would need to be substantially better than their opponents to achieve a win.

---

7 *The Cricketer*, Spring 1954, page 7: 'MCC Tour in the West Indies' by Philip Thomson.

Hutton lost the toss – as he had done throughout the previous summer – and the West Indies unsurprisingly chose to bat. In the press box there was discussion about whether Hutton would have put the opposition in, tempted perhaps by the hard, glassy look of the pitch which according to Alex Bannister, with an image from an earlier age, shone as if it had been polished by a zealous housewife. It proved blander than it looked, however, and the West Indies lost only one wicket in the session through to lunch.

For more than two days West Indies batted on inexorably – disciplined and painstaking – intent on not relinquishing the level of control that winning the toss had given them. What drama there was in the cricket stemmed from early signs of crowd unrest, initially when John Holt, in his first Test match, was given out leg before to Statham when only six runs short of a century. The dismissal took place before lunch on the second morning and stirred the crowd into unprecedented disapproval of the umpires, Perry Burke and T.A. Ewart, not only at the time but when the players returned after the interval, and later on, when the Burke's family was threatened with violence.

The new batsman was the Jamaican George Headley, some 20 years after he had been named a *Wisden* Cricketer of the Year and playing what would be his final Test match. The mood worsened as a direct result of a courteous gesture by the captain of the bowling side. Most unusually, and in an apparent gesture of respect for Headley's long-standing career, Hutton appeared to give Headley an uncontested single to begin his innings. Brian Statham, a man whose accuracy was one of his greatest strengths, bowled a full toss down the leg side. Headley ambled a single and all seemed well enough. The mood in the crowd – already fired up by the earlier dismissal of Holt – saw the move by the

Englishmen as both patronising and cynical, the latter with some justification since the ball had been Statham's last of the over and Headley was immediately faced with an over from Fred Trueman, who would be all too aware of the Jamaican's recent struggles against the short ball. Indeed, the afternoon session saw a barrage of bouncers. The gift of 'one off the mark' to George Headley was, to some eyes, the single most inflammable incident of the entire tour. Cricket on this tour was always played against a politically sensitive background: the Englishmen were 'almost afraid to talk to a white man' for fear of what it might elicit, while Hutton was weighed down by the social demands and political intensity of the whites. As for the home side, 'the selection of the West Indies Test team was bedevilled by inter-island rivalries'.[8]

The West Indies total of 417, made over two days and a bit, put them in a strong position and England's reply on the third day was decidedly limp, with the batsmen seemingly unable to cope with the spin of Valentine and Ramadhin. Jim Swanton shook his head at the way the Englishmen attempted to play the turning ball anchored to the crease, although the issue was less to do with turn on the cracked strip and more the result of flight and length on a pitch so hard that inserting the stumps required the holes to be wetted.

Not only was England's batting feeble in the face of the West Indian spin attack, but it was also painfully slow. West Indies themselves had been decidedly pedestrian, scoring their 417 at around 2.7 runs per over, but England's rate was a snail-like 1.9 during a painfully eked out and inadequate 170. All the top order, with the exception of the unfortunate Willie Watson,

8 Miller, op. cit., page 86.

got into double figures, but then faltered, leaving Peter May's 31 as England's top score. With a West Indian lead of 247 it seemed highly likely that England would have to follow on, but in the event Stollmeyer chose to bat again, an understandably cautious approach which suggested that he anticipated the wicket would deteriorate significantly in the fourth innings. It was not, however, a decision welcomed by a section of the simmering crowd: he was roundly booed when he came out to bat.

From then on the game slipped away from Hutton's men, although there was a glimmer of hope with West Indies at a nervy 119/6. But an unbroken stand of 90 for the seventh wicket was a decisive blow from which the English never recovered. Somehow the no-balling of left-arm spinner Tony Lock for throwing symbolised the visitors' disarray. That no-ball was the only one of the West Indian innings but was of considerable significance given the growing conviction that the Surrey man occasionally threw his faster delivery. Its occurrence at that moment in the game was timely for the home team, but a blow for the struggling visitors.

West Indies chose not to declare at their overnight score of 203/6 but batted on briefly in the morning for a further six runs, presumably because of calculations about the runs required and the time left in the game. The target set was a tall order – 457 runs – which at the rate of scoring through the game to that point would be very challenging. Courtesy of Watson and Hutton's opening stand, England started well and were 220/1 at one point but fell away in the final afternoon of the game as 282/4 faded ingloriously to 316 all out. The loss of Compton, bowled by Ramadhin for only 2, was the turning point. Swanton was disapproving, contending that each Englishman had 'devised his own method of suicide'.

The *Telegraph*'s man stumbled away from the press box dismayed by what he had seen, hoping that a few days watching golf in Jamaica's Open Championship might dispel the gloom and the sheer size of the defeat. There he exchanged the view from the Sabina Park press box (over mid-off and looking north) with a view of palm trees and distant mountains, for an idyll of green fairways stretching away from the ocean towards the Blue Mountains. He found himself comparing the healthy competitiveness of the golfers and their followers with the 'dangerously inflammable' atmosphere at the Test. The experience of umpire Burke, who was approached on a Kingston railway platform by someone wielding a knife cursing the man who had given John Holt out six runs short of his hundred, somehow symbolised that unhealthy state of the series with four Tests still to play. The clean swing of golf clubs and the patter of polite applause was a blessed relief to Swanton's troubled soul.

Hutton's strategy for that disappointing first Test had been based on a misguided assumption that the Kingston wicket was so benign that completing four innings on it over six days was very unlikely. Maintaining the morale of his bowlers was a priority and he did not want to see his spinners demoralised so early in the tour by a flamboyant West Indian batter like Clyde Walcott or Everton Weekes, hence the decision to play four pacemen. While 11 of the 16 wickets to fall had gone to those quicker bowlers, only the reliable Brian Statham had respectable figures (6-140 in the match). He had bowled with great control of length and direction, making him the pick of the England attack. The other three had removed just five West Indians between them while conceding 335 runs. The much-heralded young tearaway Fred Trueman was markedly less fearsome or successful than had been hoped, taking just two wickets (both tailenders) for 139. The Hutton plan had clearly misfired and on the thousand-mile flight east to Antigua, the captain had much to consider and some of it not about cricket. The aircraft was searched for bombs and it was no consolation that the plane carrying Stollmeyer's men was also scoured for explosives.

The hangover of the Jamaica Test was blown away by a gentle outing against the Leeward Islands played over two days on a damp wicket. It was everything that the Test had not been – light-hearted, unchallenging and dominated by the English spinners. Wardle and Laker hustled the islanders out for 38 in the first innings. It was clear that Hutton's use of the two mainstream spinners, with Denis Compton being given 13 overs in the second innings (he took 5-50 with his quirky mix of chinamen and googlies) hinted at a change in strategy for the upcoming Barbados Test. Hutton was seen to be in close discussion with his 'selection advisers' – the manager Charlie Palmer, Bailey and Compton – and Swanton assumed part of the discussion involved a shared conviction that the batting in Kingston had been weakened by the misjudged selections. There was talk too about Trueman's disappointing shortage of genuine pace and, Swanton surmised, his fiery, unreliable temperament.

In Barbados the sugar cane drifted at the whim of the on-shore breeze, the harsh light from a remorseless sun was reflected off gleaming white buildings and the eye was drawn to the blue of the ocean, the waves capped with surf. The beauty of the location did not dispel the uncertainties in the England camp. There were injuries already (Statham was plagued by an outbreak of boils on a knee and wicketkeeper Evans had needed a shoulder operation). Equally worrying was the fact that Tony Lock was no-balled again (twice) in the match against Barbados which was narrowly won by MCC.

The Barbados Test began on 6 February 1954 and was marked by unexpected and significant changes in the England XI, with Moss, Trueman and Johnny Wardle omitted and Charlie Palmer included for his first (and last) Test. His selection had been made while he had absented himself from the selectorial meeting. He hadn't 'had a bat in [his] hand for three weeks'.[9] There was a strong sense of déjà vu about the ensuing game. Hutton lost the toss for the seventh time in a row, West Indies batted and the English bowling was patchy at best: Lock, perhaps disconcerted by the spectral threat of umpires beadily looking at his action, bowled too short and Trevor Bailey broke a finger. Things did not improve as the game wore on.

After the rest day, England played soporifically – it was, thought Swanton, the feeblest English performance for many years. The batting was tedious in the extreme, grim and deeply unattractive and the crowd was unsettled, calling loudly and regularly for a refund of the entry money. Through that miserable third day England managed a funereal 128 runs with only the captain getting past 50. The tail folded abjectly with the last four Englishmen adding only 14. Swanton was left bewildered by what he had witnessed. On the fourth day England took just the one wicket (a run-out); John Holt got his hundred (166*) and England were set 495 to win.

There were still more than nine hours left in the game so, given the pace of England's batting thus far, a draw was the more likely target and Hutton and Peter May contributed to an

9 Miller, op. cit., page 91.

encouraging start. It didn't last and the final day saw another humiliating collapse, the new ball proving too much in the afternoon session with five men, Watson, Palmer, Laker, Lock and Statham, all failing to score. That miserable defeat by 140 runs at Jamaica was followed therefore by an even more dispiriting loss by 181 runs at Bridgetown's Kensington Oval. In less than a month of Test cricket the West Indies appeared to have every hope of securing a series win, two up in a five-match series.

Over the ten Tests during 1953/54 Len Hutton's team-mates would watch him walk out to the middle to contest the toss with mounting pessimism about what would follow. The bowlers would be warming up and stretching, and the wicketkeeper (usually Godfrey Evans) would be buckling on his pads. Nine times the ill-starred Hutton looked down at a coin on the turf to see that he had called incorrectly once again and was at the mercy of his opposite number. That meant, almost always, that England would bowl first. Since June 1953, England had bowled first in six out of seven Tests. The exception was at Georgetown, British Guiana, on 24 February, which saw two English batters putting on the pads, Willie Watson and, with slightly more haste, the captain after hurrying back from the middle. As the two Yorkshiremen walked out to face Gomez and Worrell, the West Indian opening bowlers, the conversation was more likely to be about the need to take full advantage of batting first, rather than airy comments about the sun glinting off the mosques behind the stands, or the breeze tousling the palm trees. They would have been all too aware of the difficulty of coming back from 2-0 down.

The happenstance of how the coin falls is a telling factor in determining how a cricket match will unfold. The pitch and the weather are important factors too, but clearly none of the three are within the control of the visiting captain. Over such things Hutton would shrug his shoulders, but what he could do was lift the mood of his men, hone their preparedness and define the broad strategy to be followed – the team's attitude to run-making (free-spirited attack or a dour accumulation of run upon run?) and bowling (high, aggressive pace or artful, patient spin?) Underlying such considerations was the issue of team selection.

How much change should there be after the two comprehensive defeats in Jamaica and Bridgetown? Would Hutton have regretfully cast his eye back to those left behind in England – batters Raman Subba Row (average 50.6) and Bill Edrich (47.35) for example, or bowlers Alec Bedser (162 wickets at 16.7 each) or Lancashire's Roy Tattersall (164 at 18.1) perhaps? He would certainly have considered, with variable degrees of enthusiasm, those omitted from the Barbados Test – Trueman, Moss, Spooner, Suttle and Wardle – but neither of the quick men had covered themselves in glory in Jamaica (Trueman's two wickets had cost him 139 runs) and Spooner and Suttle had not done enough to merit selection.

Hutton's options were very limited in truth, so he simply went for Wardle at the expense of the hapless Charles Palmer. An analysis of the statistics from the first two Tests reveals some harsh truths. Only Brian Statham had averaged below 30 with the ball; only Hutton averaged over 50 with the bat. England's tail had been inept in the two Tests: Evans, Lock, Laker and Statham had contributed just 42 runs in 14 innings. The solution then was plain: play a spinner who can bat (Wardle) and drop the man who shouldn't have played in Bridgetown (Palmer). That was the only change. Improvement must come from the existing underperformers in the team: Bailey (18.75 with the bat and two wickets at 96.5); Compton (average only 30); the spinners (ten wickets between them, but at a cost of 468 runs). The catches needed to be held; the fielding had to be sharper and runs needed to come from every man in the chosen XI.

Georgetown, British Guiana was a place to win the toss, count your blessings and bat, head down for the next two days. Hutton's pleasure in calling correctly was tempered slightly by the residual damp in the air after the series of tropical storms that had swept in over the past week. That had left a hint of green to the outfield, and looking out from the pavilion as the English openers padded up, they could see clouds in the sky and sense a distinctly humid atmosphere. The trees encircling the ground were swaying in a cool breeze. The cricket that day had a cheerless feel to it: implacably dour and unconscionably slow, as befitted a team that dare not lose again and whose selection of five specialist bowlers meant a long and vulnerable tail. In the press box, Jim Swanton scowled and, while admiring Hutton's stubborn and cautious accumulation of runs, he took the view that the approach was attritional, tedious and did England's cricketing reputation no favours.

During the afternoon session, when only 67 runs were scored, sections of the crowd became increasingly restless, the mood soon manifesting itself in loud and angry barracking. After tea England's batting was even slower, but at the close of play a near-flawless Hutton had survived, on 84 not out, with Compton staunchly accompanying him and the score at 153/2. Through the day England had scored at a pedestrian 1.4 runs per over. Perhaps a six-day match encouraged slow batting and certainly there was a slow outfield and a two-paced wicket to contend with, but it was a day that won few friends and none of them West Indian. Interestingly, West Indies bowled 106 overs that day, far more than the modern-day requirement of 90 – a target which is rarely achieved.

Given the uncomfortable history shared by the two cricketing nations and the attitudes of each to the other at this time of dying British imperialism, it might have been anticipated that when the cricket turned churlish and stony-faced then the West Indian supporters around the fence might recall past resentments and wish to voice their dissatisfaction with the English way – both of playing cricket and otherwise. On that first day, there had been no more than rumblings of angry discontent, but there were hints of something more sinister in the heat and humidity of Georgetown in the days to come.

Gradually England cemented their slim advantage, even managing to accelerate the rate of scoring on the second day. West Indies used seven bowlers as they struggled to bowl England out. The spin bowler Sonny Ramadhin (6-113) was the most successful, while Hutton (169) and Denis Compton put together a stand of 150. The second day closed with England well set at 401/8. On the following morning a further 34 runs were added before West Indies began their reply. The English innings had lasted for 220 overs, the run rate a fraction under two per over, enough to test the most patient spectators at Lord's, let alone those in the stifling heat of British Guiana.

When West Indies batted they ran into two storms, the first courtesy of Brian Statham who took three quick wickets in an exemplary spell of quick bowling. The second came from the heavens during the lunch break, a violent tempest that drenched the outfield and washed out play for the day. At the start of day four, with half the game over, England found themselves with a good chance of securing a much-needed victory; their bowlers chipped away, with the metronomic Statham taking 4/64.

But then, as the end of the West Indian innings drew to a close, the undercurrent that had been in the air throughout the game turned violent and dangerous. What began it was the run-out of Clifford McWatt, courtesy of a rapid piece of fielding by Peter May out on the leg-side boundary. There seems little doubt that the West Indian wicketkeeper was sufficiently far out of his ground to make an umpire's decision straightforward. Indeed, McWatt had simply carried on running towards the pavilion, resigned to the inevitable. But it was enough of a trigger to provoke a section of the crowd into throwing bottles, wooden boxes and beer crates towards the square leg umpire, Badge Menzies. Soon the air was thick with flying glass and angry voices, threatening enough for the fielders to move rapidly towards the playing strip. Play stopped for ten minutes as mounted police moved in on the rioters. West Indian officials came on to the pitch to plead for calm and chaos reigned. Len Hutton, at his most obdurate, ordered his men back to their fielding positions. 'We want another wicket or two,' was his response it seems and, with a brave pretence that all was well, play was resumed with fielders' eyes uncertainly flicking to the area of the ground from where the bottles had first been hurled.

The sense of civil unrest was heightened by news of a fire over the weekend at the Queen's Park Oval, Port of Spain, Trinidad – venue for the fourth Test – which destroyed two stands. Arson was suspected and the prevailing mood was not helped by threats made to Menzies – a local man who doubled as the groundsman at Bourda – which resulted in a precautionary police guard being placed around his house. England's manager Charles Palmer, suddenly caught up in a political situation far beyond his experience, contemplated asking for military support from the Argyll and Sutherland Highlanders, but in the end settled for ringing Government House to ask for an increased police presence. Palmer's position on this tour was never easy: 'I was subordinate to the captain and sometimes he was subordinate to me.'[10]

By Monday things had calmed down and England soon secured a position of strength in the match, enforcing the follow-on and then dismissing the West Indies for 256 with the wickets shared amongst all five mainstream bowlers. Watson and Graveney were unbeaten at the end with England winning by nine wickets. Spirits were higher when they flew out of British Guiana than when they had arrived, but the images of broken glass and the cacophony of riot stayed in the touring party's minds. There was no mistaking the tensions beyond the green of the cricket field and it added to the sour atmosphere surrounding the tour, the result of a sense that the English were increasingly beleaguered. Not for the last time, the unsavoury episode in Georgetown raised the question about the wisdom of cricketers playing the game in situations where political tensions are high. This was, after all, a context where British Guiana had recently seen its constitution suspended, a 'state of emergency' announced (on 9 October 1953), and its chief minister, Cheddi Jagan, summarily removed from power. He would be arrested early in April 1954, a month after the third Test. It was widely reported that by mid-April police powers were greatly increased

10 Miller, op. cit., page 87.

with assemblies of five or more people, for example, deemed illegal. By then the tourists had left the Caribbean for home.

In England spring was drawing nearer and the nation's cricketers were, for the most part, contemplating early season nets and wondering when the weather would turn to something less chill. For the tourists in the West Indies, by contrast, there were two Test matches still to be played in a series where, not so long ago, all had seemed lost. Two-one down and with two to play, clearly things could still be saved. What complicated matters was the nature of the wicket at Port of Spain, Trinidad. The batting strip comprised jute matting, not grass, with the result that the contest between bat and ball became weighted hugely in favour of the former. The game began badly with Evans, suffering from a foot infection, having to cede wicketkeeping duties to Dick Spooner then early in the morning of the first day Brian Statham injured a rib. He would not bowl again on the tour. As for Spooner, he failed to take a catch in the entire match, though he was involved in one of two 'catches' not given by the umpires Ellis Achong and Ken Woods, whose performance baffled and infuriated the Englishmen and caused considerable controversy. On that unforgiving concrete-like surface, the bowlers needed things to run their way and, in their view at least, competent umpires.

West Indies batted on into the third day before declaring at a massive 681/8, with the 'three Ws' – Clyde Walcott, Everton Weekes and Frank Worrell – all scoring hundreds. Those days of bowling, according to Fred Trueman who bowled 33 overs, resembled 'hard labour' for prison convicts. Later, while watching the England reply from the pavilion in temperatures approaching 90 degrees as May and Compton batted serenely on, those waiting to bat could savour the beauty of the setting – distant, green-tinged mountains, a heat haze, and best of all, sitting idly by while the England innings stretched over several days towards the safety of a draw. In truth, there was never much hope of a result in a game where bowlers were the underclass and batters given free rein.

Up next was a 1,200-mile flight to Jamaica for the final Test.[11] England, without the injured Statham, opted for Trevor Bailey to open the bowling rather than Alan Moss. Unusually the Essex man would also open the batting. After Hutton had lost the toss once more, Bailey's medium pace proved highly effective – he took seven wickets for 34 – and that was enough to put England in a strong position which they never relinquished. Hutton's 205 out of a total of 414 proved as decisive as Bailey's earlier, unanticipated spell. Fred Trueman took five wickets in the match, unaware of Swanton's cold disapproval. From an apparently shaky position a month or so before, England had contrived to draw the series.

For those final days in Jamaica some of the players now had their wives in attendance. In those very different times, 'permission' had been given for their presence, but no help offered in terms of the necessary travel arrangements or expenses. It was the first time that Godfrey Evans' wife, Jean, had travelled out to a series. He had spent five out of eight post-war winters touring one or other of the world's cricket-playing countries. In his end-of-tour report, Len Hutton confirmed his comments on the Kent wicketkeeper: 'I feel that you know all there is to know about

11 It was the first Test match in the illustrious career of the West Indian all-rounder, Garry Sobers. He scored 14* and 26 and took 4-75 in England's first innings of 414.

him.' It was the kind of laconic, undemonstrative, throwaway remark that typified England's Test skipper.

Hutton's batting on that West Indian journey had been exemplary (he averaged 96.7 in the Tests), and Swanton admired his 'stout backbone' but there were widely held doubts about his suitability for the forthcoming tour of Australia and New Zealand – now just over six months away. The West Indies tour had been only a 'qualified success', the newspaperman thought. The objection seemed to be that there was not enough of the officer class about the Yorkshireman. With his most set and grim-faced expression, the *Telegraph*'s man faced his typewriter and tapped out his considered opinion about what the England captaincy required down under. 'The tour will be a searching test for modern professionalism's powers of leadership.'[12] Without the correct background and antecedents, Swanton opined, the professional cricketer might not have 'quite the right stuff'.

---

12 *Swanton in Australia: With MCC 1946-1975* by EW Swanton, page 89.

3

The SS *Orsova*

Autumn, 1954

IN SOME way or other they were all marked by the war, the cricketers and the newspaper correspondents caught up in England's tours of the mid-1950s. Jim Swanton, for example, had been a prisoner of war for three years, captured by the Japanese when Singapore fell; *The Observer*'s Alan Ross had sailed in the Arctic convoys to Russia; while Ian Peebles (*Sunday Times*) had lost an eye during a German air raid. As for the cricketers selected to tour Australia in the winter of 1954/55, the effect of the war years was, at the very least, to shorten the span of their cricketing careers. Moreover, there had been injuries, distant postings, hardship, decorations and the loss of both friends and rivals. The war cast a long shadow: even those cricketers who had not served in the war were no strangers to military uniform. For example, Yorkshire's Fred Trueman was only demobilised at the end of 1953. He had made his Test debut the year before. As the 1954 home season drew to an end he would have been hoping that, despite a mediocre and troublesome tour of the West Indies, he would have been included in the party for Australia.

The summer of 1954 was wet – the worst, Alan Ross believed, of his lifetime – so the prospect of blue skies and heat over the coming weeks would have appealed to the touring party, even those challenged by the confinement of the ship and the long six-month separation from home. The 17 cricketers – two more than flew to the West Indies – sailed from Tilbury on 15 September 1954, on board the *Orsova*, a new 27,000-ton liner making only its second voyage to Australia. The players had met in London the previous night and were addressed over dinner by the MCC president 'as if we were just off to Agincourt'.[13] The next morning, the day of departure, the party took the boat-train to Tilbury and, before the ship sailed, the shipping company provided a valedictory lunch at which Len Hutton took time to reassure Colin Cowdrey's parents that he would 'look after' their son on his first tour. He was 21 years old.

Heading down the Channel, the autumn weather was clear and bright while the sea was calm. They would be sailing south and east for just over three weeks before docking in Fremantle on Australia's west coast. An 18th selection, the Middlesex batter Denis Compton, was to fly out later after an operation on his troublesome knee. He had been visiting Charing Cross Hospital three or four times a week for treatment. The press contingent easily outnumbered the players: *The Observer*'s correspondent, Alan Ross, put the figure at about 20, while the England captain, Len Hutton, named almost 30.[14] Amongst them were former

---

13 *MCC – The Autobiography of a Cricketer* by Colin Cowdrey, page 57.

14 *Just My Story* by Len Hutton, page 143. The pace bowler Frank Tyson listed EW Swanton, John Woodcock (*The Times*), Crawford White (*News Chronicle*), Frank Rostron (*Daily Express*), Alex Bannister (*Daily Mail*), Len Bailey (*Evening Star*), EM Wellings (*Evening News*), Alan Ross (*Guardian*), plus another dozen or so. See *In The Eye of the Typhoon* by Frank Tyson, page 14.

players – the retired pace bowlers Bill Bowes of the *Yorkshire Evening News* and Alf Gover, *Sunday Pictorial*; an ex-captain of England (FR Brown, *Daily Mail*); freelancers (Eric Bedser); doyens of the art of sports writing (Neville Cardus, *Manchester Guardian*) and EW Swanton (*Daily Telegraph*). There was only one woman – Margaret Hughes of the *Sydney Daily Telegraph*. She noted that it was 'the largest press party yet to tour Australia'; and that with their typewriters and briefcases they looked 'more important than the players'. Swanton, she thought, 'had all the presence and grandeur of a great Maharaja'.[15]

Prior to the sailing, there had been much speculation about the nature and composition of the touring party, even about its leader, despite the fact that Hutton, England's first professional captain, had led the team which recaptured the Ashes in the summer of 1953 before the tour of the Caribbean. Yorkshire's Hutton had skippered that tour as if it were a Roses match against Lancashire – uncompromising and dour – and the reaction in the Caribbean was predictably one of disenchantment with the tourists.

Predictably, the selection for Australia revealed some consequences of the controversies of the 1954 West Indies expedition. The left-arm spinner Tony Lock and quick bowler Fred Trueman were both omitted. The latter had been the only player whose £50 good conduct bonus was not paid, a decision confirmed at an MCC Cricket Committee meeting on 25 May 1954: 'The reward for discipline during the tour should be given to all the professional cricketers of the team with the exception of FS Trueman.' £50 was some 10% of the player's tour salary. Hutton, as captain, was part of the group that approved the sanction on

15 *The Long Hop* by Margaret Hughes, page 22.

his fellow Yorkshireman. Trueman's omission prompted a flurry of protests: 'I should like to know,' wrote Wilfred Aldersley from Kendal, 'how long the MCC has been the arbiter of a person's morals and social caste.' The letter went on to wonder if 'one of the qualifications for selection is to be found drunk in charge of a motor car', a thought prompted by a recent, much-publicised indiscretion by a senior official at Lord's.[16]

The controversy over whether Hutton should continue as captain sold newspapers and the press worried away at the issue in the days and weeks before the appointment was finally confirmed. Even as the party sailed there were doubts about whether the Yorkshireman was the best man for the job. It was, after all, a daunting task – until the home series of 1953, Australia had held the Ashes for more than 20 years. England had last won in Australia in the Bodyline series of 1932/33 when the tourists had been led by an equally flinty captain in Douglas Jardine. He was as tough as Hutton but from a very different background, what Swanton might have dubbed 'the right side of the tracks'. Jardine was Hutton's boyhood hero.

The man whose name had been in the frame to lead the MCC party was of that same public-school background as Jardine, the Sussex amateur batsman David Sheppard. He was soon to be ordained as a priest and with his Sherborne School pedigree he fitted the MCC establishment view of the ideal England captain. *The Observer*'s Alan Ross dismissed the amateur/professional debate – only 'a complete moron' would think that of any relevance – while Ian Peebles expressed doubts about Hutton's frame of mind for the battles ahead. The previous

16 MCC Archive, 1954/55 tour file.

summer had seen him struggle, both physically and mentally. He had batted, according to Ross, as if the batting crease was 'the equivalent of the dentist's chair'.[17] As the *Orsova* forged south, Ross contemplated Hutton's captaincy with unease: it lacked, he thought, the firm determination of his batting; was over-cautious at times; he seemed reluctant to use spin; and somehow did not bring out the best in other batsmen.

Three weeks at sea gave plenty of time for those on board to look at the players charged with retaining the Ashes: there were natural groupings – men who had toured together before (Peter May, Trevor Bailey, Brian Statham for example); county team-mates (Surrey's Alec Bedser, Peter May and Peter Loader); and those who had played in the Ashes-winning series of 1953 (Hutton, Simpson, Compton, Graveney, May, Bailey, Wardle, Bedser, Evans, Statham, Edrich). Players shared cabin accommodation: May with Cowdrey, Andrew and Tyson, Graveney and Statham, for example.

But there was no hiding the fact that the bowling looked weaker without Jim Laker, Tony Lock and Fred Trueman. It was not a young squad either, with an average age of just over 28, six players aged 34 or over and only one (Cowdrey) under 24. There were worries about the reliability of the English close catching, an area in which the Australians were much the stronger. There weren't enough good close catchers, Alan Ross noted, and 'few quick movers'.

There were brief stopovers on the long voyage to Australia. The *Orsova* paused at Naples, allowing the Yorkshiremen in the party – Hutton, Bob Appleyard, Vic Wilson, Wardle and

17 *Australia 55* by Alan Ross, page 14.

Bowes – to visit Hedley Verity's grave at Caserta, where they laid white roses to mark the loss during the war of the great England and Yorkshire spin bowler. Three correspondents – Swanton, Ross and Peebles – hired a car and drove into the mountains to visit Pompeii, returning to eat lobsters and rice in Santa Lucia. Swanton and Peebles had once been flatmates in London and 'got along splendidly' – a few years later Peebles would be Swanton's best man when the confirmed bachelor got married on his 51st birthday.[18] Ross sat with both at dinner on board ship, enjoying their conversation and ribaldry. Like Peebles, he was a newly appointed cricket correspondent, in his case at *The Observer* where he had taken over from the legendary RC Robertson-Glasgow.

Soon the ship passed through the Suez Canal, where English troops on its banks provided a musical accompaniment. 'The pipes and drums of the 1st Battalion Scots Guards were formed on a green sward on the last tip of land to play us out to the strains of "Will ye no come back again?" To Margaret Hughes it showed "that cricket is still the binder of the Empire".'[19] The canal kindled memories of wartime journeys for some, while Alan Ross was reminded of his schoolboy travels to and from India, as well as 'the strange disenchanted summer of 1948' when the Australians were proving themselves invincible and he was living temporarily in Corsica.[20] Later there was a brief stay at Colombo in what was then Ceylon for a match played over four hours and during which Colin Cowdrey top-scored with 66 not out in 'Turkish-bath heat' and where the effect of being at sea for so long made him feel the ground was moving under his cricket boots.

---

18 Swanton was godfather to Ian Peebles' son. *Spinner's Yarn* by Ian Peebles, page 89.

19 Hughes, op. cit. page 29.

20 Ross, op. cit., page 23.

After Colombo the old shipboard routine returned, the round of mealtimes, deck games, desultory conversation, walks along the length of the ship, or idly leaning on the rail watching the ocean roll by. For his part, the rookie England paceman, Frank Tyson, from the moment that the *Orsova* sailed, 'pounded the decks before breakfast, even in the torrid heat of the Red Sea'.[21] Bare-chested and in shorts he would be up betimes with his skipping rope. This was not his only eccentricity: Tyson was a man who, when walking back to his bowling mark on the pitch, could be heard reciting lines from Wordsworth. As for Len Hutton, despite his other preoccupations, he took time to take the young Colin Cowdrey aside and warn him about the Australians, in particular their preference for 'rough' tactics and their aggression when a new man came in to bat. 'You'll find,' the captain said, 'that the language can fly in the Test arena.'[22]

After a month at sea English autumn was exchanged for springtime in Western Australia. The *Orsova* docked at Fremantle's Victoria Quay on Thursday, 7 October. Ian Peebles was struck by the vivid blue of the Swan River and its breadth, like a 'small loch' he thought, while Alan Ross could see a Caledonian influence at work in the architecture, 'as though an affluent but eccentric Scottish laird had been given a free hand'. With its hotels resembling cricket pavilions, Ross was struck by Perth's 'graciousness'. Tyson, by contrast, was less enthusiastic, judging Fremantle to be a 'shabby ghost town.'[23]

On the dockside the English party were greeted by an eager Australian press corps. They were duly invited on board for a

---

21 *Fifty Years in Cricket* by Len Hutton, page 119.

22 Cowdrey, op. cit., page 58.

23 Tyson, op. cit., page 39.

briefing and were unexpectedly charmed by the England captain's dry humour and willingness to talk. If Hutton was initially warmed by the attitude towards him of the Australian press, it did not last. By the end of the tour he would observe that they were 'very hard on failures', noting that 'encouragement [was] a commodity which is almost non-existent in the Australian press'.[24]

Overall it seemed that the tour was getting off to an auspicious start, a feeling that quickly faded when one of the England players received some bad news. At the Palace Hotel in Perth there was a pile of mail awaiting Colin Cowdrey. At the top was a telegram with the news of his father's death. Thereafter Hutton 'made certain that [he] was occupied every minute of the day'.[25] The manager, Geoffrey Howard, was also told of Cowdrey's loss in a telegram from the MCC committee which sent 'heartfelt sympathy to Colin', adding that his mother wanted her son to know that 'all arrangements at home [were] going satisfactorily'. She sent her love and was 'most anxious Colin carries on with as little worry and sadness as possible'.[26] The following Sunday the older man partnered the young England batsman at a golf match. In very different ways the two men would have been keen to get started with the cricket and forget the wider world.

The tourists were soon at work, with nets at the Western Australia Cricket Association ground (WACA) the following morning, a warm one tempered by a gentle breeze off the sea. Already there were reservations about what lay ahead, with one of the team's best batters, Denis Compton, still in London; doubts

24 MCC Archive, 1954/55 tour file, captain's report.

25 Cowdrey, op. cit., p. 59.

26 MCC Archive, 1954/55 tour file.

about the quality of England's fielding (the best fielders, it was thought, would not make the Test XI); Alec Bedser, the likely mainstay of the pace attack, was suffering from shingles; and the quality of the spin attack, missing both Lock and Laker, and with no leg-spinner in the party. That omission troubled Hutton in his preparation. Later, wanting to ready himself for the Australian leg-spin attack, he was obliged to recruit two pressmen, Ian Peebles and Freddie Brown, to bowl at him in the nets. The watching Alan Ross thought both temporary recruits did well and admired the 'grace and limpidity of Ian Peebles's action'.

Just four days after the *Orsova* had docked the MCC party was in action. They travelled to Bunbury, on the coast a hundred miles to the south along a ruler-straight road. It was a friendly workout, a match against a Country XI providing relatively gentle competition during the day and a steak and beer barbecue in the evening. The match was a comfortable draw – a hundred from Bill Edrich (129) and a five-wicket haul for Glamorgan's diffident off-spinner, Jim McConnon. The novice Northamptonshire fast bowler Frank Tyson, preferred to Fred Trueman for the tour, despite his lack of Test experience – he had made his debut only months before at the Oval against Pakistan – was certainly quick, if erratic. His run-up to the wicket was unsettling for batsmen. Ian Peebles judged the distance between his bowler's mark and where the wicketkeeper stood to be some 70 yards. Disappointingly, he took just one wicket in 15 eight-ball overs. It was Brian Statham with nine wickets in the following game against Western Australia in Perth who took the plaudits. They headed east unbeaten, but well aware that the real business was about to begin.

4

'The Experience of Australia'

Autumn, 1954

ALAN ROSS was interested in both Australia and cricket – hence his choice of DH Lawrence's novel *Kangaroo* as his reading on board the *Orsova*. He read the book with great interest, although the sleepy, relaxed life on the ship was such that he had not finished it when he stepped on to the Fremantle quayside. He had 'lain mostly in the sun … book open but unread'. Those weeks at sea were an elysian round of day-dreaming, eating and sleeping, with entertainment provided at the dinner table by Swanton and Peebles – they would have been good enough for music hall, Ross thought, while Peebles 'would fit decently into an early Waugh novel'.[27] At one point the cricket correspondents played cricket against the ships' officers on a matting wicket, with Swanton cutting 'a lordly figure at the crease'. The writers' XI was bolstered by the ex-players amongst their ranks – Ian Peebles (13 Test caps), Freddie Brown (22) and Bill Bowes (15). Thus strengthened, the correspondents demonstrated to the defenders of the Ashes how to stroll to an emphatic victory.

---

27 Ross, op. cit., pages 22–23.

Kangaroo is set in New South Wales and Ross warmed to the way the book made 'the experience of Australia real'. The book's central character was similarly a new arrival in Australia who found himself struck by the 'fume of Perth and Fremantle', the city's seashore and the distant lighthouse, the 'crystal blue' of the sky, the clarity of the air, the sense of distance and 'that peculiar, lost, weary aloofness of Australia'.[28]

Ross was resolved to 'travel the breadth of Australia by the slowest route possible' and left Perth on Sunday afternoon, 24 October, missing the final day of the game against a Western Australia Combined XI. Instead, he caught the train – diesel-driven and air-conditioned – heading east, initially through a landscape of jarrah trees, clouds of red swirling dust and then thinning vegetation before there was only desert. The railway track was arrow-straight for hundreds of miles, not the ghost of a curve, while the landscape scarcely changed from one day to the next. Over the journey the time zone changed twice; the engines too, since there were variations in the track gauge from state to state. There was little comfort to be had on board: no bar and the food was distinctly unappetising. There was comfort though in the 'lazy beauty of the old Australian place names en route, Bookaloo, Tarcoola ...' Approaching Adelaide, with the Nullarbor desert finally conceding ground to the city's unexceptional northern suburbs, implausibly it began to rain.

Ross's background was not an obvious fit for a cricket correspondent. He was born in May 1922 in Calcutta and as a child spoke Hindustani more confidently than he did English. It was coming to England for his schooling that triggered his interest

---

28 *Kangaroo* by DH Lawrence, page 5.

in cricket. After attending Haileybury School, he briefly read Modern Languages at St John's College, Oxford (from October 1940 to March 1942), doing little or no work, but gaining blues in both cricket and squash. He was a contemporary at Oxford of both the novelist Kingsley Amis and the poet Philip Larkin, with whom he 'played hockey ... for St John's and Worcester on one occasion'.[29] Turning his back on wartime Oxford, Ross joined the Royal Navy and, at the end of 1942, was fortunate to survive the Battle of the Barents Sea, an engagement off the north Norwegian coast, at one point being trapped in the flooded hold of HMS *Onslow*.

When the war ended Ross contemplated playing county cricket for a 'season or two'. He was good enough as a medium-pacer to open the bowling with Alec Bedser when the great Surrey paceman was merely 'an unknown aircraftman'. Ross was on leave from his ship and the two men dismissed an Army side for 70, sharing the wickets in an unchanged bowling attack. Ross would long regret being 'robbed of the only hat-trick' of his cricketing career. He played one wartime game for Northamptonshire against Leicestershire, was bowled by Tom Goddard of Gloucestershire and England when playing for Oxford, and first played at Lord's aged 15.[30] Any prospect of a career as a cricketer was ruled out by the delay in getting out of uniform and Germany where he was stationed in the months after the war ended. Instead, spurred by the publication of a poetry collection, *The Derelict Day*, in 1947 and the award of an Atlantic Award by the Rockefeller Foundation, he took the first tentative steps towards a literary

29 It was, it seems, Larkin's only game of hockey: the poet 'found the strokes too dangerous.' See *Philip Larkin: A Writer's Life* by Andrew Motion, page 38.

30 See the *Cricket Archive* for his full record (11 matches in all).

career. He wanted, he wrote, 'to reconcile ... sport and poetry'.[31] Coincidentally, the £500 associated with the Rockefeller award was the same as the salary for an England cricketer on the recent West Indies tour. Instead of academia or the county cricket circuit he went to Corsica with the painter John Minton and published a travel book on the experience in 1948, when Australia's cricketers were retaining the Ashes. He married Jennifer Fry in 1949. He was 'exceptionally attractive – dark-eyed, black-haired, slim and athletic'; she was six years older than him and when he met her at Cyril Connolly's house he fell for her 'huge dark eyes and long dark hair, wearing a black dress'. She had previously been married to the 'Mad Boy', Robert Heber-Percy, the 'wildly physical, unscholarly young hothead' with a liking for galloping naked on horseback. Heber-Percy was the lover of the eccentric peer, Lord Berners, who was some 28 years his senior.[32] The as yet undiscovered Russian spy Donald Maclean was a guest at Ross's wedding. In 1953 the family, now including the new-born Jonathan, moved to Sussex and Alan became *The Observer*'s cricket correspondent. The landscape of Sussex and the exploits of its cricketers would become powerful influences.

***

On 27 October, three days after Ross had left Perth, the rest of the tour party, cricketers and writers, flew the 1,600 miles to Adelaide in a Dakota of Australian National Airways. The exception was the tour's only female correspondent, an Englishwoman, Margaret Hughes, writing for the *Sydney Daily Telegraph* and visiting friends in Adelaide. Hughes had been

31 *Blindfold Games* by Alan Ross, pages 65–66.

32 *The Mad Boy, Lord Berners, my Grandmother and Me* by Sofka Zinovieff, page 7.

appointed after a meeting at London's Savoy Hotel with Frank Packer, the paper's owner – and father of Kerry Packer.[33] At Sydney, where she changed planes for Adelaide, she saw Denis Compton looking 'tired and drawn' who told her that he had not slept for nearly a week.[34] He had been travelling for seven days. Compton was arriving late for the tour after knee surgery at Charing Cross Hospital and an eventful, dangerous journey. He had flown via Beirut and Karachi where the pilot had been unable to lower the Constellation's nose-wheel. Eventually the navigator had emerged from the cockpit after a few unnerving circuits of the aerodrome and announced that 'they would have to throw the plane about a bit' in an attempt to loosen the wheel. They circled for 45 minutes while a landing strip 'was ploughed and lit in preparation for an emergency landing'.[35] In the end the pilot – a former flying boat captain – managed, against the odds, a perfect landing, although Compton remembered that there was 'a tearing, grinding, scraping noise and a fair amount of bumping'.[36]

After the Nullarbor desert, Adelaide had variety, greenery and a certain elegance. It had hills, including the stony bulk of Mount Lofty, and was skirted by a fringe of beaches on an ocean inlet. Alan Ross was reminded of both the Mediterranean and the countryside around Clayton where he lived, beneath Ditchling Beacon on the Sussex Weald. Ian Peebles, staying at the Adelaide Club, enjoyed its old-fashioned, leathery comfort and

---

33 Packer had confided that in his view cricket was 'dying out'; 23 years later Kerry Packer was instrumental in creating World Series Cricket, which led to one of the most tumultuous periods in cricket history.

34 Hughes, op. cit., page 43.

35 *End of an Innings* by Denis Compton, page 134 and Peebles, op. cit., p. 35.

36 Compton, op. cit., page 135.

warmed to the city's graciousness and its inhabitants' kindness. Perhaps soured by aspects of MCC's overall performance against South Australia at Adelaide, Ross was more critical of the city, disconcerted by its angularity and lack of curves, the impermanence of the buildings and the absence of a coherent style. At times, it reminded him of a 'provincial cattle town'.[37] For all the doubts, his spirits were invariably uplifted by the approach to Adelaide's cricket ground which reminded him of Worcester, a bucolic parade of 'spires, water, swans, trees and grass'.

As for the cricket, most of the tourists' performance was less than convincing, lethargic and cumbersome. In particular the middle order was a worry. Tom Graveney, for example, got out twice when well set. Only Denis Compton impressed in the first innings, less than two days after being met at Adelaide Airport by Godfrey Evans and fellow Middlesex cricketer, Bill Edrich, a man with his own stories of flying, courtesy of his RAF wartime service. Compton duly top-scored for MCC with 113 out of the side's disappointing 246 all out. The bowlers – notably Tyson and Bob Appleyard – saved the day and MCC left Adelaide with the game won by 21 runs. The outcome was close enough to make the tourists realise that the crossing of the Nullarbor marked the divide between those wide-eyed early days of the tour and uncertainty about what was to come.

***

Heading south on the night sleeper for Melbourne, Alan Ross reflected upon recent days and Adelaide's unexpected greenness, its pale wheatfields and the quality of the light. Then darkness

37 Ross, op. cit., page 48.

fell and his thoughts turned towards Melbourne and cricket, his spirits buoyed by the promise of Frank Tyson's six wickets in the previous match, the young man's explosive, gathering pace. Added to which the tourists remained unbeaten after the opening four games. The train trundled 'on through the warm Australian night' as the sleeper slowly climbed through the hills surrounding Adelaide.[38] Sleep did not come easily: Tyson found himself wandering along the corridors trying to borrow something to read. This was a man, Margaret Hughes noted, who had a penchant for Wordsworth, played bridge and was unlike other English professional cricketers because he studied at university.[39] It was 9.30 in the morning before the tourists stepped out on the platform at Melbourne's Spencer Street station.

It was 4 November, nearly a month since they had arrived in Australia during which time they had played 13 days of cricket. The tourists might not have lost but there were significant concerns. The batting, in particular, was a major issue and Hutton's reaction to that aspect of the narrow win against South Australia was to order extra net practice. The *News Chronicle*'s Crawford White was not alone when he suggested that the English batters could learn something from the 'skill, fight and confidence' shown by their bowlers. As if to underline the concern, the squad buckled down to a second bout of extra nets at the Melbourne Cricket Ground (MCG) in the afternoon after a reception at the Windsor Hotel.

There were still three weeks – and three games to play – before the Test series began in Brisbane, more than a thousand miles to the north. Hutton was very keen to get his batters into

---

38 Ross, op. cit., page 59.

39 Hughes, op. cit., page 20.

some kind of consistent form and chose to leave himself out of the Melbourne fixture against a strong Australian XI. The heir apparent, Peter May, captained the side instead, won the toss and chose to bat. The MCG was a behemoth of a stadium and Margaret Hughes, Ross, Peebles and the rest were all struck by its size and atmosphere. Part of one stand had been removed, like a tooth from a jaw, in order to enlarge the ground for the 1956 Olympics. Instead of the old tight claustrophobia there was now a view beyond the ground's confines. Ross was unpersuaded by the MCG's look, but he liked the approach to it, the palm trees, the lily ponds and lakes, flower borders and the lingering aroma of roses and cedar. Hughes, by contrast, thought, with the revelation of green fields and trees following the removal of part of the stand, that it now had a touch of the village green about it. At all events, the cricket emphatically had no such bucolic feel.

It began well enough. Reg Simpson and Bill Edrich put on 48 for the first wicket; Simpson made a graceful and dashing 74 before an ill-judged stroke was caught and bowled by Richie Benaud. Bill Edrich by contrast was evidently out of touch and the middle order fell away alarmingly: 135/2 soon became 168/7. Alan Ross watched the collapse with dismay, both the thin pickings from the middle order and then the way the tail '[folded] up as abruptly as a deckchair under an obese man'.[40] The outcome was a feeble 205 all out, the damage done by the Australian spinners, Benaud and particularly Ian Johnson with figures of 6-66. An old English weakness revealing itself again, some thought.

40 Ross, op. cit., page 62.

England's spinner, Johnny Wardle, was wicketless in the Australian XI's reply. Rather it was Trevor Bailey's persevering medium pace which reduced the Australians to 167/7 before the weather, grey and louring for most of the day, deteriorated further. The final three days saw unremitting rain and no more cricket in the vast bowl of the MCG, now gloomy, unoccupied and puddled.

Compensation for Alan Ross was the comfort of the Melbourne Club where he was staying and enjoying Lawrence's *Kangaroo* and its truths about the Australian landscape and the country's distinctive essence. The rain was unexpected and reminded Hughes of Manchester and wet English summer days of bleak rain. Looking out over the grass as the rain fell, she thought the pitch resembled a black pudding. For his part, Ross enjoyed the horsey feel of the city. It was Melbourne Cup week, and time passed in a warm cycle of drinks and billiards long into the night. Occasionally he would spare a thought for the cricketers confined to their shared hotel rooms. Days and nights like these were not the best part of touring. Perhaps prompted by having too much time on his hands Hutton revealed more of himself to the press, telling them that he would not want his sons to play cricket, citing the absence of home life. 'I might as well not be married,' he said.[41]

With no cricket to watch, Ross found himself intrigued by the 40 or so members of the press box, variously passing the time as the rain fell: the clatter of typewriters, the cable-boys scurrying to and fro clutching sheets of typescript; the Australian ex-players losing their hair but not their 'wits, legend or stamina',

41 Hughes, op. cit., page 53.

a bespectacled Bill Bowes and his 'air of pity', the old hands' air of 'golfing cronies' Crawford White and Charles Bray, the 'brooding' Ian Peebles; and Jim Swanton, suavely elegant as ever. Later he would remember the press box as 'a very jolly place' despite 'the odd sourpuss'. Over time he would become friends with Peebles, Robertson-Glasgow, Cardus and Swanton.

There was no more cricket to be played in Melbourne for now at least – they would return for the third Test, beginning on New Year's Eve. The rain was unceasing, and the city flooded in parts. It was a place of dripping tarpaulins, puddles, scudding clouds and reluctant travellers. Margaret Hughes, due to fly out for Sydney, was obliged to take a three-hour bus ride to an alternative airport. When she finally reached her accommodation in Sydney, at one in the morning, the room was infested with cockroaches. The tour party itself left for Sydney on another night sleeper.

Alan Ross, towards the end of a long night's journey, looked out of the train window as the outskirts of Sydney unreeled in the early morning: an unromantic spread of bungalows, neat patches of sun-baked lawn, red roof tiles, washing hung on lines, a pyjama-clad girl sipping coffee in the sun and then, scrawled on a white wall, a stark reminder of a wider world, 'Terror and Violence in Soviet Russia'. Soon after, in a fleeting moment as the train was about to enter a tunnel, he saw a silvered glimpse of the Harbour Bridge.

Selection for the game against New South Wales in Sydney told a story – within the next fortnight England needed to find an opening batter to partner the captain in the upcoming Test. In Sydney Bill Edrich would be given that role. As far as the bowling was concerned, it seemed Hutton would be relying on pace – no Wardle or McConnon in the XI. Keith Miller won the toss and asked MCC to bat first on a wicket with its greenish tinge hinting at an overnight watering.[42] It proved to be a lively and disconcerting opening hour or so – Edrich, Simpson, May and Vic Wilson all blown away, leaving the tourists on the brink of losing the game by lunch on day one. It was a familiar story of brittle batting against the new ball. Alan Ross saw the batting order as a 'still digesting snake', thin at the top and bottom, but bulging in the middle.[43] Hutton himself, however, was anything but brittle and he and Colin Cowdrey stood firm long enough to post a total of 252. Both men scored hundreds, but otherwise only Godfrey Evans (11) got into double figures.

MCC had a deficit of 130 runs after Frank Tyson and Alec Bedser had taken four wickets each. True to type Hutton relied predominantly on pace, with some 81% of the overs bowled by his three seamers. Hutton and Cowdrey opened MCC's batting in the second innings, the pair scoring nearly 60% of the runs. The Kent man had thus scored a century in each innings of a game for MCC before he had done so for his county. The game meandered towards a draw with no greater clarity about how England would manage to win a Test match, not just at Brisbane in a fortnight, but over the coming few months. If there was a silver lining it was that the Australian batting looked similarly flaky. There was much to contemplate as bags were packed and the journeys north to Brisbane begun, the tour party by air and Ross, true to his

---

42 This was the first toss that Hutton had lost since the start of the Australian tour. He would have mixed fortunes with the coin in the Tests, losing three tosses and winning two.

43 Ross, op. cit., page 70.

predetermined wish to see as much of the Australian landscape as possible, by train. It would take 19 hours.

There was one final warm-up game, against Queensland, before the Test at Brisbane's Woolloongabba Ground. Unsurprisingly, it was scarcely a classic, sinking latterly into a mood more akin to siesta than first-class cricket, or so Margaret Hughes thought. Reg Simpson scored runs in convincing fashion, making 136 and for the first time on tour 'not batting like a man with a high temperature'.[44] On the down side, Trevor Bailey had split a finger, and Jim McConnon was in hospital after being struck in the groin when fielding close in. The Glamorgan spinner would remain hospitalised for a week.

There were two days left before the Brisbane Test and Hutton remained preoccupied by a string of concerns. He had needed to prop up the batting for weeks – neither Graveney nor Edrich had yet made any significant runs; the Englishmen's best fielder, Wilson, had scored 22 runs in four innings; there was uncertainty about who would open the batting with the captain; the batting order was by no means fixed; and while the pace attack was clear enough, the decision about a spin option was unresolved. That was made more complex by the fact that the flimsy batting necessitated playing a sixth specialist batter. The signs were that, should he win the toss, the England captain would ask the Australians to bat first since bowling last required a potent spin option. Arguably all possibilities of that had remained behind in England.

44 Ross, op. cit., p. 86.

5

Best Laid Plans

Brisbane and Sydney, 1954

ON THE evening before the Test on 25 November a committee comprising Len Hutton, the manager, Geoffrey Howard, Peter May, Bill Edrich and Godfrey Evans met to pick the men to face Australia. The skipper had spent most of the day sitting outside the pavilion watching every ball like a hawk, avoiding conversation and concentrating hard. The issues were familiar: the balance between spin and seam; who should open with the captain; the fallible middle order; and whether England should put them into bat if they won the toss. That was the most troubling. Hutton kept mulling over the apparent uncertainty of the states' batters against Statham and Tyson and reflecting on the 'expected liveliness of the wicket on the first day'.[45] There was concern too about the well-known threat of the Australian quicks, Lindwall and Miller, on such a wicket. Hutton was not a man for changing his mind or being much influenced by those around him.

The morning was one of bright sun and a gentle breeze 'sufficient … to ripple the players' shirts'.[46] Significantly there

45 *Just My Story* by Len Hutton, page 90.

46 *The Urn Returns* by AER Gilligan, page 67.

had been no rain in Brisbane for a week and humidity was low. Putting the opposition in to bat on the first morning of an Ashes Test was very rare. In the years from 1903 to 1954, Australia had always chosen to bat, while England had inserted the opposition on just two occasions, in 1908 and 1912, the latter occasion resulting in an innings victory. England captains were less than fortunate in winning the toss in this fixture. In the 48 games between December 1903 and November 1954 the England captain called correctly just 18 times – 38% only.

Hutton's decision to bowl if the toss went England's way necessarily flowed from the selected XI, with its emphasis on pace bowling. Jim Swanton, in his lordly way, would later describe it as a 'sort of midsummer madness'. The sense of general unease amongst the English press grew as they watched the visitors step out on to the baked grass of the Gabba. Look where you might in the England XI there were concerns, some more obvious than others. Hutton himself was carrying the double onus of being captain and principal batter; Reg Simpson was an 'enigma', in Ian Peebles' eyes at least; Peter May was averaging under 40 on the tour and Edrich only just over 30; Colin Cowdrey was in his first Test; Alec Bedser was ill with shingles; Denis Compton's knee was only weeks away from the cut of a surgeon's knife. Then early on Friday morning, hours from the start of the Test, Godfrey Evans fell ill – variously diagnosed as a severe chill, flu or 'sick with sun stroke' in John Arlott's judgement. The Northamptonshire keeper Keith Andrew was called up for his first Test. He would only play one more, almost a decade later.

In the next hotel bedroom to Evans was John Arlott on his first (and only) trip to Australia. He had arrived in the second half of November after a circuitous journey via Karachi,

Hong Kong, Tokyo and Korea, before heading north for the Brisbane Test. The visit to Tokyo was 'to see Edmund Blunden who was then a professor of English Literature in Japan'. Blunden wanted his students to hear Thomas Hardy's work read in a West Country burr'.[47] Arlott was not enamoured of the Australian weather, preferring a cool breeze from the west off the Bristol Channel. In Sydney, where he shared a flat with Bill Bowes, he found he liked the city and Brisbane, he thought, was somewhat milder than the 'hothouse temperature and humidity' he had anticipated. He was not one for 'sun-baking'. Nor did he warm to Australian taxi drivers, who were unimpressed if fares did not sit beside them in the front of the cab. His excursions with Bill Bowes to Australian vineyards were, however, a comfort.

Margaret Hughes, for her part, sitting on the tram taking her to the Gabba that first morning of the series was rereading the telegram from Colin Cowdrey suggesting a trip to see *The Mikado*. She thought the match conditions were 'clammy and sultry'. Thankfully for the English correspondents the press box was in the shadiest part of the ground, but Hughes was struck by two things, the grubby surroundings – 'the dirtiest I have been in'[48] – and the levels of anxiety amongst the English.

It started badly and got worse. In Alec Bedser's second over, Keith Andrew failed to take a chance down the leg side off a faint edge by Arthur Morris. The Australian would go on to make 153. The dropped catch was symptomatic of a poor day for England generally, with only one wicket falling, 12 catches being dropped and Denis Compton fracturing a metacarpal of

---

47 *Arlott in Conversation with Mike Brearley*, page 114.

48 Hughes, op. cit., page 65.

the fourth finger of his left hand crashing into a boundary fence while fielding. Even Frank Tyson was obliged to leave the field with cramp towards the end of the day. It could not have been much worse, but at least the new ball was due in the morning. Australia were 208/2 as the players left the field.

As the days wore on, the weather seemed to get hotter. Certainly England's fielding became ever more slipshod and later, when all trace of optimism had faded, it was plain lethargic. Meanwhile, the Australian grip on the game never wavered. At the close of the second day they were still batting (503/6), Neil Harvey having played himself into form and emulating Arthur Morris with a big hundred. At one point an Australian wicket had not fallen for some 24 hours. Too late the England bowlers found an appropriate line to bowl – outside off stump – but by then the absence of a spin option was painfully evident. Both Tyson and Bedser had each conceded well over a hundred runs for just one wicket each.

By contrast the Australian bowling attack when England batted on the third day was balanced: incisive 'clinking' pace and varied, right- and left-arm spinners bowling off and leg breaks and googlies. By close on the Monday (day 3) England were tottering at 107/5, the cream of the batting long gone. The visitors' parlous state was somehow emphasised by the unexpected appearance of the injured Denis Compton, left hand voluminously bandaged, stepping down the pavilion steps when it seemed that the England first innings was over. He survived an equal number of balls and minutes (15) before Trevor Bailey was out for 88, his hopes of a century gone. Only four Englishmen reached double figures, and Bailey had scored almost half England's runs. The Essex all-rounder was a man, according to Hutton, who 'didn't wilt under pressure'. He was less well regarded by the Australian opposition. Keith Miller, in 1953, had commented that when he was dead 'they'll find the name of Trevor Bailey written on my heart' so large did he figure in those days of English resistance.[49]

The decision by Ian Johnson, the Australian captain, to enforce the follow-on was not a difficult one, with English morale so low. The deficit was 411 runs. Hutton and Simpson were soon out and, even when rain fell, it offered no prospect of saving the English cause. It merely served to spice the wicket up. By the first day of December, approaching 4.15 in the afternoon, with rain in the air, the England second innings ended on 257: defeat by an innings and 154 runs. Thanks to Bill Edrich (88) and Peter May (44) the English had made a marginally better fist of it second time around. But prospects for the remainder of the series did not look good. It had been a game, in Alan Ross's phrase, of 'five wounding days' but he could see scope for a change of fortunes: 'No-balls in this match cost us around 50 runs, dropped catches 200, slow running between the wickets another 30.'[50] Ross would remember Brisbane for many reasons: being 'soaked in perspiration'; having dinner with Peebles at the Queensland club; Surfer's Paradise with Freddie Brown; and most of all 'drinking beer late into the small hours with John Woodcock and Ronald Roberts', the three correspondents reflecting on what had gone wrong that day on the pitch.[51] After the event, John Arlott saw Hutton 'standing alone in the bar with a half pint of beer in his hand'. Arlott put an arm around the beaten captain's shoulder and

49 Cardus, op. cit., page 162.

50 Ross, op. cit., page 105.

51 Ross, op. cit., page 107.

commiserated. It got 'the wryest of smiles' in return, but Hutton 'refused a second half'.[52]

As for Len Hutton's decision to bowl first at Brisbane, it would be 48 years before an English captain followed the same perilous course: in 2002 Nasser Hussain put Australia in and watched in increasing dismay as the home side amassed 362/2 on the first day against a pace attack of Andrew Caddick and Matthew Hoggard.[53] It did not end well then either, with Hussain's England going on to lose the series 4-1. The question for Hutton and his men was: did they have the ammunition to come back from the humiliation at Brisbane?

***

In 1952 Roger Kahn, then a sportswriter with the *New York Herald Tribune*, toured the United States with the Brooklyn Dodgers baseball squad. It was, he thought, far 'beyond undertaking a newspaper assignment'. He believed he was 'joining a team'.[54] A young and impressionable New Yorker with a passion for the game, as well as being a Dodgers fan, he was in no doubts about the pleasures of the long assignment. 'The road with the Dodgers was a lonely, thrilling chaos, at once seductive, free and wild. There were no telephone bills to pay, no relatives to meet, no office to visit and no planning to suffer.'[55] Perhaps it was his youth that encouraged this sense of unalloyed freedom 'on the

52 Arlott, op. cit., page 234.

53 In the same period, Australia, by contrast, won the toss and chose to bowl first on three occasions at Brisbane: in 1982, 1986 and 1990. They lost once (1986). The Australian captains who made those decisions were Greg Chappell (1982) and Alan Border (1986 and 1990).

54 *The Boys of Summer* by Roger Kahn, page 4.

55 Kahn, op. cit., page 125.

road', whereas the cricket correspondents of 54/55, travelling alongside Hutton's men, were older, more hard-bitten and less likely to be seduced by the novelty of co-existing with the team, being an additional squad member. Many of them had played the game at the highest level: Peebles, Brown, Bowes. That and the chequered experience of wartime journeys necessarily coloured their perceptions of the crossing and recrossing of Australia, rendering them more phlegmatic.

John Arlott noted the difference in the relationship between players and writers when on tour, believing that, 'The reporter becomes more at one with the team.'[56] He thought it a by-product of being 'one of a small company in "enemy" territory'. Kahn was constantly struck by the novelty of his experiences when travelling and observing the players, whether it was the informed proximity to individual 'boys of summer' and the team management; the novelty of what could be seen of the American South viewed from the railroad; the eye-opening impact of the press box with its segregation of white and black writers; or the crowds. In Mobile, for example, 'most of the grandstand was reserved for whites … the black humanity … stood and squatted and bent and sat wedged two to a seat'.[57] The United States, South Africa, the West Indies: each country's sport manifested too many such images of injustice.

The men and one woman travelling with MCC in 1954/55 across the vast land mass of Australia were dutiful and thorough in their accounts of the cricket they saw. Beyond the boundary fence and the press box there was also much to hold their attention, although necessarily what made its way into despatches

56 Arlott, op. cit., page 10.

57 Kahn, op. cit., page 107.

home was restricted by the needs of demanding editorial staff behind their London desks. Nonetheless, beyond the dutiful prose about weather, pitches, selection and the day-to-day combat between bat and ball, a picture emerges of 1950s Australia from their accounts of the game. Thus there are observations about landscape – the 'heavy palm trees' at Sydney and the weather with its sudden variations of temperature; the cities – John Arlott thought Adelaide was a 'city of churches' and observed 'shop window announcements in German', while Margeret Hughes thought Melbourne was 'staid and stuffy' and fleas were 'commonplace' in Sydney.[58] The crowds in Brisbane were 'almost truculently Australian', Arlott thought, while Evelyn Maitland Wellings (known as 'Lyn" or EM Wellings) was critical of the 'numerous larrikins' in the crowd and the effects of too much beer.[59] Margaret Hughes commented on the legislation obliging bars to close at six in the evening, remarking on the difference between bars in Australia and pubs back home. Its consequence, she wrote, was that 'in the cities there was no nightlife after eight-thirty' and that Australian men arrive home at night after work 'so full of beer' that dinner is invariably spoiled.

The issue of excessive drinking was a matter of current debate in the country. After the debacle at Brisbane was over, Hughes flew back to Sydney, then went on to Melbourne where she was struck by the debate about the Liquor Referendum, a vote on the 6pm bar closure. The main party, meanwhile, was soberly travelling in the opposite direction, all too aware that there were just over two weeks before the principal battle was to be rejoined at the Sydney Cricket Ground. Whatever recovery and planning

58 Hughes, op. cit., pages 49 and 55.

59 *The Ashes Retained* by EM Wellings, page 95.

time Len Hutton would have wished for in the aftermath of that sorry affair in Queensland, it would not have chimed with what the stony-hearted tour planners had determined. England's cricketers and their shadows, the press, were obliged to fly north some 300 miles to Rockhampton in Queensland, just inside the Tropic of Capricorn. It was hot – average temperatures are in the early thirties in December – humid and frequently wet. Air travel, it was felt by the cricket authorities, was 'more restful and cheaper'. Hutton was certainly of the view that too much air travel was 'not a very good thing for touring teams'.[60] The preference was for it to be an option 'only for the very long intermediary journeys – Perth to Adelaide and Australia to New Zealand'.[61]

Faced with the reality of the tour schedule, Alan Ross abandoned his personal commitment to travel by train which he still thought the best way to see the true nature of Australia. Instead, he flew in a DC3, then struggled to sleep that night, sweating heavily beneath a mosquito net. The cricket ground at Rockhampton was rustic, the pitch itself dropped in and the outfield was 'dusty and uneven', while the fielders would need to tread with care since 'various kinds of cattle had left their cards'.[62] Game won, there was little respite in the schedule: rather a long flight south to Canberra for a one-day game; then to Melbourne before travelling to Sydney for the second Test beginning on 17 December. Between the two Tests the MCC party had been required to travel some 2,000 miles.

Something in the way England played their cricket needed to change if the sad outcome at Brisbane was not to be replicated

60 MCC Archive, 1954/55 tour file, captain's report.

61 MCC Archive, 1954/55 tour file.

62 Ross, op. cit., page 108.

through the rest of the series. Margaret Hughes, with the benefit of hindsight, pinpointed the moment when the tide turned. The crucial day was Monday, 13 December when, with the next Test just four days away, Frank Tyson cut his run-up by half and still bowled at the highest pace with significantly greater accuracy and no loss of venom. It had been Alf Gover, the former Surrey and England quick bowler (and in Australia working for the *Sunday Mirror*) who first suggested the change. Len Hutton, when facing Tyson in the Perth nets, had noticed that the fast bowler lost no appreciable speed when using a shorter run. Moreover, he gained greater accuracy and could bowl significantly longer spells. After a gruelling second day in the Brisbane Test the England captain – heeding Gover's advice – suggested that Tyson use a shorter run and the Northants man was happy to give it a try, being used to such an approach from his days playing league cricket and in both the army and at university. MCC put in a solid batting display against Victoria after winning the toss, making 312 on a rain-affected wicket. Then Tyson took six wickets (for 68), with five of the dismissals being with deliveries that hit the stumps. He was suddenly not only blisteringly quick but accurate as well. His 6-68 was his best return to date and one correspondent at least thought his pace faster than the great Harold Larwood in his prime.

The bad weather that had taken time out of the drawn game in Melbourne was a factor in Sydney too where there had been violent storms that week. Before the Test began there was an intense thunderstorm overnight and the first day was one of drizzle and indifferent light. Correspondents drew muttered comparisons with Manchester's Old Trafford while outside the ground's locked gates there were long queues, people disconsolately wearing raincoats and holding umbrellas. On a day which would have suited Alec Bedser's medium pace – dark, heavy cloud and a green top – he was judged unfit, his shingles taking much longer to clear up than had been expected. On the plus side England named a more balanced side with the spin option of both Wardle and Appleyard, a third seamer, Bailey, opening the batting with Hutton, Edrich at number six and Evans back behind the stumps. The wicketkeeper was, in many ways, the ideal tourist. Len Hutton described how 'he'd be keeping wicket all day in Sydney, 95 in the shade, and never miss a thing … [then] … have a bath, get dressed, have a drink, sit down at the piano in the hotel and start to play. He was ready for the evening.'[63]

Blithely ignoring the lesson of Brisbane, when Hutton had put the opposition in, the Australian captain Arthur Morris chose to do the same. Arlott, for one, was amazed by the decision. England were soon 19/2 with Bailey and May both gone, but Graveney and Hutton managed to survive till lunch when the score was 34/2 – 'surely one of the slowest openings in all Test cricket'.[64] Progress was achingly slow with England 'cautious in the extreme' according to Ian Peebles.[65] Somehow in the early afternoon batting seemed fraught with risk and watching England trying to establish themselves in the session was nerve-racking, with the batters not entirely to be trusted. Alan Ross, for example, thought Tom Graveney to be 'a player of yacht-like character, beautiful in calm seas, yet at the mercy of every change of weather'.[66] Then the more resilient of the two, Len Hutton, was caught at leg slip playing an authentic

63 *Cricket: Wit, Wickets and Wisdom,* ed. Richard Knott.

64 Arlott, op. cit., page 61.

65 *The Ashes 1954-1955* by Ian Peebles, page 78.

66 Ross, op. cit., page 131.

shot, the catch by Alan Davidson so good that Hutton walked off slowly, in apparent disbelief. That was soon followed by the end of Graveney's innings and thereafter wickets continued to fall, leaving England in disarray at tea on 94/7 and glad of a flurry of rain which took them off the field. A last-wicket stand of 43 between Wardle (35 runs of 'rustic comedy' according to Arlott) and Brian Statham saw England reach 154, hardly an improvement on the grim events at Brisbane. Before the close Trevor Bailey had claimed the wicket of the Australian captain, leaving the home side at 18/1 and apparently firmly in control.

There was change in the air, evident before play started on the Saturday, with the dampness of that gloomy first day gone, and the atmosphere altogether lighter. On a pitch whose colour reminded Ian Peebles 'of an unpolished tan shoe' it was Trevor Bailey who made the first inroads, taking two wickets either side of lunch after Tyson and Statham had failed to make an early breakthrough. At lunch the Australians were only 66 behind, with eight wickets standing and seemingly retaining control of the game: perhaps nothing had changed since they had taken that initial stranglehold at Brisbane.

During the course of the afternoon the game – and the series – was turned on its head. By tea Australia's top five were all gone and Richie Benaud and Ron Archer were left as precarious as 'curates on a dowager's Regency chairs'.[67] The key figure was Frank Tyson with a spell of whirlwind pace produced from his shortened run and reducing the normally boisterous Sydney crowd on the Hill to an uneasy quiet. England took the new ball after tea and Australia fell away to 228 all out at the

67 Ross, op. cit., page 135.

close of the second day, a lead of just 72. The old black and white footage of Tyson does not do him justice: he seems to struggle to the wicket on a curved run-up, slightly leaning forward, each gathering step almost tentative, as if his feet hurt, while his head leans back over a wiry frame lost in a voluminous shirt. There is no mistaking, however, the speed at which the unhelmeted figure at the other end is hurried by the pace and bounce the slim Englishman delivered. It was Frank Tyson who changed the course of the game in one afternoon of the highest pace.

On Monday, the third day, it seemed for a time that despite the bowlers' efforts, the batsmen would not be able to drive home the advantage. Bailey soon went, while Hutton was no more than 'ruminative' as England slowly chipped away at the Australian lead. By lunch with the sun appearing for the first time for days the deficit was still 16, with Bailey, Hutton and a runless Tom Graveney all gone. On balance the Australians were still in the ascendancy. Cold lobster at lunch did not warm the spirits of the English press contingent, whose overwhelming view was that the heroics of Tyson and the other bowlers was not enough to stave off a second defeat. Then, against the odds, May and Cowdrey built a partnership and after the latter was out for a well-made fifty, the day ended at 204/4 (May 98*) with England's lead standing at 130.

May got his hundred early on the next day. But it was an unpromising morning, drizzle obscuring the view over Botany Bay for a while and there was a brief stoppage of play. When it resumed Arthur Morris delayed taking the new ball until the outfield had lost its slick wetness. But there was no denying Australia's gathering dominance, a feeling reinforced by the sickening blow that Frank Tyson took on the back of his head courtesy of Ray Lindwall. Two ambulancemen escorted the

Englishman from the field. Wickets continued to fall, five of them for just 28 runs. The much-shaken Tyson surprisingly returned, following an X-ray in hospital, only to be bowled by Lindwall. On what had become a placid pitch the target of 223 set by England looked eminently achievable. At 72/2 at the close, Australia looked to be back in control.

A corn-coloured pitch, blue sky and a gentle breeze suggested the day would be one of a slow English death. That it wasn't stemmed from a remarkable spell of bowling at extreme pace from a bruised Frank Tyson, a veritable typhoon on this fine day of Australian summer. His 6-85 in the Australian innings of 184 gave England victory by 38 runs and, to the surprise of the lobster-eaters of the day before, levelled the series. Hutton had exorcised his flawed decision at Brisbane by captaining with 'patience, skill and admirable control'[68], although for those basking in the English success that night over oysters and fizz, it was interesting that the English spinners, seen as unwisely omitted from the Brisbane Test, only bowled 17 overs at Sydney, taking just one wicket. Johnny Wardle's contribution was a token four overs in the second innings. The game was won by raw English pace. Arlott's view was that the English bowlers were now bowling like Australians, 'putting the ball up to the bat ... along the line of the off stump'.[69] It had ended two days before Christmas and the celebrating Alan Ross 'felt an elation altogether out of proportion', the result he surmised of 'being present at a rebirth'.[70] Certainly Hutton's men had come back from something close to cricketing death.

---

68 Ross, op. cit., page 149.

69 Arlott, op. cit., page 83.

70 Ross, op. cit., page 150.

6

A Tale of Three Cities

Melbourne, Adelaide, Sydney, December 1954–March 1955

ENGLAND'S CRICKETERS' gift to themselves that Christmas was to finish the Sydney Test a day early, giving them four clear days before the contest resumed. On Christmas Eve Frank Tyson and the kitman, George Duckworth, paid a visit to Harold Larwood's home in the Sydney suburb of Kensington. Larwood was a boyhood hero to Tyson after the former's crucial role in the 'Bodyline' series and had emigrated to Australia four years earlier. There was an unfortunate backdrop to the meeting, since it seemed that Larwood had been shunned by the England tourists of 1951, the captain Freddie Brown allegedly shutting the dressing room door in Larwood's face.[71] Tyson and Larwood, however, shared a couple of beers together, some from Larwood's fridge and some brought by Duckworth.

The tourists ate Christmas lunch together at the Oceanic Hotel, dressed as if by decree in white shirts and ties, wearing a variety of party hats. A photograph from the *Sydney Morning*

---

71 See *Harold Larwood* by Duncan Hamilton, page 293.

Herald shows them sitting cheek by jowl in a room of draped streamers, pulled crackers, balloons and assorted bottles on the table. It looks a long way from home and not everyone is smiling, the broadest grin belonging to Trevor Bailey. Later, they had the chance to speak to their families over the phone, disembodied voices thousands of miles distant.

The brief window between Tests also benefited the travelling correspondents. Ian Peebles spent Christmas Day at Eleanora near Sydney with friends, at the home of someone he had met in India before the war. He was entertained with a 'turkey and plum pudding' lunch, and beguiled by the two daughters in the house who still believed in Santa Claus and reminded him of his own family at home. Once they had eaten they 'went and had a warm dip in the sea, just below' the house.[72]

Peebles was a much-travelled man. The first Scot to play cricket for England, he was tall and had the perfect spinner's action, though later he was much troubled by shoulder problems. Early in his career he had played cricket for Hampstead in London, thanks to the help of Cecil Beaton's father, Ernest. His career as a cricketer included being named a *Wisden* Cricketer of the Year in 1931; bowling once in tandem with a future prime minister of England (Alec Douglas-Home); and having a dismissal reported in the South African *Cape Times* as Peebles absent bathing, 0.

Peebles had been briefly 'one of the most formidable bowlers in the world'. Don Bradman, writing about a series between Australia and England more than two decades before, noted Peebles' splendid bowling, admitting that he 'gave us (but

72 Peebles, op. cit., page 115.

particularly myself) a very anxious time'.[73] Peebles was a veteran tourist who would later recall that, when sailing from England to play cricket, they 'danced, played desk games, fed like fighting cocks and enjoyed brief shipboard romances'.[74] This was the same tour in 1930 that prompted Lady Astor in the House of Commons to remark that 'if the MCC drank less they would win more matches'. He captained Middlesex in 1939 but missed the last game of that season in order to go to the local army recruiting centre, with Jim Swanton.

Alan Ross, struck by how different an Australian Christmas was compared to life in the chill north, drove with friends an hour northward out of Sydney to Palm Beach, a confusion of sandy beaches on gently curving bays, secret inlets and wooded slopes, with in all directions the clear blue water of the Pacific and clean, white surf. The weather was no more than pleasantly warm with a sharp breeze ruffling the ocean as far as the horizon. How different from the intense bustle of pre-Christmas Sydney with its noise, swirling crowds, and on Christmas Eve, the wail of fire-engine sirens across the city. 'Instead, here in late afternoon the sea turns silver, the trees blacken above the rockline,' wrote Ross. Less than a week before, he had been caught up with thousands in the unfolding drama at the SCG; now he felt a sense of serenity, something 'rare in the Australian landscape'.[75]

On Boxing Day Ross and Ian Peebles flew down to Melbourne together with cricket at the front of their minds once more. It was a bumpy, turbulent flight culminating in a

73 *Farewell to Cricket* by Don Bradman, page 32. Bradman's comment relates to the Manchester Test match in July 1930.

74 Peebles, op. cit., page 80.

75 Ross, op. cit., page 152.

nervy landing as a crosswind swept the runway. Melbourne was disturbingly hot, the sky dull, headache-inducing, and the atmosphere heavy. As if to underline the strange threat of the weather, the temperature rapidly plummeted, falling some 30 degrees between its noontide peak and the early evening. Beyond the city's boundaries bush fires burned, smoke clouding the sky. The third Test, due to start at the MCG on New Year's Eve, would be played it seemed in unforgiving heat.

Hutton felt unwell on the first morning of the Test – suffering from 'fibrositis and a cold, white as a sheet and shivering'.[76] He needed to be encouraged out of bed, by Godfrey Evans for one and by the manager Geoffrey Howard. Howard was nothing if not conscientious: 'Ambassador, press relations officer, selector, travel coordinator, banker (albeit operating from a personal overdraft), gentle disciplinarian, convenor of the boisterous Saturday night club, even psychologist.'[77] Hutton had been insisting, it seems, that Peter May should assume the captaincy and that he should stand down. Evans was unflinching. 'Exactly what the Aussies want,' was the wicketkeeper's response. It was enough to drag Hutton out of his despondent state. Not long after he was padding up prior to walking out with Bill Edrich to open the England innings.[78]

Hutton's decision to bat after winning the toss restored some normality to the proceedings. With Denis Compton in the side for Graveney the only change (and Bedser once more omitted), the expectation was that England, buoyed by the events at Sydney and in clear, blue light, would drive their advantage

76 *Len Hutton: The Biography* by Gerald Howat, page 156.

77 Chalke, op. cit., page 258.

78 *Godfrey Evans* by Christopher Sandford, page 129.

home. Instead, they fumbled their way to 41/4 within the hour, the doughty heart of the batting – Hutton, Edrich, May and Compton – all blown away by Miller and Lindwall.

Without 102 from Colin Cowdrey in his second Test match, England would have been contemplating defeat by the end of the first day. Even then the total of 191 was 'a sorry show' according to *Wisden*, partly excused by the 'sporting' nature of the pitch. From the start it was cracked and had a distinctly glassy look, while the ball seemed to retain its red sheen for longer than usual. It was unpredictable and spiteful too. The second day was windless and blisteringly hot, a day when being in pavilion shade was infinitely preferable to fielding under an unforgiving sun. Hutton wisely had England's bowlers bowling in short spells and they slowly chipped away at the Australian batting order. At the close the home side were only three runs behind with two wickets remaining. Throughout the series the Australians outshone the visitors in several areas of the game. One was in fielding, while the other was the contribution of runs from tailenders. On the third morning, the last four batters eked out a 40-run lead.

Sunday's rest day was anything but peaceful, with accusations of the pitch being watered and a subsequent inquiry denying any such malpractice. There were suspicions of dark curatorial arts before the game, Ian Peebles writing in the *Manchester Evening Chronicle* that the MCG had recently seen 'some bother about the pitches here'.[79] He noted on the Monday morning that, while the weekend had seen no rain and the pitch had been dry on the Saturday, it had become 'so moist that [players'] spikes sank into it and left a black mark'.[80]

---

79 Peebles, op. cit., page 95.

80 Peebles, op. cit., page 104.

He was not alone in his suspicions. Hutton, in his end-of-tour report, noted that 'the pitch was certainly showing signs of breaking'.[81] As well as the playing strip, there were problems with the weather. Margaret Hughes would never forget the Sunday: 'The scorching heat reached 107° … [with] a blistering dry northerly gale.'[82] It had been 94° at midnight.

The third day was even hotter – the 'hottest day ever recorded', Alan Ross claimed – but slowly England, led by the 'commanding' Peter May (91 in almost three and a half hours) batting with the captain, took some control of the game. England's slow progress was greeted by 'fans banging empty beer cans on the MCG's concrete terracing'.[83] The fifth day began with the home side needing 165 to win, with eight wickets remaining. The sun was relentless, shining 'like a searchlight through low sultry clouds', testing the England pacemen's endurance but on a wearing pitch with uneven bounce the Australians were dismissed for 111, falling short by 128 runs. Appleyard and Wardle might have been expected to cause problems on that pitch, but in the event it was Frank Tyson whose fiery pace destroyed the Australians. Eight wickets fell for 36 in 80 minutes; Tyson's seven wickets cost only 27 runs, and *Wisden* described him as having 'blazed through them like a bushfire'.[84] In his diary on 5 January the fast bowler wrote, 'Perhaps the luckiest and certainly the happiest day of my life. I bowled out Australia before lunch!'[85] After the win, the players attended a barbecue, the MCC men in jackets and ties.

---

81 MCC Archive, 1954/55 tour file, captain's report.

82 Hughes, op. cit., page 107.

83 *Spirit of Cricket* by Mike Brearley, page 154.

84 *Wisden Cricketers' Almanack, 1956*, page 841.

85 *A Typhoon Called Tyson* by Frank Tyson, page 117.

Alan Ross had struggled through the Test, having been under the weather, literally and metaphorically, for several weeks. The pain he was in detracted from a famous victory and hindered his ability to share in the celebratory mood in the English section of the press box. He was eventually diagnosed with appendicitis and faced the prospect of an operation, a sobering proposition as he roamed anxiously around the streets of Melbourne on foot or by car. His thoughts were divided between England's cricketing rebirth and an Australian surgeon's knife.

There were more than three weeks before the next Test during which time MCC found themselves on the road – and at sea – for the traditional week's cricket in Tasmania, where MCC seemed keen, like the Royal Navy, to fly the flag. There had been official concerns after the 1950/51 tour that the England captain would not play on the island – Compton had stood in as captain in 1951 – but Hutton played in both fixtures, at Hobart and Launceston. Preoccupied by the lingering discomfort of his grumbling appendix, Alan Ross took time away from what was run-of-the-mill cricket to visit friends on a sheep station in the remote territory halfway between Hobart and Launceston. He was not enamoured of the island's hot and dusty interior, best suited he thought to 'ascetics [and] solitaries' and for people so keen to socialise that it was enough to galvanise them into driving 'a hundred miles along bad roads to a cocktail party'.[86]

However, by 24 January he was in Adelaide's Calvary Hospital about to lose both his appendix and crucial days at the cricket. He would not be at the Adelaide Oval on the 28th to watch Australia win the toss and choose to bat.

---

86 Ross, op. cit., page 189.

The Adelaide Test was played over five days of great heat – 'unbearable' for John Arlott. There had been no rain for 22 days and the only solace for cricketers and spectators was a variable breeze. To make conditions worse for the persevering and perspiring English bowlers on the first morning, the wicket proved to be placid, while the atmosphere was humid. No wicket fell before lunch, and by the end of a slow day, Hutton's instinctively defensive tactics and cautious Australian batting had resulted in an unconvincing 161/4.

The weather was slightly cooler on the following morning with a few scattered grey clouds. Despite Brian Statham struggling with a damaged toenail, the English bowlers grafted away, taking three more wickets by lunch when the score had reached 221/7. At one point it looked as if the home side would be dismissed for under 250, but a minor recovery saw them make a competitive total of 323. The England reply began auspiciously and Hutton and Edrich put on 60 together in what proved to be the best opening stand of the tour. With the exception of Peter May, out for a single, the English batting was comfortingly secure with Hutton's 80 the top score. The sense of calm was soon blown away on the fourth morning, however, courtesy of the new ball and the overall lead at the end of the England innings was only 18 when it had promised to be significantly more.

The fifth day saw 12 wickets fall, ten Australian (all out for 111 with the wickets shared) and two in the England reply – Hutton and Edrich gone early chasing only 94 to win. Three more wickets fell on the final day, but May, Compton and Trevor Bailey saw the visitors through to a third successive victory. The Ashes were retained. On that concluding day, Alan Ross, out of his hospital bed, was able 'to walk, rather sedately, to a seat in the sun and watch'. Much of the Test he had followed on the radio to the background of whirring fans in his hospital ward, the soothing rustle of the nuns' robes, the footsteps of nurses as they drifted through the ward, and the astringent smell of anaesthetic. He had seen many solicitous visitors including Colin Cowdrey, the manager Geoffrey Howard, Alf Gover and other members of the press box, including Swanton, complete with 'his admirable daily accounts' of play, as well as Lyn Wellings and John Woodcock, whom he had last seen in a Hobart hospital suffering from a duodenal ulcer. Ross's wife, Jennifer and his stepdaughter had arrived by sea, unaware that he was hospitalised, and they enjoyed a post-Test, post-operative convalescence at a friend's house by the sea, looking out over a beach under yellow cliffs, the light crystal clear, a sparkling ocean and 'waves curling on sand the colour of bronze'.[87]

And so to Sydney for the final Test where persistent rain – even occasional ice – fell from an indigo-coloured sky. There was no play at all for three days and large areas of New South Wales were flooded. Sydney was a city of 'grey light, dripping foliage and shadowed waters'.[88] The cricket, after so much time had been lost, was notable for a fine hundred from Tom Graveney amidst a solid England first innings, declared at 371/7. Len Hutton asked the Australians to follow on. It was the first time that had happened since August 1938 at the Oval when the Yorkshireman had scored 364 out of England's 903/7 declared. Some 16 years later, another Yorkshireman, Johnny Wardle, took eight wickets in a match where, in Ross's words, 'Australia were

87 Ross, op. cit., page 206.
88 Arlott, op. cit., page 213.

again made to look a shabby side.'[89] Shabby and ashen, he might have added.

***

The tourists and their followers had been away from home for six months and in England the spring was drawing ever closer. The tour schedule, however, remained unforgiving: instead of a rapid return to the northern hemisphere, there was a further journey south across the Tasman Sea, for most of the squad at least. Jim McConnon had returned home early because of a hand injury suffered in Hobart, soon after he had recovered from a blow to the groin when he had been fielding close to the bat.[90] Alan Ross summed up the spin bowler's miserable tour: 'He travelled some 25,000 miles to bowl 83 first-class overs and take eight wickets.'[91] Alec Bedser and Denis Compton also went directly home.

On the final evening of the Sydney Test John Arlott invited Frank Tyson to dinner with the girlfriend the fast bowler had met on the boat. The couple had met just two days out of Tilbury on the journey to Australia back in the autumn. Arlott and Tyson had developed a friendship spending time together on tour trawling Australia's second-hand bookshops. It was an emotional evening with Tyson's Australian girlfriend extremely upset by the imminent parting. The England man would later describe it as 'one of the worst nights of my inexperienced existence'.[92] She was, he said, his 'first real girlfriend', not a phrase that seems to chime with the image of a fiery quick bowler. Arlott had also

---

89 Ross, op. cit., page 225.

90 He would retire from the game before the 1955 season, for 'business reasons', see *Wisden Cricketers' Almanack 1956*, page 567.

91 Ross, op. cit., page 236.

92 Tyson, op. cit., page 214.

invited Charles Fortune and his wife who found herself consoling the young girl, the evening overshadowed by Tyson's imminent departure with the rest of the tour party on a plane leaving for New Zealand at half past midnight. The pain of the parting was made worse by the fact that Tyson was obliged to travel to the airport on the team bus while the sobbing young woman made her own way out to the airfield. A long wait followed: TEAL flight 576 was postponed due to fog at Christchurch Airport.

They eventually landed in New Zealand in the morning, after a difficult flight. MCC would play two Test matches as well as games against Canterbury and Wellington. All four games were won comfortably and so the 1954/55 tour was over. There was no direct return home, nor another ocean sailing. Instead, a series of air flights circling the globe: a Pan Am Constellation to Fiji on 29 March, then Honolulu, San Francisco and arriving in New York on 4 April. As for the press, a number returned by boat – the *Orsova* again – Peebles, Swanton, the Bedser twins and John Woodcock: 'entertaining company' sharing the same table for dinner.[93]

A month later Frank Tyson found himself playing in Bradford for Northamptonshire against Yorkshire, no doubt part of him pleased that he was required to bowl just eight overs in the match on a spinners' wicket. There would be time enough to build up speed for the summer of 1955.

93 Peebles, op. cit., page 191.

7

The Accession of May

South Africa, 1956/57

'A CRICKET tour,' wrote Alan Ross, 'is a series of these transitions.'[94] As he wrote that he was contemplating the Sussex landscape around his house in Clayton – the Downs, the land 'grazing-green, corn-coloured and splashed with trees', the sprawl of country from Ditchling Beacon down to the coast at Brighton, its gradual shift in look and feel. He was reflecting too on the impact of travelling with cricketers across the wide spread of the country and what that teaches the cricket correspondent. For the returning England players after so long and distant a journey back from Australia there was much to reflect upon with a new cricket season, with both its anticipated and unforeseen changes, only weeks away. Frank Tyson – one of five England men to have had an outstanding tour along with Statham, Cowdrey, May and Godfrey Evans according to Ross – was wondering whether his Sydney girlfriend would indeed write to him as she had promised. Others like Compton and Edrich were contemplating whether form and fitness would be good enough to make the next tour

94 *Cape Summer* by Alan Ross, page 13.

given their ages. Denis Compton was to have a kneecap removed in November 1955. By contrast Colin Cowdrey was concerned about the fact that he was in line for National Service on his return to England and would soon find himself required to report to RAF Cardington in Bedfordshire.

As for the captain, having been the critical pivot for his England team through the last tour, he had much to preoccupy him on his return. He and his wife Dorothy did not fly back home with the rest of the tour party, returning instead by boat. Yorkshire had given him permission to miss the opening of the new English season. He arrived back in early May 1955, feeling fit and well, but aware that he would be 39 on his next birthday, alive too to the fact that his batting form in Australia – he had averaged only a shade over 24 in the Tests – had been far below his high standards and markedly less impressive than his obdurate, focused captaincy had been.

May's appointment as captain for the home series against South Africa was announced on 23 May. He had not captained before, either at Cambridge or for his county. Len Hutton had played only his second game of the season five days before – under Norman Yardley's captaincy – in a convincing win over Somerset at Headingley, scoring 11 and 66. But at the end of the first day against the South Africans he had retired ill with his score at 2 not out and he did not bat again in the match. In his resignation letter he wrote that 'after a few days' cricket in this climate my pains returned'.[95] He revealed the extent of the problem in a letter to Ross. 'I am writing this at 3am unable to sleep,' he wrote, blaming the pain down his right leg. It was the

95 Howat, op. cit., page 168.

end of an era and marked a return to England playing under an amateur captain. This changing of the guard meant a young man in his mid-20s stepping into the studded white boots of a tired man approaching 40.

The summer of 1955 saw England play five home Tests against South Africa, a series eventually won by the home side by three Tests to two. Inevitably, the Ashes-winning side of the previous winter had begun to break up: no Hutton; Frank Tyson could only play in two Tests; there was a continuing problem over the choice of opening batsmen – Alan Ross referred to their 'unvarying moderateness', while Tom Graveney was unable to turn his great promise into consistent success.

There was no full-blown MCC tour in 1955/56, although Jim Swanton took a group of players to the West Indies in March 1956 for 'an auspicious frolic' under the captaincy of Colin Cowdrey and including Frank Tyson and Graveney from the Ashes-winning squad. There was also an 'A' team tour to Pakistan led by Derbyshire's Donald Carr, a series more noted for the bad blood created than for the quality of the cricket. Sparked by the touring party's resentful anger over a series of what it judged to be dubious umpiring decisions, a group of English players poured a bucket of water over one of the umpires. Predictably there was fury, resentment and an exchange of anxious cables between London and Pakistan including a suggestion that the tourists might end the tour forthwith. It would not be the last time that tensions threatened to bring an abrupt ending to a tour in Pakistan.[96] Moreover, the amateur/professional divide was still very much in evidence. At one point on the tour the players took the train

96 See *The Tour* by Simon Wilde, pages 183–4.

from Lahore to Bahawalpur. The professionals and amateurs were segregated, the former given inferior accommodation for the night. When Carr 'let the troops [professionals] out' they emerged 'coated in red sand and gasping'.[97]

The struggle for the Ashes was resumed in the summer of 1956. After the away success of 1955 the expectation might have been that the English pace attack would be the decisive factor once again, but in the event it was the off spin of Jim Laker – not selected for the winter tour in 1955 – that proved decisive, the Surrey man taking 46 wickets at 9.6 each, including all ten in the second innings at Manchester – while Tyson, having fractured his foot in the first game, only bowled 14 overs in the series.

***

At the end of the summer of 1956, three days after England's decisive Ashes victory at the Oval, Frank Tyson was in Scarborough playing for the Players against the Gentlemen in the town's cricket festival. The game was won by the Players – the professionals – against an XI that was demonstrably weaker on paper, though perhaps more gentlemanly. Intriguingly, the two batsmen who scored hundreds in the game – the amateur Bill Edrich (133) and the professional Tom Graveney (124) – were both omitted from the 16 names in MCC's party for the winter tour of South Africa which was due to set off in a month's time. Tyson had a quiet game, taking a couple of wickets and scoring just a single when he batted. On his mind, apart from his cricketing form (injury had limited him to a bit part in the summer's Tests), was a love affair. The letters from the woman

97 Wilde, op. cit., pages 183–4.

he had met on the boat out may have dried up, but he had also met someone else during the rain-soaked match in Melbourne in December. Ursula had come over to England and was at the Scarborough Festival where the couple made a pact: 'There we decided that if, at the conclusion of the South African tour … we still felt the same way about one another, we should become engaged.'[98]

The party selected for the tour differed markedly from its predecessor to Australia: no Hutton, Bedser, Reg Simpson, Graveney, Bob Appleyard, Jim McConnon, Vic Wilson, Keith Andrew or Bill Edrich – about half of the successful Ashes-winning group of just two years before. There were two extremely contentious omissions which the press took pleasure in highlighting. Gloucestershire's Tom Graveney, who had topped the country's batting averages, was left out; so too Fred Trueman, who had taken 135 wickets in the season at an average of just over 17. Graveney believed that his omission stemmed from the veto of the chairman of selectors, Gubby Allen, who 'ran MCC as his personal fiefdom' and who was regarded as much preferring players with the 'right' background.[99] Despite the evidence to the contrary, his elegance as a batter, and his proven record – those 2,397 runs at 49.93 that summer – there was something about the Gloucestershire man that the all-powerful Allen could not stomach.

The squad included the two spinners surprisingly omitted from the previous tour: the Surrey pair of Jim Laker and Tony Lock. The remaining places were taken by a left-handed wicketkeeper/batter from Essex, Brian Taylor; his county

98 Tyson, op. cit., page 257.

99 *Touched by Greatness* by Andrew Murtagh, page 139.

captain, another batter, Doug Insole; two Sussex men – Jim Parks and Alan Oakman – and the Worcestershire opening bat Peter Richardson. Taylor, Parks and Oakman would not play in any of the Tests. The squad's average age was 28.6, much the same as the group setting out on the *Orsova* two years before.

Jim Swanton warmed to the fact that the captain, Peter May, vice-captain (Doug Insole) and manager (Freddie Brown) were all Cambridge men. There were those, however, who raised an eyebrow at Insole's elevation to the vice-captaincy. He had played only three Tests to date and averaged an underwhelming 15.2 with the bat. Neither Swanton nor Alan Ross were convinced by Insole, the former doubting the Essex man's technique while Ross took the view that he wasn't of Test class. For the tourists' selection group there were some tricky decisions: who should open the batting with Richardson? Lock or Wardle as the left-arm spinner? Was the 16-man squad able to cope with one or two serious injuries?

The MCC party sailed from Southampton aboard the *Edinburgh Castle* at the beginning of October 1956 with the prospect of being away for six months, not returning until late March 1957. Amongst the correspondents on board were Swanton, John Woodcock (*The Times*), Charles Fortune and Rex Alston of the BBC.[100] Neither John Arlott nor Margaret Hughes were among the party. The ship was the same one in which Ian Peebles had travelled to South Africa back in 1930 when, among the professionals in the squad, was George Duckworth of Lancashire, now MCC's scorer and baggage-master. The tour tradition of evening dances, quoits and deck

100 In his book about the tour, *The MCC Tour of South Africa 1956–57,* Charles Fortune listed 16 names in the 'official Press Party'.

tennis, brief flirtations and committed eating for England was carried on. Godfrey Evans, wicketkeeper by profession and wag by inclination, would have assumed his traditional role as master of ceremonies, leading the MCC team on fancy-dress night. He would appear as Carmen Miranda 'beautifully made up, carrying a basket of fruit precariously balanced on his head' and then, with team victory assured, he would lead a 'never-ending dance through every corner of the ship'.[101] After two weeks at sea when time seemed to have slowed down and cricket had been briefly set aside, the MCC squad arrived in Cape Town. It was 18 October 1956.

Alan Ross was a member of the official press party but he travelled separately, arriving in time for the first Test in early December. He had moved to a new house in Clayton in Sussex shortly before the tour to Australia in 1954 and the pull of the place was understandably powerful. He had paid £6,000 for the house and relished that fact that it was in Sussex, somewhere that he had dreamed of when he was at sea in wartime. The very word 'Sussex' would send a shiver down his back.[102] He fondly remembered that the best part of the summer of 1956 had been before the Test series against Australia had got under way. The month of May in Sussex meant 'meals on the terrace, the wistaria rioting above us, tulips and polyanthus striping the walls as the daffodils and narcissi died down at the foot of the apple trees'.[103] But cricketing tourists do not choose when or where their work must be done. The Australians in that same month were faced

101 The description is from Colin Cowdrey's address at the memorial service for Godfrey Evans at Canterbury Cathedral on 30 September 1999. See *Wisden, 2000*, page 83. Evans had died that May, aged 78.

102 *Coastwise Lights* by Alan Ross, page 192.

103 *Cape Summer* by Alan Ross, page 23.

with cold winds and rain in the opening games of that summer tour at Worcester, Leicester and Bradford. The *Observer's* cricket correspondent will have reflected on the idyll that was Clayton in springtime when he faced the oven-like heat and gales the following autumn in South Africa.

Ross travelled out to South Africa by sea a month after the MCC party. On 23 November, while the tourists were playing Rhodesia in Salisbury, his ship was in Grand Canary. He missed Peter May's chanceless 206 in MCC's heavyweight total of 501 that day as well as the subsequent overwhelming victory. For Jim Swanton that win marked the end of the tour's honeymoon period. Meanwhile, Ross's ship continued south over a blue ocean, the correspondent seeing dolphins, the occasional shark, gulls and porpoises, as well as the dark hulls of oil tankers diverted from their usual waters by the political uproar over the Suez Canal. The midnight hours encouraged the ship's rats to frolic and gambol in the darkness.

It was 5 December when Ross's ship docked in Cape Town, where a fierce south-easterly gale was blowing and the heat was unforgiving and inescapable. The city reminded Ross of Australian cities, both Adelaide and Sydney which he thought seemed to be 'British-Colonial', rather than being overtly African.[104] He left Cape Town on the Blue Train to Pretoria, a near thousand-mile, 27-hour railroad journey marked by a series of six-course meals and with an observation car that would sell you 'almost anything including sherry at 9d. a glass and gin at a shilling'.[105] The train steamed across the semi-desert of the Karoo which reminded Ross of the Nullarbor desert in Australia.

104 Ross, op. cit., page 131.

105 Ross, op. cit., page 132.

Alan Ross reached Pretoria on 13 December, two days after MCC had lost to a South African XI. The tourists by then had travelled on to Durban, recovering from the low-scoring defeat where the South African spinner, Hugh Tayfield, had taken 12 wickets over both innings. The experiment of employing Alan Oakman as an opening partner for Richardson had signally failed with a total of eight runs in his two brief (56-minute) visits to the crease. Swanton's jaundiced view of the overall state of play after the win in Salisbury was proving prophetic, with concerns over slow play, negative tactics, the lack of sufficient opportunities for batting and bowling in the nets, the undue amount of time spent travelling, and the lack of challenge provided by the early one-sided games. The issue of batting and bowling in the nets on a regular basis was a major one. In Australia Colin Cowdrey would have a net every day, sometimes two. Here it was weekly at best. The amount of time spent travelling was not good for working cricketers either. A train meandering two miles up across the high veld, while the players were in the observation car 'reading, writing letters, playing bridge and bickering amiably'[106] did not help to win Test matches.

There were concerns too over the failure to find an opening batter; the evident English susceptibility to spin; and, out of the blue, the illness of Jim Parks, whose attacks of migraine were bad enough to see him hospitalised in a nursing home for some days. From time to time the outside world intruded. In the early part of the tour, for example, Jim Swanton was much exercised by the almost total absence of 'news of the great events directly to the northward' – the military (and doomed) action in the Middle

106 *Report from South Africa* by EW Swanton, page 38.

East over Suez by French and British forces. By the time of the first Test the 'great events' had become a political embarrassment. The failure of the Anglo-French action was arguably the reason that so 'many of us who were children in 1956 have memories of our fathers coasting down hills to save a drop of petrol'.[107] The heading of Swanton's piece on Sunday, 9 December, *The Shadow of Defeat*, may well have struck the *Telegraph*'s man as relating to a wider conflict than MCC versus a South African XI, or indeed the Test match battles that lay ahead.

The timing of Ross's arrival at Pretoria meant that he missed the critical moment when the leisurely peace of the tour was broken. Charles Fortune later described the game with a South African XI as 'a dogfight' and both Ross and Swanton were unsettled by the events on the penultimate day.[108] An unseemly row had blown up over the regulations, their meaning and their interpretation by the umpires. MCC had been set what seemed a relatively straightforward 148 to win, but the innings soon fell apart, with wickets falling regularly, and with none of the top four batters getting into double figures. Batting 'miscalculations' were the problem, Jim Swanton thought, rather than any undue difficulties with the wicket. Doug Insole, standing in for May as captain, was out without scoring and the tourists fell away to a dismal 88/7, with Bailey and Lock struggling to survive.

The light was fading fast and the looming shadow cast by the grandstand was troubling the batters. After the eighth wicket

---

107 *1956 The Year That Changed Britain* by Francis Beckett and Tony Russell, page 266. Petrol rationing was announced on 29 November 1956 and was planned to run for four months from 17 December until April 1957. It immediately caused shortages and panic-buying.

108 *The MCC Tour of South Africa 1956/57* by Charles Fortune, page 74.

fell, the incoming batter, Peter Loader, appealed against the light. The umpires duly turned it down. Soon after the South African captain, Jackie McGlew, left the field to discuss the situation with his counterpart, Doug Insole. Coincidentally, both had been named *Wisden* Cricketers of the Year that summer. In a somewhat more leisurely fashion the MCC batters and the umpires started to walk off the field, leaving the fielders in position but non-plussed. Eventually 'the batsmen had to return, having been under a misapprehension about the rules existing for extra time'.[109] By then the light had worsened. Finally, the players came off in 'semi-tropical light' with the score at 95/8; 53 still needed and just Loader, Statham and Bailey left. Next morning the end was quick, the MCC tail blown away inside 30 minutes and a first defeat of the tour confirmed.

There had been other mutterings and exchanges on the pitch over what the MCC players deemed a dubious decision by the umpire when Peter Richardson was dismissed caught at short leg, the bowler's appeal having been for lbw. Richardson did not 'walk' and he was known to do so as a matter of principle when out caught. He left the field slowly and the non-striker made his feelings all too clear. The episode made newspaper headlines in South Africa and 'did not reflect too happily on MCC', Alan Ross for one believing that MCC 'appeared to be losing with bad grace'.[110] Later Peter May admitted that some MCC players had been 'censured for certain practices indulged in on the field.'[111]

Dubious light and bad blood were not the sole concerns of the MCC party with the Test getting uncomfortably near.

109 *Wisden Cricketers' Almanack, 1958,* page 823.

110 Ross, op. cit., page 138.

111 *Wisden*, op. cit., page 823.

Problems apparent in October had not gone away. The batting was fragile and too often strokeless, apart from the captain whose batting was exemplary and, for Alan Ross, 'a joy to behold'. There was no certainty about who would partner Peter Richardson and while selection of the bowlers was straightforward, so far on the tour Frank Tyson had 'lain pretty low'.[112] There was also the continuing issue of the squad size: May had stated to the press that no replacement for the absent Jim Parks would be countenanced. But the Sussex man had collapsed at London Airport on his way back out to rejoin the squad. No matter – once Bailey was installed to open and Wardle chosen rather than Tony Lock, the England XI for the first Test contained no surprises.

112 Ross, op. cit., page 144.

8

Start of a Cricket War

South Africa, 1956/57

ALAN ROSS, Jim Swanton, Charles Fortune and the rest looked down over the hastily constructed Wanderers ground in Johannesburg and watched the blazered formalities that preceded the opening day of the Test series. It was Christmas Eve 1956 and, while snow fell in England over the festive period, in South Africa it was a glorious morning. The view from the press box took in the golf course, the deep shade of assorted trees and in the far distance, the Rand mountains, a sharp ridge of blue-smudged haze. Peter May's back, however, was turned to the distant landscape and his attention was firmly on his opposite number, Clive van Ryneveld, about to spin the coin. It fell kindly as May probably anticipated: allied to his grace with a cricket bat, he had a sorcerer's luck with the tossed coin. This would be the fifth win out of six since becoming captain.

The expectation had been that Jackie McGlew would be the man leading out the South Africans, but his shoulder injury had been a well-guarded secret. The news that he would not play only emerged 'in the stop-press column of the city edition' that hit the streets early on Christmas Eve. The radio commentator Charles

Fortune, all too aware of the disruption to news deadlines of the timing of the announcement, saw a troubling shadow on the near horizon in the South African 'obsession with secrecy' and the troubling prospect, not of 'a game of cricket', but rather 'the start of a cricket war'. It all had the feel, he thought, of 'a battle communique of the wartime years'.[113]

New South African captain Van Ryneveld was an Oxford man – indeed he and Peter May had been on opposite sides in the 1950 varsity match. On that occasion Hubert Doggart, fresh from his two Tests in June against the West Indies, had won the toss for Cambridge.[114] The varsity match had ended in a draw, but Van Ryneveld had had the better of things, taking 5-78 in the first innings while May had only scored 7 and 39.[115]

On that morning in Johannesburg six years later Peter May predictably opted to bat and the makeshift pairing of Trevor Bailey and Peter Richardson set the tone for what was to come. The two openers eschewed risk and ground out 28 painful runs before the first wicket fell – Bailey, after 97 minutes at the wicket – for just 16. The Essex man's bat, Alan Ross thought, made 'a coffin-like sound', perhaps heralding its brief life and certainly fitting the funereal mood.[116] That first day of the series, the correspondents agreed, was deeply disappointing. It was a 'melancholy day' (Jim Swanton); 'wretchedly dull' (Charles Fortune) and the batting 'badly out of touch' (Alan Ross). The home side had made things difficult by what some thought was negative bowling and Fortune for one believed too much was

113 Fortune, op. cit., pages 95–96.

114 The Oxford captain Donald Carr also played in just two Tests.

115 Van Ryneveld was an international rugby player too, winning four caps – for England.

116 Ross, op. cit., page 147.

pitched wide of the stumps. On an easy-paced wicket, a day of painstaking batting had produced an underwhelming score of 157/3.

When the undefeated Richardson (69*) and Cowdrey (51*) left the field at the end of that first day, they would have contemplated the Christmas Day rest with some satisfaction and welcomed the temporary relief. Players and press, having geared themselves up for the start of the series after weeks of preparation, found themselves idle for a day. Alan Ross, for one, was struck by the strangeness of celebrating Christmas in the glaring sunshine of high summer, what with 'the shops full of tinsel and Father Christmases wagging their white beards'.[117]

As well as a Test match, Johannesburg was also seeing the opening formalities of the 'treason trials' at which some 156 people – Nelson Mandela among them – were accused. They would last some six years and, at their conclusion, every defendant was found not guilty. Ross was much exercised by this uneasy juxtaposition of sport and the politics of injustice. In the same city as the Test, police were wielding batons and firing shots at a peaceful crowd demonstrating against what it saw as the growing existence of a police state – freedoms being rapidly eroded. 'How long,' he wondered, 'will Parliamentary democracy survive in South Africa?' Jim Swanton was less voluble on the issue in his account of the tour, but he 'abhorred apartheid' and would opt out of the subsequent tour to South Africa in 1964/65.[118] For now, his trenchant views, in print at least, tended to focus on the imperfections of Doug Insole's stance at the wicket and slow over rates, rather than social or racial injustice.

---

117 Ross, op. cit., page 161.

118 Rayvern Allen, op. cit., page 263.

Each day once the cricket was over and with the evening light fading, Ross would motor the 35 miles or so to Pretoria across the high veld, soothed by the Blue Hills, the air flecked with the smoke of fires from the shanty towns of Johannesburg. He welcomed the prevailing – if misplaced – sense of peace. On Christmas Day he was with established friends enjoying a little gentle swimming, a set or two of tennis and a liberality of cocktails.

Twenty-four hours away from the South African attack however made little difference to the overall approach of the batting side and when Peter Richardson was finally out, lbw to Goddard for 117, he had been at the crease for eight and three-quarter hours. It was very hot under a blistering sun and at one point Alan Ross noted that 'heads had been nodding like marigolds in the shadeless stands'.[119] Richardson and Cowdrey (59) between them had made two-thirds of England's total of 268. Despite the length of Richardson's worthy innings, it was evident that his form was just as scratchy at the end as it had been before the first ball had been bowled two days previously.

If England were to defend what was a less than convincing total their bowlers needed to put the South African openers, Taylor and Goddard, under real pressure from the start. Instead Brian Statham tended to overpitch, while Frank Tyson was perhaps less quick than usual and certainly finding little in the way of movement off the pitch or in the air. When the first wicket fell at 54, it was to a spinner, courtesy of a stumping by Evans off Johnny Wardle. South Africa's 215 all out was scored at a pedestrian 2.4 runs per eight-ball over (England's rate was

---

119 Ross, op. cit., pages 148–9.

2.3), while Wardle, Statham and Bailey each took three wickets. Champagne cricket it was not.

The flat nature of the play tempted some correspondents into drawing parallels with warfare and its slow, painful and attritional qualities. Jim Swanton described Christmas Day as the 'Christmas Armistice' and bemoaned the colourless, dirge-like quality of the cricket. Nonetheless, England plodded their way to an overall advantage, despite losing Frank Tyson, who spent the third day in bed with tonsillitis. The art of batting had become increasingly problematic and England's second innings fell away to a shoddy 150 all out, with Compton top-scoring with 32.

Set to make 204 to win, South Africa collapsed to 72 all out, with Trevor Bailey (5-20) inflicting the most damage. Towards the end, the disarray of the South African innings was mirrored by gathering bad light and an ink-dark sky, followed by a sudden dust storm, the chaotic cricket somehow symbolised by a confusion of sightscreens being toppled over by the wind, bails spirited away from the stumps, hats and litter billowing around the ground, all accompanied by savage gusts of rain and hail. The end when it came was strangely low-key, the home side hanging on grimly for a while, but then giving it away ineptly, the last two wickets seeing Heine and the captain, Van Ryneveld, both run out. England, players and press, headed off for Cape Town on an early morning flight, having won by the comfortable margin of 131 runs.

There was to be little respite from the struggle, however, with only two days between the end of the first Test and the start of the next on New Year's Day, 1957. Take out travelling time and there would be little opportunity for practice or the considered changing of plans before action was resumed. As for the touring press, at least they were blessed with enough time for some serious celebration: it had been, after all, an emphatic win – a 'windfall English victory', so Alan Ross thought – and a night of revelry began for him and others with dinner at Dawson's before progressing to Ciro's. At some point the idea of a night's sleep was abandoned in favour of the earliest of morning departures. The hotel where Ross and the MCC party had been staying was thought unsatisfactory, 'very noisy', with both poor food and service,[120] so Ross was glad to be on the move, driving 'up the steep ramp of the Victoria Hotel and out of the waking city'.[121] He left in the limousine splendour of his newly acquired Nash Rambler as the dawn light began to spread across the distant Rand.

The prospect of the 900-mile road trip south attracted Ross and he was greatly looking forward to watching cricket at Newlands in Cape Town, with its oak trees, sprawling, tumbling mountain ridge just beyond the ground's perimeter and fine pavilion. He hadn't warmed to the 'architectural mess' that characterised the Wanderers. Within ten minutes Johannesburg had been left behind and Ross settled back for the long drive across the featureless and empty red plains – 'more or less desert' – a relentless journey on flat, ruler-straight roads to Cape Town. From time to time there were dust devils, roadkill, cattle towns, birds of prey, large lizards asleep on milestones and – always – the enticement of distant hills. Spooked by the thunder of the car's engine, the lizards scuttled away 'with the alacrity of hotel guests surprised in unauthorised bedrooms'.[122] On arriving in the hazy

---

120 MCC Archive, 1956/57 tour file: Freddie Brown's manager's report.

121 Ross, op. cit., page 162.

122 Ross, op. cit., page 163.

dust of Cape Town, along with the lava-coloured sea and the bulk of Table Mountain, Ross saw placards announcing the news that Frank Tyson was out of the forthcoming Test.

It was clear from early morning that the first day of 1957 would be hot: Cape Town's weather was set fair. Of the England party, Tony Lock was suffering with a heavy cold and so, unsurprisingly, Johnny Wardle kept his place. Tyson's absence with tonsillitis was confirmed and Peter Loader stood in, with the visitors' batting line-up marginally weakened as a result. A swirling south-east wind ruffled the trees and promised some relief from the heat of Africa. Peter May continued his good fortune at the toss, winning the sixth out of seven, and soon after Peter Richardson and Trevor Bailey walked out to face Heine and Adcock. In the press box, Jim Swanton took an aristocratic view of what might ensue, earnestly praying 'that the slower side may lose'.[123] He feared a reprise of dour batting and wide, leg-side bowling and was predictably right: the cricket was grimly sterile all day, with the openers setting the tone, Bailey batting robotically and Richardson serenely competent.

It was after lunch before the first wicket fell, but then both openers fell quickly, prompting an afternoon that tested the patience of most on the ground, fulfilled Swanton's worst fears and caused a disgruntled crowd to demonstrate their frustrated disappointment. Tayfield came on to bowl his slow spin at midday and proceeded to wheel away for hours, churning out 41 eight-ball overs for only 69 runs – and three wickets. It was hard going, however, with even the cavalier Compton diminished by a combination of a slow-paced wicket, defensive bowling and

123 Swanton, op. cit., page 106.

English ultra-caution. Alan Ross would long remember Compton batting against Hugh Tayfield as if he was 'tied to his crease like a dog in his kennel'.[124]

Little changed on the second morning, with only Godfrey Evans achieving a respectable run rate. Wickets fell steadily; Cowdrey made an inhibited, occasionally soporific, 101 and once he had reached his century he was out, deemed leg before wicket, 'the umpire presumably having had enough of a good thing'.[125] England's total of 369 would, in May's mind, certainly have justified the ponderous approach.

The South African reply was equally slow, their runs made at around two per over. The weather was scorchingly hot, with the merest whisper of a wind. Swanton fulminated about batters with a 'two-eyed or two-shouldered stance', harking back to the great days when batting was 'a sideways game'.[126] As the match unfolded, the wicket began to turn and the wind – the 'Cape Doctor' – took the edge from the Newlands heat. It was Johnny Wardle with match figures of 12-89 who broke the South African resolve, but the English relentless, measured pursuit of runs on the first two days had proved crucial. England's winning margin was 312 runs and the game was soon over on the fifth morning. By 1pm, with Table Mountain 'giving off a powdery blue heat', Alan Ross was back in the sweltering city.[127]As for Jim Swanton, despite the crushing victory, he brooded how, by the halfway mark on a full-length tour, the cricket writer feels the need of some kind of break. No doubt the English cricketers, so

---

124 *Green Fading Into Blue* by Alan Ross, page 3. Ross and Compton 'quarrelled regularly about South Africa'.

125 Ross, op. cit., page 171.

126 Swanton, op. cit., page 116.

127 Ross, op. cit., page 177.

far from the comforts of home, and who had played Test cricket for 10 days out of the last 13, felt much the same.

Freddie Brown's 'Manager's Report' of the tour, held in the archives at Lord's, makes a passing reference to the slow scoring issue: he notes the financial success of the tour before commenting that this was 'in spite of all that was written in the press condemning the slow rate of scoring'.[128] He was at pains to attribute some of the cause to 'Goddard's accuracy' as well as the South African pacemen directing 'a high percentage of balls down the leg side'. He could also have drawn attention to the fact that the English pace of scoring in the series was little different from other tours: 2.4 runs per over compared to 2.2 in the West Indies (1953/54) and 2.9 in Australia (1954/55).[129]

Two up in the series, courtesy of implacable batting, adroit use of a powerful bowling attack and Peter May's good luck with coins, the MCC party moved on, contemplating the luxury of 20 days before the next Test, to be played in Durban, a thousand miles away. True to form, Alan Ross climbed back into the Nash Rambler and headed east, along the 'garden route', initially to East London, making 300 miles on the first day, his attention caught from time to time by the orchids and agapanthuses on either side of the dusty highway. Later his road trip, begun in a kind of paradise, acquired a nightmare quality, a perfect storm of winding coastal roads and brutal weather, the tired correspondent peering uneasily through the windscreen at fog, lightning, biblical rainstorms and landslides. He battled on, troubled by a broken fuel gauge but fortified by occasional halts for 'a couple of

128 MCC Archive, 1956/57 tour file, manager's report.

129 The equivalent figures for the opposition are: West Indies 2.8; Australia 3.8; and South Africa 2.3.

scotches' and some sandwiches, before he finally rolled thankfully into Durban and the sanctuary of the Edward Hotel. As a reward for his endeavours, the Edward proved to be the best hotel that the MCC party stayed in throughout the tour.[130]

Durban proved to be a turning point, although initially, the first day seemed to follow exactly the same pattern with Peter May winning the toss and choosing to bat on a hot and cloudless morning; the England XI was unchanged and Peter Richardson and Trevor Bailey batted through till lunch (103/0). The correspondents nodded in agreement over the predicted retention of Loader for Tyson, with Charles Fortune of the opinion that 'Frank Tyson had ceased to be a world beater.'[131] There were rumours too of trouble in the South African camp, player 'brawls' Fortune thought, and there were mutterings about the connection between slow play and the rows of empty seats around the ground.

The Durban pitch was shorn of grass and unquestionably fast. It was hot enough too for the flowers on the pavilion to droop and wilt. English wickets started to fall inexorably after lunch: 115/0 became 186/6 with Richardson out for 68 (lbw yet again), May gone for just 2 and the tail folding.[132] Cowdrey had suffered a bout of dysentery and felt weak; Tayfield bowled 14 maiden overs in a row; Swanton despaired of Bailey's 'dead-bat forward stab' and complained bitterly of May's 'cynical' approach – the ruthless determination to take time out of the game by slow, painstaking batting; 'A joyful, sunny morning', Swanton wrote, 'gave way to toil and gloom.'[133]

130 MCC Archive, 1956/57 tour file.

131 Fortune, op. cit., p. 156.

132 May's Test scores on the tour to that point were: 6, 14, 8, 15 and 2: 45 runs averaging 9.

133 Swanton, op. cit., page 144.

From England's point of view the series never reached the heights of Cape Town. Instead, Durban would be remembered for humidity, sunless days, low scores, bad light ending play, Bailey breaking a finger and May making 'no bones about saving the match, rather than take any risk in winning it'.[134] The draw achieved at Durban, however, ensured that the series could not be lost. It was as well that the English captain had shown his Hutton side in his captaincy: once he lost the knack of winning the toss, things fell apart. The South African captain, Van Ryneveld, won the remaining two tosses, at Johannesburg in February and Port Elizabeth in early March and England lost both games, by a slender 17 runs at the Wanderers and by 58 runs in the fifth and final Test match. Frank Tyson's 6-40 at Port Elizabeth was a poignant reminder of his potent pace, but it was too little and too late to edge the series in England's favour.

When MCC toured Australia in 1954/55, the final Test of that series did not conclude the tour. The party had been away from home for more than 170 days, but the schedule required an onward flight to New Zealand to play two further Tests as well as two other games. It would be three more weeks before they could leave for home. The series against South Africa ended less punishingly with a single match after the final Test – against the Combined Universities on 9 March. It was still a long time to be away – half a year, more or less – and the length of tours remained a challenge for players. Johnny Wardle, for example, had received an invitation to tour South Africa in the early autumn of 1956. Previously, however, he 'had made a vow when I was in Australia 18 months before that never again would I be away from my wife

134 Ross, op. cit., page 204.

and family at Christmas. I hated the very idea of it. I still hate the idea, but … I went.'[135]

The day before the last game of the tour, Alan Ross had begun his journey home. Looking down from a Skymaster airliner he noted blue ocean, surf, sand and later 'the kopjes and lakes like bits of broken glass and smooth brown humps of the Karoo'.[136] He felt a deep affection for the country, while recognising its paradoxes. 'It is a place of pain and suffering, of prejudice and competition and violence, but it is also mysterious and various and ceaselessly beautiful.'[137] Also on that flight to Johannesburg were Trevor Bailey, Doug Insole, Brian Statham and Johnny Wardle, none of them required for the tour's last act in which their understudies, Alan Oakman, Brian Taylor, Tony Lock – and the manager Freddie Brown, batting at no. 9 – did enough to ensure a winning end to the tour.[138] With that completed they travelled to Cape Town to board the *Stirling Castle* on 15 March 1957.

It had been a series where both sides' bowlers out-performed the batters. The one disappointment amongst the visitors' bowling attack was Frank Tyson, whose pace seemed visibly to have declined. May's leadership had been valued but his batting in the Tests was disappointing (he averaged 15.3 with a top score of 61). Only one South African (McLean) had scored a century (exactly 100 at Durban). Doug Insole, despite Swanton's doubts, topped England's batting averages, while another Essex man, Trevor Bailey, with 19 wickets at 12.21, was the most successful

135 *Happy Go Johnny* by Johnny Wardle, page 181.

136 Ross, op. cit., page 243.

137 Ross, op. cit., page 252.

138 The 45-year-old Brown scored 0 and bowled briefly in both innings – 0-6 and 0-20.

bowler. Frank Tyson had bowled only 49 overs, taking eight wickets, all in the final Test. Johnny Wardle's spin had taken 26 wickets (at 13.80), outgunning both Laker and Lock. South Africa's Hugh Tayfield's 37 wickets (at 17.18) was the outstanding performance over the five Tests.

Freddie Brown, in his report of the tour, recommended that full bonuses should be paid to all; expressed his admiration of the skipper; and noted the excellent team spirit and popularity of the players. He pointed out the drawbacks of train travel. While being 'reasonably comfortable', there were problems on sleeper trains since they stopped during the night at each station, thereby constantly waking tired cricketers. On one occasion the touring party was delayed by 'heavy rains [which] caused a landslide on the line between Durban and Johannesburg', delaying the start of the match against North East Transvaal. Brown also worried that a playing day of six hours imposed 'a heavy strain especially on fast bowlers' and he thought a Test of six five-hour days would be preferable. His final concern was about players' wives accompanying the tour – three of them had been there for part of the time. This needed 'careful consideration' and it had been evident that when Jim Laker's wife and children arrived, the spinner's 'keenness and interest in the cricket had flagged'. He was also concerned over a consequence of the amateur/professional divide – you couldn't impose a financial penalty on amateurs, he argued, and believed that 'sending them home' was the only option.[139]

There were two further issues, one sporting, the other political. First there was the marked falling away of the tourists'

139 MCC Archive, 1956/57 tour file.

cricket, which Colin Cowdrey among others attributed to the 'open-handed welcome' of the South Africans. The result of such hospitality was that the tourists were 'certainly reduced to something well short of the fitness that a Test team must maintain'.[140]

The second issue was race, in particular the South African government's treatment of its black population. Before the MCC party left home, Viscount Monckton had reminded the tourists 'of South Africa's problems, and told us that colour, as a topic of conversation, was strictly out'. Later, on the tour, Laker and Alan Oakman had seen the problem at first hand when a policeman attending a car accident involving Oakman and a cyclist had automatically blamed the latter, a black South African. 'This, thought Alan [Oakman] too bemused to do anything, is what white men call justice.'[141]

As chance would have it while MCC were on tour, playing elsewhere in the country was a cricketer who would later greatly affect, not only cricket, but also relations between South Africa and Britain. While MCC were playing a South African XI in Pretoria in early December, a young Basil D'Oliveira was playing for South African Non-Europeans in Cape Town. He was of the same broad age group as the South African Test XI but was not selected because of his colour. Some seven years later he would be playing county cricket in England – and it was a cricket correspondent, John Arlott, who helped facilitate that change. By the end of that decade D'Oliveira's selection for England and his potential return to South Africa would throw cricket into turmoil.

---

140 Cowdrey, op. cit., page 114.

141 *Over to Me* by Jim Laker, pages 90–91. Cited in *Basil D'Oliveira* by Peter Oborne, page 15.

9

'This Most Disappointing of Cricket Teams'

Australia, 1958/59

IT IS mid-January 1959, almost two years on from England's drawn Test with South Africa in Durban and the current MCC touring side is fielding against Victoria in Melbourne and looking uncomfortably hot and bothered. The team is captained by Colin Cowdrey in Peter May's absence and is much changed from its predecessors. There is no Trevor Bailey, Godfrey Evans, Jim Laker, Brian Statham or Denis Compton in the XI and some of the 1957 tourists are now retired from the game. Their replacements have, for the most part, yet to confirm their standing as Test cricketers. Gloucestershire's John Mortimore has yet to play a Test match, while his team-mate Arthur Milton has played just two Tests against New Zealand, making 104 not out on debut. The batter Raman Subba Row has played a single Test match; so too Roy Swetman, replacing Godfrey Evans as wicketkeeper, while the all-rounder Ted Dexter, a late call-up to the squad, has played in two (scoring 64 runs in three innings and scarcely given a chance with the ball). The first three Tests of the series have come and gone and here in this state match in Melbourne, on a day of ominous weather, Cowdrey has lost the toss. It means a long day in the field for the Englishmen and even at the start of the day it is searingly, dangerously hot. The temperature will reach 109 degrees in the shade, with little respite over the next three days.

In the press box Alan Ross – who had witnessed six overseas tours and never seen England lose a series – had been replaced by Michael Davie and in his report of the day's play in *The Observer* the new man emphasises the physical challenge of playing first-class cricket in such brutal heat. Victoria scored 270/5 that day, an unremarkable score, but the batting side was infinitely the happier. When play ended several of the fielding team were physically sick. It had been the hottest day in Melbourne for seven years and the city's streets were melting into putty. MCC's bowlers, particularly the pacemen, struggled and Cowdrey strictly limited the number of overs each man bowled. The captain himself was sick after play ended for the day while off-spinner John Mortimore collapsed in the heat, having bowled well for 17 overs before doubling up in pain and then vomiting. The Gloucestershire man had been brought over as a replacement, arriving 'in the middle of the Australian summer, looking very white'.[142] Minutes after being sick he left the field. Davie thought playing cricket in such conditions was 'pointless', not least because the gate money for the day was a paltry $A748. 'It is to be hoped,' he wrote, 'that not too much of MCC's share had to go on doctors' bills.'[143]

In the Test-playing countries other than England, the climate was often extremely hot and prior to the tour to the

---

142 *May's Men in Australia* by Alec Bedser, page 208.

143 *A Hot and Futile Day* by Michael Davie, in *The Observer on Cricket* ed. Scyld Berry, pages 118-120.

West Indies in 1954 MCC had commissioned a report, *Cricket in Hot Climates*. It dealt with seasickness, sunburn, the body's adjustment to heat, hangovers and diet, as well as suggesting exercises for loosening up and relieving anxiety. Advice was proffered on dealing with 'liberal hospitality': take two Alka Seltzer, the report said, or crushed aspirins, a lot of water, have breakfast, then lie down for 30 minutes, remembering to defer smoking for a short while. As well as ignoring the perils of smoking, the report suggests that the medical advisers were highly sceptical of cricketers' self-discipline. 'It is a rare cricketer who will do physical training by himself, or take salt tablets, or refuse chipped potatoes.'[144]

The weather had been out of kilter ever since the tour party had left England on 20 September 1958, sailing from Tilbury. Aboard the P&O liner, *Iberia*, was the MCC party of 16 cricketers and some 20 or so pressmen – and they were all men, no Margaret Hughes. A number of former players were on press duty, including Alec Bedser who travelled up to Tilbury from Woking on a fine autumn morning with his twin brother Eric. Alec was looking forward to some balmy Australian weather, thinking that 'sunshine would be beneficial' after his recent serious illness. Early in the voyage the weather was predictable enough: blazing hot through the Red Sea, but after Aden the cloud descended and later, when the squad flew from a steamy Bombay to Colombo, monsoon rains resulted in the two days of planned cricket being limited to just two hours. The rain would be falling too when they finally reached Australia in the second week of October.

---

144 MCC Archive, 1953/54 tour file: *Advice on 'Cricket in Hot Climates'*.

The MCC squad had a core of experienced Test cricketers who had toured four years before, but ten of that group were not on this tour.[145] The press reaction for the chosen 16 was positive – EM Wellings had never remembered 'a team chosen for Australia meeting with such approval'.[146] There were some raised eyebrows at the selection of Swetman as Evans' deputy keeper – he was not Surrey's first-choice wicketkeeper after all – and there were concerns about the lack of an established opening pair of batters. But the squad had a strong bowling line-up and the batting included two men of the highest quality and others with potential.[147]

Life on the *Iberia* was one of rest and relaxation – deck tennis but no formal physical training until after they had left Colombo when Peter Richardson, an army PE instructor in earlier days, led the exercises. Earlier Yorkshire's Willie Watson had seriously damaged a knee getting out of a deckchair just out from the port of Aden. His knee was put in plaster and eventually he was flown to Perth for an operation. It would be weeks before he was fully mobile. The injury immediately raised concerns about England's opening pair for the Tests in December and early January. The press corps were not immune from physical problems on board the ship either. Ian Peebles' leg was poisoned after an insect bite and he spent half the voyage lying on his back.

Nor was the overall mood in the camp trouble-free. When Peter Richardson came into breakfast one morning not wearing a tie or a cravat he was disciplined by co-manager Freddie Brown.

---

145 Missing in 1958/59 from the previous tour in 1954/55 were Hutton, Simpson, Edrich, Compton, Wardle, Bedser, Appleyard, McConnon, Andrew and Wilson.

146 *The Ashes Thrown Away* by EM Wellings, page 5.

147 The 1958/59 tourists who hadn't travelled to Australia four years earlier were Laker, Lock, Trueman, Milton, Watson, Subba Row, Swetman and Watson.

Evidently peeved, Richardson took breakfast in his cabin and came to lunch in the heat of the midday sun wearing 'arctic overdress, complete with coat, muffler and hat'.[148] The incident somehow reinforced a sense that things were not quite right. There had already been the 'Wardle incident'. The spinner's county Yorkshire had revealed late in the summer that they would not re-engage him for the 1959 season. His selection for the tour was cancelled as a result and he subsequently wrote 'a series of somewhat pungent articles in the *Daily Mail*', criticising his new county captain and adding some unsavoury details about his own behaviour.[149] The outcome was that Wardle's selection was cancelled. The *Mail* duly appointed him to cover the tour.

Heavy rain in Perth denied the visitors valuable net practice which meant that the first tour match against Western Australia which started only a few days after the *Iberia* docked was played without adequate preparation. The weather was decidedly unseasonable too with a cold wind and a temperature of only 60°.

Alec Bedser, once of Surrey and England and now working for the *News of the World* and the Australian Broadcasting Company, was one of the pressmen keen to question his former team-mate, Peter May. The Surrey batter was now a highly experienced captain of his country – only Wally Hammond had skippered the national side as often – and he was determined to deal only with questions through Freddie Brown or Desmond Eagar, the two England co-managers. May believed that his disappointing form in the South African Tests two years before had been the result of undue press demands. So, at press conferences he ruled out questions about the 'Wardle situation' – the Yorkshireman was

148 Wellings, op. cit., page 19.

149 *The Fight for the Ashes 1958/59* by Ian Peebles, page 17.

unavailable because of 'domestic difficulties' was the official line. Instead, he offered insights on the uncontroversial: no, his players would not be subject to a curfew; Tom Graveney's part-time leg breaks might be useful; the squad was in fine fettle and yes, quite adequate in numbers to complete the job. May was perhaps more fluent with the bat than when confronted by the press. He 'evidently feels that talking to writers is as unpredictably risky as throwing an egg into an electric fan'.[150]

Each tour seemed to raise the question of the optimum number of tourists, an issue made more complex when players were injured or became ill. Should a replacement be flown out or can we manage with what we've got? The injury to Watson temporarily reduced the pool of available players to 15 but, despite suggestions that Sussex's Ted Dexter might be sent out as a replacement, no additions were made at this stage. Ian Peebles, drawing on his experiences as a tourist took the view that, 'There is nothing more wearisome than travelling as an unemployed member of a touring cricket team.'[151]

It didn't take long for doubts to arise and weaknesses to emerge; who would open with Richardson? Was one all-rounder enough? Anyway, was Trevor Bailey fit enough and was his weight a problem? Was playing four pace bowlers in a Test sensible? Is the unexpectedly slow pace of Australian pitches a problem? Which of the battery of fast men would settle for bowling into the wind? The most telling question of all would centre on Frank Tyson. Peebles thought the Northamptonshire quick bowler was 'at rather a low ebb', seeming to be off-colour and having lost

---

150 *Richie Benaud's Blue Suede Shoes* by David Kynaston and Harry Ricketts, pages 6-7. They are quoting from *The Observer*, probably written by Michael Davie.

151 Peebles, op. cit., page 18.

weight. The fast bowler was also 'worried by his newly married wife's ill health'.[152] At Lord's in the summer against New Zealand the Kiwi batters had punished him without mercy.

Lingering doubt began to sharpen into warning signs once the cricket began on 17 October against Western Australia. There were runs for Graveney, Cowdrey and May but neither of the opening games was won and the MCC party flew to Adelaide with renewed concerns and worrying about an injury to Peter May, who had torn a knee ligament. A further cloud on the horizon was that Norman O'Neill, the latest Australian to be branded the next Bradman, scored an ominous 104 for a Combined XI. There was some encouragement in that MCC remained unbeaten before the first Test at Brisbane which began on 5 December, but concerns would not go away. Watson remained injured; Subba Row was also unfit; Fred Trueman was suffering from lumbago and Peter Loader had problems with a tendon as well as having flu. It was a sign perhaps of unease that, as the Brisbane Test loomed, John Mortimore of Gloucestershire had been rushed out to Australia to bolster the bowling options.

Back in the English autumn it had been thought that the touring party was more than strong enough to resist Australian attempts to reclaim the Ashes. But by tea on 5 December in Brisbane that assumption was proved to be mistaken. May had won the toss, chosen to bat and watched the optimism fade fast: when tea was taken England had been reduced to 83/6 and were already fighting to save the first Test.

The Brisbane Test began some seven weeks after the *Iberia* had docked, time which had not fully prepared the MCC party

---

152 Peebles, op. cit., page 15.

for the series that lay ahead. Net practices had been limited by bad weather, injuries had hindered team selection, and the dubious form of potential opening batters was problematic. For once it might have been a good toss to lose, but despite unease about the long English tail, with Godfrey Evans batting at number seven, followed by four bowlers, May elected to bat, on what was a warm and humid day. Lyn Wellings, Ian Peebles, Jim Swanton and the rest looked down from the press box on to a light-coloured, shorn pitch, sensed the heaviness of the atmosphere and wondered whether the ball might swing. It did, and lifted too.

In Wellings' account of the Brisbane debacle – with its charmless ground, its grim, plodding cricket and the evident English weaknesses – it was the trees that provided some comfort: 'Thank goodness for the poincianas during … those five days.'[153] There was not much else to lift the spirits during that Test, a match that Swanton described as 'the dullest and most depressing I have ever watched'.[154]

It began ominously with the Australian pacemen, Alan Davidson and Ian Meckiff, troubling the untested opening partnership of Arthur Milton and Peter Richardson with both pace and lift. Milton was uneasy against Meckiff from the outset and was soon dismissed, yorked for 5, and Richardson quickly followed. England reached lunch with no further wickets falling, though with precious few runs either: 36/2. The pitch continued to show an unnerving level of lift.

After lunch, it was soon clear that the pitch retained some life. As if that wasn't enough, Meckiff was presenting

153 Wellings, op. cit., page 71.

154 *Swanton in Australia* by E W Swanton, page 108.

considerable problems, partly arising from his erratic sense of direction – his 'incomprehensible spraying' as the Australian pressman and former Test cricketer Jack Fingleton put it.[155] A Meckiff over might include a few whistling down the leg side, a full toss or two, a couple of yorkers and, every so often, a near-wide down the off side, before a straight delivery that lifted disconcertingly. As wickets fell – May and Colin Cowdrey both falling to Meckiff – the talk in the press box centred on the bowler's 'dubious' action. Was it legitimate, or was Meckiff actually throwing the ball? Alec Bedser took the view that when Meckiff 'brought his arm over quickly' there was 'a suspicion of a throw'.[156]

The umpires, however, thought otherwise, and Meckiff ended the day with three wickets, all of them in England's top five. The visitors were all out for 134 before the end of the day's play, with Trevor Bailey, batting at six, top-scoring with 27. It had been profoundly slow going by the batting side and Alec Bedser for one wondered whether the first day would prove to be the best to bowl on. For a cautious man like Peter May, putting the opposition in – as Len Hutton had done not so long ago on the first day of a series – was anathema. It would not take many weeks, however, for his side's position to require such a gambler's throw of the dice.

The second day was warm and there had been some overnight rain. England's bowlers persevered, working in short spells – Swanton judged their efforts 'worthy' – and Australia made only steady progress: 55/1 at lunch and 110/4 at tea. By the end of the second day they had achieved a slim lead of 22, still

155 *Four Chukkas to Australia* by Jack Fingleton, page 48.

156 *May's Men in Australia* by Alec Bedser, page 64.

with four wickets in hand. Sunday, a rest day, was scorching hot, more than 90° in the shade, but on the Monday it was marginally cooler. England did well to limit the Australian first-innings lead to 52, with Peter Loader taking 4-56. It could not be sustained, the dubious technique of the English openers once again laid bare. Richardson (8) and Milton (17) were both gone by tea, which was taken at 49/2. Soon after Peter May was adjudged lbw for 4 offering no stroke to his opposite number, the leg-spinner, Richie Benaud.

The cricket was soporific: ponderous batting from Trevor Bailey amid a wild barrage from Ian Meckiff. At one point a heckler in the crowd, frustrated by Meckiff's continuing inaccuracies, demanded loudly that Benaud 'put Harvey on … he can at least throw straight!'[157] The bowler managed some deliveries that were straight enough, getting Cowdrey caught by Lindsay Kline at short fine leg, although the catch was contentious – had it been scooped up off the ground? – with the raised finger of umpire Mel McInnes condemning Cowdrey. McInnes had begun an unwanted sequence of being the principal figure at the heart of controversy. Trevor Bailey plodded on, his 68 made in seven and a half hours seeming to the despairing Peebles as 'dull to the point of anaesthesia'.[158] He 'played doggo to 388 deliveries'.[159] Jim Swanton was sickened at the 'deadly tedium', his 'gorge rising' at what he saw as cricket played with 'no tactical or technical justification whatever'.[160] 'It will go down in cricketing

157 Peebles, op. cit., page 84.

158 Peebles, op. cit., page 85. *Wisden* reported it as 7 hours and 38 minutes.

159 Fingleton, op. cit., page 59.

160 Swanton, op. cit., page 108.

history,' wrote Jack Fingleton, 'as the Battle of the Snooze.'[161] At the end Australia were left with a relatively undemanding 147 to win on a pitch that remained benign. Norman O'Neill's 71* took the home side through to a comfortable victory by eight wickets with a day and a half to spare.

The English correspondents' inquest blamed the dreary cricket on leg-side fields and accurate leg-side bowling, but there was a broader context to the malaise: 'The modern cricketer,' Lyn Wellings argued, 'is a curious mixture of shrewdness and puerile stupidity.'[162] Some blamed the timidity of England's approach. Peter May came in for much criticism, including personal attacks for 'neglecting his team and devoting his attention to his fiancée'. Virginia Gilligan had recently arrived in Australia to be with her future husband and 'the tabloid press pack hounded May on personal as well as cricketing grounds'.[163] Wellings regretted the 'small section of the English press' that raised the issue, but argued that, 'Experience has shown that the presence of wives among a touring side is unhelpful and a barrier to team spirit.'[164] The captain was seen to have made errors, including pushing Bailey up the order, and showed a 'streak of caution'. Wellings was also 'astonished' by the way co-manager Desmond Eagar and four England players went off to the Barrier Reef during the Test – days on the beach rather than watching their colleagues struggle on the field. The *Daily Mirror*'s Brian Chapman caught the mood of the press corps, writing that England needed 'a pride of lions, not a bunch of

161 Fingleton, op. cit., page 47.

162 Wellings, op. cit., page 71.

163 Kynaston and Ricketts, op. cit., page 17. May and Virginia Gilligan married soon after the tour, on 24 April 1959.

164 Wellings, op. cit., page 74.

pussy cats'.[165] Above all, there were the related questions of the legality or otherwise of some Australian bowlers and the poverty of English batting technique.

It was three weeks before the second Test which started on New Year's Eve at the MCG. It was Peter May's 29th birthday. The weather was cloudy with a cold south-east wind while the wicket seemed to be unduly grassy. The 'chucking' row had escalated to the point where Swanton was calling for the umpires to no-ball Meckiff. The chosen England XI was the same as for the match at Brisbane except that Willie Watson replaced Arthur Milton. May won the toss again and elected to bat. Richardson and Bailey opened with Watson coming in next. Richardson was soon out, caught behind for 3 and both Watson and Tom Graveney followed and the visitors were 7/3 in 17 minutes of cricket. There was a slow recovery centred upon the captain and the close came at 173/4.

The second day was cloudy and May completed his hundred before falling to Meckiff for 113. There was no doubt in May's mind about the reasons for his dismissal. He blamed Meckiff's 'dubious action' which made it 'exceedingly difficult to pick up the line of flight'.[166] That was 'a characteristic of chuckers', Swanton complained, insisting that he 'never saw anything as blatant as Meckiff's action'.[167] Thanks to May, the England batting performed better, making 259 all out, but the Australian reply that day – 96/1 – showed what was possible on that easy wicket. They consolidated on the next day, Neil Harvey (167) and Norman O'Neill putting on a

---

165 Fingleton, op. cit., page 64.
166 Peebles, op. cit., page 107.
167 Swanton, op. cit., page 111.

fine display of batting and England sticking to the task with 'élan' (such a Swanton word), with Brian Statham taking 7-57 in an Australian total of 308, a lead of 49, very similar to Brisbane (52).

What followed in England's second innings was a lamentable rout: Richardson gone for 2, one of seven Englishmen who failed to reach double figures. The captain's 17 was the team's top score as they fell to 87 all out and, soon after, an eight-wicket defeat – again. In short order England were 2-0 down with three to play and crucially needing to avoid defeat in the next Test.

Sydney was overcast and the pitch was lightish in colour, offering little pace. There had been rain about and England's preparations had once again been hindered. May won the toss for the third time and unsurprisingly opted to bat. The team showed four changes with Richardson dropped, Swetman replacing the injured Evans, and Trueman, Dexter and Milton all playing. Bailey opened with the Gloucestershire man – but both were gone by the time the score was 23. The overall pattern was unchanged: Meckiff bowling with 'very dubious legality'; slow scoring; wickets falling regularly. The recently arrived Ted Dexter – he had been working with an insurance firm in Paris – was out lbw for 1, without offering a stroke. The reserve wicketkeeper Roy Swetman – a slight, boyish figure – and his Surrey team-mate Tony Lock dug in and England were 190/6 at the close.

The second day was grey and wet and play didn't begin until 4.15. England subsided to 219 (Benaud 5-83). It would get worse: chances were dropped (two by Swetman); Laker and Lock were overused (89.2 overs between them). When England batted again Milton and Bailey posted the best opening stand of the series thus far (just 30). On day six England declared at 287/7 with May 92 and Cowdrey 100*. It was a cautious declaration: Australia were set 150 in 110 minutes to win, a challenge that Benaud understandably declined. The game was saved, however, and, in a second sign of hope for the England players, Meckiff was declared unfit, suffering from a bruised heel and an Achilles tendon problem.

Writing about the state of play in Melbourne a few days after the end of the third Test, Lyn Wellings was torn between complaining about the 'outrageous heat' and bewailing the poverty of England's cricket. 'A fan wafts hot air towards me which does nothing to cool the typewriter I am using,' he wrote, troubled by the approaching bush fires and the intensity of the north wind blowing in from the interior. Such heat 'does not aid thought', he typed, but he could not escape thinking morosely about 'this most disappointing of cricket teams'.[168]

There were two weeks between the end of the Sydney Test and the fourth Test in Adelaide. In the intervening state games, Trueman had taken wickets (5-42 against Victoria); Watson had scored 142 against the same opposition; and Tyson had taken 4-55 against New South Wales. Promising, you would have thought. In hot sunny weather England duly made changes for Adelaide, prompted by previous disappointments. Admittedly Richardson for Milton was founded on hope rather than history – one flawed batter exchanged for another – but Watson for Dexter and including Frank Tyson made sense. Evans came back for Swetman. Jim Laker, however, was suffering from an arthritic finger and hadn't bowled for a fortnight. Laker's omission

168 Wellings, op. cit., page 150.

prompted supposition and rumour. The off-spinner underwent a long pre-match net before declaring that his finger would not manage a six-day Test. Wellings was sceptical: 'Men have bowled in important matches with far worse fingers,' he wrote, arguing that most of the party took the view that 'the Laker finger did not represent an undue risk'.[169]

Laker's decision to stand aside left May with two key decisions. What would he do if he won the toss? In his first 29 Tests as captain, Peter May won the toss a remarkable 20 times. Invariably he would choose to bat – until suddenly on 30 January 1959, in Adelaide, he opted to put the opposition in, despite having suffered the grim consequences along with his team-mates when Len Hutton did the same thing in Brisbane four years earlier. May clearly felt that the risk was necessary to keep his side in with a chance of saving the Ashes. By this halfway point in the tour it was clear that the fourth Test was crucial and needed a show of courage from the tourists, an embracing of risk, considerable good fortune and a strong batting performance. What should his bowling attack be? A third issue concerned the batting: how could the side put together a match-winning total, given that May and Cowdrey typically were scoring over 50% of England's runs?

In the event May opted for a four-man pace attack – like Hutton in Brisbane four years before – with only Tony Lock as a mainstream spinner. He won the toss – and, like Hutton, elected to bowl first. It was a quixotic decision made perhaps in the heat after Laker's withdrawal – there was an historical impasse between the two men – but given the placid look of

169 Wellings, op. cit., page 158.

the pitch (it was no 'green top') it is little wonder that the press corps was deeply critical. 'Madness' was Wellings' view and while Alec Bedser suggested that England, in difficult circumstances, needed to gamble, the overall view was the skipper's 'judgement had deserted him'.

Frank Tyson got most out of what was an easy wicket but no Australian was out before lunch (58/0). Already there was a dispirited feel to the England showing. Tony Lock was checked for 'rubbing the ball in the dust' and then officially cautioned for running on the wicket.[170] It was late in the afternoon before a wicket fell and by then the realisation was that the Ashes had been surrendered. The score mounted with the heat: 200/1 at the end of the first day; 268/1 at lunch on day two; 403/6 at the close (the temperature over 100°) and 476 all out by early afternoon on the third day. The unfortunate Richardson was soon gone, strokeless and lbw to Ray Lindwall (4).[171] Bailey followed and England were 11/2. Next came the usual May/Cowdrey rescue operation, until the skipper was out for 37, leaving his side 115/3 at stumps.

The fourth day was overcast and cooler – better for bowling and, once Cowdrey was dismissed (84), the usual collapse ensued (170/3 rapidly becoming 188/9) until a defiant Statham and Watson put on 52 for the last wicket. Once again May and Cowdrey had made half of England's runs. Following on, Richardson and Watson put on the best English opening stand of the series, leaving the visitors 87/0 at lunch. It was a fleeting moment of success. What immediately followed was the dismissal of Watson off a long hop and then a predictable decline to 270 all

170 Peebles, op. cit., page 150.

171 Richardson's scores in the series at that point were 11, 8, 3, 2 and 4.

out and a third defeat, this time by ten wickets. It left the English press blaming Australian umpires who made errors, Australian quick bowlers who threw, injuries, the England captain, the England batters, Jim Laker, the selectors and those members of the team who underperformed.

Changes were made for the final Test at Melbourne beginning on 13 February. Two of those were the result of a car accident in which Loader and Statham suffered injuries. After overnight rain the atmosphere was humid. As if to mock the English captain's earlier misjudgement at Adelaide, Australia fielded four quick bowlers then Benaud won the toss and chose to bowl. The *coup de grâce* was dismissing Trevor Bailey for a first-ball duck – caught by Davidson off Lindwall. May was soon caught at slip off Meckiff, the bowler's 'arm flexed like a pennant in a gale'.[172] Ted Dexter failed to score and 112/5 became 205 all out, despite a good stand between Mortimore (44*) and Fred Trueman. When England bowled there were problems with the run-ups necessitating more sawdust to firm the footholds. The wicket, however, remained plumb. Nonetheless at 209/6 there was still hope until a stand of 115 between Benaud and Wally Grout. The Australian innings ended at 351 with England 146 behind. The final hours were a microcosm of the series: early inroads against flawed batters, partial recovery, and then the innings folding rapidly. Bailey fell for nought, and May was dismissed by Lindwall for 4. The total of 214 was enough to make the home side bat again, but it was all over on the fifth day.[173]

172 Peebles, op. cit., page 176.

173 The England totals in the five Tests were nothing if not consistent: 134, 198, 259, 87, 219, 287/7, 240, 270, 205, 214. The side never made a score of 300 plus. The average was just 211.

***

Alan Ross was not *The Observer*'s man in Australia for the 1958/59 tour but his poem *Watching Benaud Bowl* is a reminder that, while regretting the scale of the Ashes defeat, he would have savoured the fact that the captain and principal wicket-taker in the overwhelming Australian victory was a purveyor of leg breaks. English Test teams in those days were more often led by batters (amateur if the name wasn't Hutton) rather than bowlers, let alone purveyors of the leg-spinning art. Ross's poem begins: '*Leg spinners pose problems much like love/Requiring commitment, the taking of a chance ...*' Commitment Peter May would have recognised, but taking chances did not come easily. Englishmen like Peter May, perhaps, do not take chances with the same bravura as the Benauds of this world and perhaps the one time on the 58/59 tour that May gambled came too late and was doomed from the outset. Jack Fingleton took the view that 'Hutton's legacy of defensive play and England's faith in "Stayput" Bailey cost May pretty dearly.'[174]

All was not well on this tour from the early days at sea with players uneasy about the atmosphere. Freddie Brown warned Fred Trueman on the boat in front of the whole squad: 'Any trouble from you, Trueman, and you're on a slow boat home.'[175] For his part the Yorkshire quick bowler thought the tour co-manager 'a snob, bad-mannered, ignorant and a bigot'.[176] The bad feeling persisted and when Trueman was suffering from lumbago in the early days in Australia Brown warned him that 'we don't want unfit people on this trip'. Tom Graveney perhaps

174 Fingleton, op. cit., page 175.

175 *Fred Trueman The Authorised Biography* by Chris Waters, p. 148.

176 Waters, op. cit., page 149.

spoke for many when he described it as 'a miserable tour'. For his part, Frank Tyson sensed that 'all was far from well within the English camp', citing the pre-tour problems over the apparently unwilling tourists, Johnny Wardle and Jim Laker, and the uneasy relationship between Laker and May. 'It is now obvious,' Tyson wrote, 'that common sense should have told Peter May he was not going to get the best out of Jim Laker.'[177] So disillusioned was the fast-bowling hero of the tour four years earlier that he felt that this group of players could not be considered a side at all. He also questioned the number of touring injuries and argued that the players were expected to exist in an over-disciplined environment – on the boat an order was made that drinks at the players' Saturday evening social club should be stopped. At one point, Tyson casually addressed May as 'Peter' to his face, only for Brown to take him aside, insisting that 'it was to be "skipper" at all times'. The troubled atmosphere in the camp was not helped by the presence of former players being part of the press corps. After Ian Meckiff had taken 6-38 in the second innings at Melbourne, Wardle 'denounced Meckiff' in the *Melbourne Herald* in forthright terms as a 'chucker'.[178]

Somehow the fact that only 12 out of 18 players were fit enough to fly out to New Zealand to fulfil the final commitments of the tour epitomised the sad state of affairs. It left the survivors obliged to play two Tests and three other games. There was no Evans, Bailey, Milton, Laker, Statham or Loader. The cricketing challenge presented by the Kiwis was much easier, however, and England won the first Test by an innings and 99 runs and drew the other in a game spoiled by high wind and rain. Peter

177 Tyson, op. cit., pages 184–5.

178 Peebles, op. cit., page 193.

May batted in characteristic fashion and Tony Lock took 11 wickets in the match at Christchurch. As a reminder of the side's problems Richardson and Watson failed again, but there was the encouragement of Ted Dexter scoring 141 at Christchurch.

A significant number of this touring party would never tour with England again: Bailey, Evans, Laker, Loader and Watson. Change was in the air and would preoccupy the selectors in the months ahead. So too would the reasons why the tour had been so disappointing: the erratic and uneven batting; the plethora of injuries; the selection errors; the unbalanced bowling attacks; the absence of adequate support for Laker; the poor throwing in by the England fielders; and May's flawed captaincy. The selectors only had to look at the stark difference between the batting and bowling averages in the two sides for the Australian and English sides to see the work that needed to be done.

	ENGLAND	AUSTRALIA
Batting	Cowdrey: 43.44 May: 40.50 Graveney: 31.11	McDonald: 65 O'Neill: 56.4 Harvey: 48.5
Bowling	Laker: 15 wickets at 21.2 Statham: 12 at 23.8 Loader: 7 at 27.6	Meckiff: 17 wickets at 17.2 Benaud: 31 at 18.8 Davidson: 24 at 19

EW (Jim) Swanton walking out to bat for the Authors' XI against the National Book League at Westminster School.

Ken Barrington of Surrey and England evades a police baton: India, November 1961.

Alan Ross, padded up and waiting to bat for the Authors in 1952. The following year he became the Observer's *cricket correspondent.*

Ian Peebles, Middlesex and England, in his playing days before becoming cricket correspondent at The Sunday Times.

15 September 1954: the MCC tourists to Australia on board the Orsova *at Tilbury.*

Denis Compton watches Trevor Bailey's dismissal in England's first innings at Brisbane, 30 November 1954. England were 411 runs behind on first innings.

Tony Lock, Jim Laker and Frank Tyson arrive at Lord's on 3 October 1956 prior to the trip to South Africa. They would be away for six months.

Australian pace bowler Ian Meckiff whose action caused much controversy. Ian Peebles thought the bowler's arm was 'flexed like a pennant in a gale.'

Sydney, 15 January 1963: the two Test captains, Ted Dexter and Richie Benaud, share a bottle after Australia's eight-wicket victory.

Dexter (captain), Cowdrey (vice-captain) and the Duke of Norfolk (manager) among those at a Lord's lunch prior to the 1962/63 tour.

Fred Titmus is met at London Airport by his family after an accident in the West Indies. He lost four toes and left the tour early on 7 March 1965.

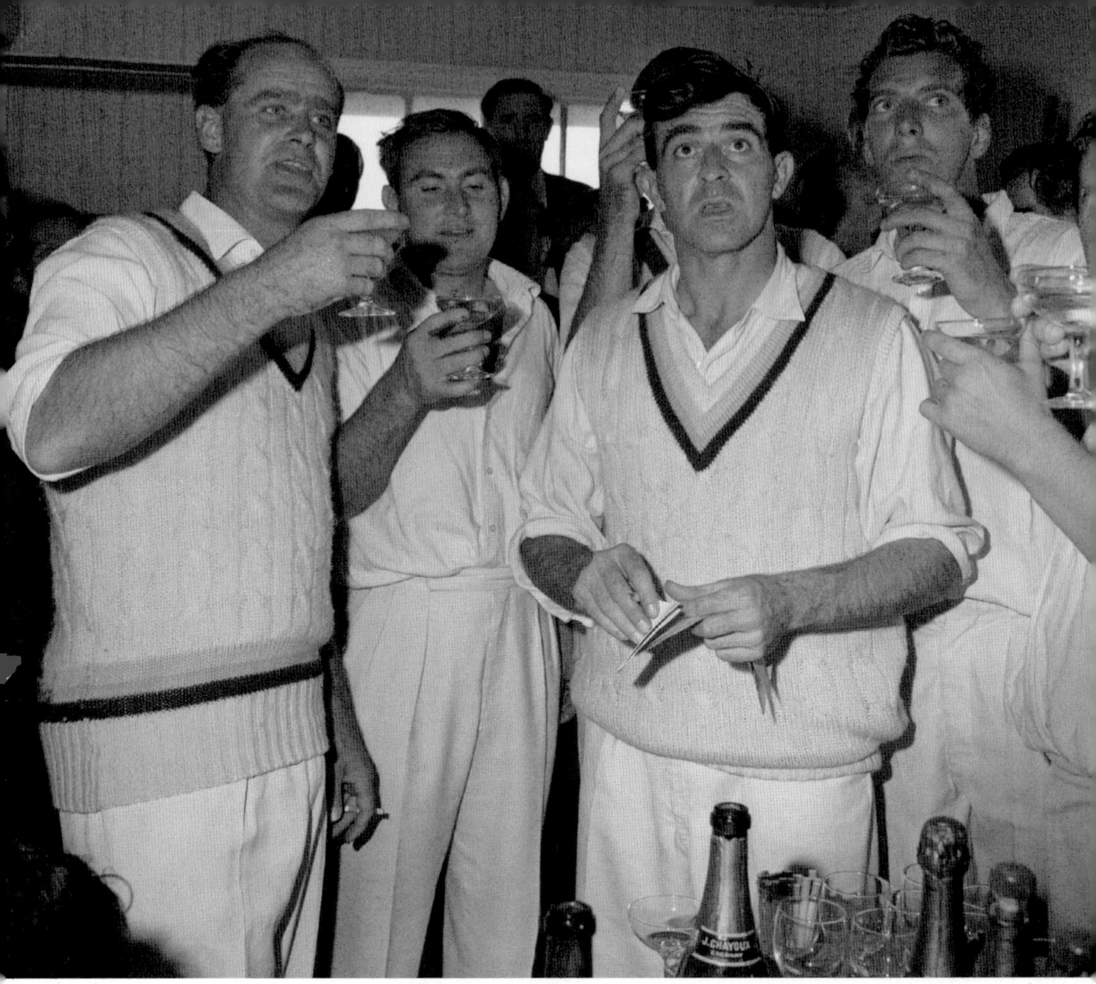

Brian Close on 7 September 1967 after Yorkshire had won the Championship. It would not be long before he lost the England captaincy.

September 1968: D'Oliveira and his wife soon after his selection for the South African tour. The decision would precipitate a cricketing and political crisis.

Part Two
The Sixties

Barbados to Karachi, Pakistan

1960–69

10

Bottle-Throwing in Trinidad

West Indies, 1959/60

TOURS OF the West Indies necessarily raised issues of colour and the decline of empire. When the Trinidadian writer and cricket-lover CLR James returned to his native country in 1958 after being away for more than 30 years, he became caught up in the campaign to 'have a black man, in this case, Frank Worrell, appointed captain of a West Indies team'.[179] In the event the series between West Indies and England played in 1959/60 saw two white men, Peter May and F.C.M. (Gerry) Alexander lead their respective sides.[180] They knew each other well from university days; both Cambridge men, they were team-mates in the 1952 varsity match against Oxford at Lord's – a game which also featured two other men from the 1959/60 tour, Colin Cowdrey playing for Oxford and Raman Subba Row in the Cambridge XI. It is noteworthy that the MCC tourists, 12 years after the passing of the British Nationality Act in 1948 and the subsequent immigration of some 500,000 people from the Caribbean, were almost without exception white. Even Raman Subba Row was born in Surrey. This was a world after all

179 *Beyond a Boundary* by CLR James, page 297.

180 Alexander was the last white man to captain the West Indies.

where Jim Swanton could, without a thought, characterise British Guiana as an 'isolated imperial outpost'. It would be another 20 years before a black cricketer played for England: Roland Butcher, Barbados-born but who played his first Test match in Bridgetown, Barbados in March 1981.

Of the 15 players named for the 1959/60 tour, two were born abroad (Colin Cowdrey in India and Ted Dexter in Milan). Of the rest, five were born in the home counties (Peter May, Ken Barrington, Alan Moss, Raman Subba Row and Roy Swetman); four were Lancastrians (Brian Statham, Geoff Pullar, Tommy Greenhough and Keith Andrew); two were Yorkshiremen (Ray Illingworth and Fred Trueman); Mike Smith was from Leicester and the young off-spinner David Allen was a Bristolian. As a group it looked short of match-winning pace bowlers and lacking an obvious replacement for Trevor Bailey as an all-rounder. All of the squad were aged under 30. Six had not been on tour with MCC previously. Alan Ross, true to his Sussex loyalties, would have opted for Jim Parks as the reserve wicketkeeper; he also felt the omission of Johnny Wardle was misguided. Jim Swanton worried that Peter May seemed 'rather stern and tight-lipped'. The appointment as manager of R.W.V. (Walter) Robins – known to be a firm disciplinarian – was perhaps an indicator that MCC was very conscious of the need to avoid political embarrassment. Robins was an enigma, 'charming' to the press according to Colin Cowdrey, but a martinet to the players. At the start of the tour he had told David Allen, 'You're not going to be playing much cricket' and, he explained, since he would be making a lot of speeches, that he expected Allen 'to look after my briefcase'.[181]

181 Cowdrey, op. cit., page 102; *Wisden Cricketers' Almanack 2015*, page 173.

The Englishmen left Avonmouth on a Fyffes banana boat, the *Camito*, on 8 December 1959, while some of the press had already sailed on board a French ship, the *Antilles*. The latter's crossing was forced by hurricane winds to lay-to outside Vigo and then became 'locked in harbour unable to get out'.[182] The correspondents of both the *Express* (Frank Rostron) and *Herald* (Charles Bray) were on board, a fact which Swanton recorded with considerable *Schadenfreude*. Nor was all well on the *Camito*: Ken Barrington on his first tour was one of several players who were seasick, while the reserve keeper Keith Andrew came down with bronchitis.

Some more cautious members of the press were spared the discomforts of Atlantic swells and weather by flying to the Caribbean in a BOAC Britannia. They even escaped spending Christmas in a hotel far from home. Instead, Jim Swanton, John Woodcock, Ian Peebles, Alan Ross and the BBC's Rex Alston flew in to Seawell Airport, Barbados on 29 December, a week or so before the first Test would begin. Headwinds had meant refuelling at Gander in bitter cold at two in the morning, an interval during which Swanton, Ross noted, remained 'a sultan islanded in sleep'.[183] In Barbados by contrast the temperature was a balmy 82° when they got there. Instead of an English winter there was salt-white sand, poinsettias, sugar cane and palm trees. Swanton was struck by how each successive touring party was accompanied by more cricket writers than its predecessor. They were busy, Jim noted, collectively filing some '332,000 words from Barbados alone'.[184]

---

182 *West Indies Revisited* by EW Swanton, page 16.

183 *Through the Caribbean* by Alan Ross, page 13.

184 Swanton, op. cit., page 19.

By 21 December the players were in action against the Windward Islands faced with a matting wicket and a slow outfield. Lancashire's Tommy Greenhough took 6-32 with his leg spin and googlies and 16 wickets fell on the first day; Fred Trueman took five in the second innings and the tourists returned to Barbados on Christmas morning with a ten-wicket win. The following day they played a Barbados Colts XI in a game which provided batting practice, but not a result.

The real business of the tour began on 30 December with a game against a strong Barbados team. May lost the toss for once and the tourists spent a torrid day in the field. Garry Sobers (154) and Seymour Nurse (213) batted on into the second day and the declaration did not arrive until the score reached 533/5. 'At times,' Swanton wrote, 'it was precious like a slaughter.'[185] MCC's reply was a limp 238 lifted somewhat by a grafting 79 from Ken Barrington against an attack in which the tall Charlie Griffith bowled with venom at a pace noticeably quicker than Trueman's. The outcome was a ten-wicket defeat, leavened somewhat by the general approval of Peter May's willingness to keep his team out in the rain while the home side completed its work. That was the only high spot: 'The fifties have not ended gloriously for English cricket,' Swanton mused in the aftermath of the emphatic defeat.[186]

He was rather more sanguine about the state of play on issues to do with race and colour. He acknowledged that 'colour distinction is more noticeable in Barbados' and 'there are two clubs exclusive to those of European descent'.[187] Nonetheless, he

185 Swanton, op. cit., page 26.
186 Swanton, op. cit., page 25.
187 Swanton, op. cit., page 38.

purred, 'the average Barbadian seems not dissatisfied with life as he finds it'.

***

There were selection issues for the tourists prior to the first Test beginning on 6 January 1960 at the Kensington Oval, Bridgetown: Brian Statham had damaged his hamstring, slipping on wet grass in the previous game. His replacement, Alan Moss, had only played one overseas Test to that point and only six all told. England's third seamer was to be Ted Dexter, who had bowled just 63 overs in his six Test matches to date. He had had a sound season for Sussex in the previous summer, taking 54 wickets at 28.3 each. David Allen was preferred to Greenhough, a decision based on an assessment of the pitch (a mirror-like strip that seemed likely to favour the batters) and a recognition of Allen's capability with the bat. It would be the Gloucestershire man's first Test.

Peter May won the toss, elected to bat and the stage was set for the opening salvos: a dozen or more bouncers at the rate of a couple every over, and slow progress by Pullar and Cowdrey. Watching from the pavilion Ted Dexter cringed at the sight of Wes Hall careering in on a 40-yard approach to the wicket and pitied the helmetless England openers under the barrage. Hall 'was ridiculously fast, faster than I'd ever seen', Dexter wrote many years later.[188] Cowdrey thought the barrage 'horrifying' and was shocked by 'the utter wildness of the attack'.[189] Predictably the English fell back on dour defence and patient killing of time: tea was taken at 131/1 and play ended for the day with rain in

---

188 *85 Not Out* by Ted Dexter, page 85.

189 Cowdrey, op. cit., page 105.

the air, May out cheaply and the score an underwhelming 188/3. The rainbow as the players walked off did not match the mood of the cricket.

In the days that followed, the batsmen prospered and the bowlers sweated, mostly in vain, despite the drama of that first morning when the English batsmen had been fending off an avalanche of short balls, with knuckles rapped and caps knocked off. On the second day Ken Barrington got his first Test century (128) while Ted Dexter's hundred was completed the following day. Dexter's 136 not out, a powerful, commanding innings, was watched by the Sussex all-rounder's parents. The England total of 482 all out made over two and a half days had made the game virtually safe; a prodigious West Indian reply would guarantee that. The home side stuttered a bit early on and day three ended on 114/3 with Worrell and Sobers at the wicket. They were still there 24 hours later after a cloudburst had broken in the late afternoon and an hour's play was lost, leaving Ross to brood over 'the palm trees mirrored in water'. He could see that only a sudden collapse on the penultimate day by the home side, or 'opulent and harsh attack by Sobers and Worrell'[190] would breathe life into 'the corpse' of the game. The partnership of 399 between Frank Worrell (177*) and Garry Sobers (216*) was a record for West Indies but the game's corpse was indeed beyond life, not least because of an unspectacular West Indian run rate of 2.5 runs per over during a total of 563/8 declared. Ross would remember the drawn Test match less for the cricket and more for the swim each morning 'at Accra Beach, the surf unrolling out of a sea of unreal blue'.[191]

---

190 Ross, op. cit., page 43.

191 Ross, op. cit., page 49.

***

Two eloquent reminders of those times: a black and white photograph of the West Indies XI – ten black men and a solitary white, the captain Gerry Alexander; and Alan Ross's passing reference to two 'colony matches' before the second Test, a phrase which jars six decades later. This was cricket in the days of a dying empire. The historian Peter Hennessy in his book *Winds of Change* refers to cricket as 'the imperial sport'.[192] We are now in Trinidad, the Queen's Park Oval in Port of Spain, with the next Test just under two weeks away. Brian Statham, recovered from his hamstring problem, gets through 30 overs in the 'colony's' first innings of 301/9 declared, taking 3-75. MCC's seamers take most of the wickets but the visitors struggle when it is their turn to bat, uneasy against spin on what was judged an easy pitch.

Subba Row and Pullar put on 53 for the first wicket and the former top-scored with 49, but thereafter five men were dismissed for single figures, including Barrington, Warwickshire's Mike Smith and Dexter, before May declared the innings closed at 171/9. Trinidad batted again, declaring at 131/6, all the wickets falling to spin. Set 262 to win in 210 minutes, the tourists secured a six-wicket victory, carried home by some powerful batting from Ted Dexter in partnership with Smith. Next up was a game at Guaracara Park, Point-a-Pierre, played amidst fields of sugar cane and the heavy smell of oil drifting in the air from the nearby refinery. Again MCC emerged victorious on a spin-friendly wicket in a game which saw runs for Cowdrey (173) and ten wickets for David Allen over both innings.

---

192 *Winds of Change* by Peter Hennessy, page 182.

Port of Spain, the venue for the second Test, was encircled by mountains, their slopes green with dense woods while the ground itself was shaded by tulip trees. Flocks of white pigeons alternately brooded and swooped over the grass. Jim Swanton was boosted by the thought that England were embarking on a second Test match for once still level in the series: in his seven visits to the Caribbean and Australia since the war he had witnessed five defeats in the opening Test. The pitch was expected to be faster than Bridgetown – the groundsman, somewhat histrionically, had promised that it would have 'pace like fire' – but May having won the toss did not hesitate to bat first, aware of the strength of the West Indian batting.

In front of a large, expectant crowd the opening overs of that dramatic first morning set the tone with the West Indian quicks, Wes Hall and Chester Watson, unleashing a barrage of blisteringly fast bouncers, an 'ordeal by fire' in Swanton's words.[193] It was enough to blow away Pullar, Cowdrey and May before lunch when the visitors were at an uneasy 57/3. Swanton was disturbed by Peter May's uncharacteristically tentative batting, the result of which was the England captain eating lunch with his first innings conclusively over. Amidst the morning's ferocity, Colin Cowdrey was hit 'amidships', while Hall was warned for 'excessive use of short-pitched balls in accordance with law 46'.[194]

When it seemed that the wave of West Indian pace would sweep away the rest of the England batting, Dexter and Barrington put on 142 runs together before England ended the first day in the relative comfort of 221/4, although the two batters had been shaken by the thunderous pace and aggression of the bowling.

---

193 Swanton, op. cit., page 94.

194 *Wisden*, op. cit., page 821.

Soon after the new ball had been taken, Barrington was hit by a delivery from Hall that 'must have got the seam indelibly imprinted on his skull'.[195] The blow left the Surrey man 'with a great lump behind the ear', but able to savour the position at the end of the day's play. He 'could lie back and take his ease, legs crossed as any Crusader's'.[196] At ease he might have seemed, but inside he was seething: in the privacy of the dressing room he had thundered, 'This is a fine fucking way to play cricket. If these bowlers don't watch out they're going to kill someone.'[197] For this outburst Barrington was reprimanded by the England manager, together with the fact that the batter, when under the barrage of Hall and Watson's fire, had 'doffed his cap' and 'pointed his bat like a rifle'.[198]

The second day saw England consolidate and work their way towards a defensible score of 382, with hundreds from both Barrington (121) and Mike Smith (108). At times the atmosphere over the first two days of the match had smouldered dangerously, but on the third it burst into flames. Fred Trueman had already had Conrad Hunte weaving and ducking in the final overs of the previous day. In the morning England's 'deadly accurate fast attack' reduced the West Indies to 98/8, a cricketing low point which coincided with the moment 'when the bottle-throwing began'.[199] The run-out of the Trinidadian slow left-armer, Charran Singh, coincided with the rapid escalation from boos to flying bottles to hordes of rioters invading the field. It was the running out of

195 Ross, op. cit., pages 91–2.

196 Ross, op. cit., page 92.

197 *England Expects: a Biography of Ken Barrington* by Mark Peel, page 44.

198 Ditto. May thought Hall and Watson 'two of the quickest I have played against'. He noted that such bowling was 'generally directed at the batsman rather than at the wicket'. His solution was not to legislate, but for the umpires to deal with the problem. MCC Archive.

199 *Wisden*, op. cit., pages 821–2.

'the obligatory local island selection' by Ted Dexter that marked the start of the madness to follow, the Sussex all-rounder noting that Singh was out of his crease by some two yards.[200] Later the blame for it all ranged from the morning's laboured cricket by the West Indian batters, the discomfort of the spectators in the tightly packed seating and, more plainly, 'sun, rum, disappointment, and sheer, evil mischief' in the judgement of the censorious Jim Swanton.[201] Walter Robins blamed the heat, the 'vast crowd tightly packed', the indifferent batting of the West Indians and 'a white umpire [giving] a few decisions in our favour'.[202]

There was, however, a potent political undercurrent to what might have seemed a boozy response to heat and looming defeat. The esteemed and radical-thinking writer CLR James, editor of the Trinidadian newspaper *The Nation*, had been campaigning fervently for a black captain for the West Indies – the replacement of the white Jamaican Gerry Alexander with the black Barbadian Frank Worrell. There were many who resented Alexander's treatment of Roy Gilchrist, sent home from the West Indian tour of India by his captain for 'dangerous bowling and disobedience.'[203] At only 24, Gilchrist's Test career was suddenly and conclusively over and somehow his summary punishment seemed symptomatic of the inequalities against which James and others railed and campaigned. Almost a year to the day since Gilchrist had bowled his last overs for his country, the English players were led off the field by their captain, escorted by police, with Statham and Trueman each armed with a stump. Geoff

---

200 Dexter, op. cit., 85.

201 Swanton, op. cit., page 106.

202 MCC Archive, 1959/60 tour file, manager's report.

203 Swanton, op. cit., page 106.

Pullar was hit by a stone and soon there were fists thrown and men fighting on the pitch amidst a hail of broken bottles and beer cans, an escalating and violent confusion which the greatly outnumbered police, armed with batons, could not control. A fire hose was turned on in an effort to clear the pitch of the rioters but 'the pressure was low and it merely sputtered out in pools at the firemen's feet like an elephant urinating'.[204] Rex Alston, commentating for the BBC, 'had no sooner denounced the insurrectionists on air in his Cambridge-educated tones' than the wooden commentary box began to burn.[205]

Whatever the causes of it all, the reality was that a Test match had been halted by several thousands of spectators spilling on to the grass, now a sea of broken glass. The outcomes were predictable. Thirty people taken to hospital; play ended for the day; the prime minister of Trinidad and Tobago, Dr Eric Williams, sending a 'telegram of regret' to MCC. For a time, the match itself seemed of secondary importance compared to the damage done to the game. The bare facts were: West Indies all out for a paltry 112 (Trueman 5-35); May opting not to enforce the follow-on but batting again, setting a mammoth 501 to win; the home side falling short by 256 runs. Two Tests; 1-0 England. However, for the players involved, it was the brutality of the cricket that would stay with them, what Colin Cowdrey (who failed in both innings) described as bowling of 'explosive violence' which was 'trying to frighten us out', and Ted Dexter remembered as 'one of the most rambunctious matches in which I've ever taken part'.[206]

---

204 Ross, op. cit., page 99.

205 Wilde, op. cit., page 332.

206 Cowdrey, op. cit., page 105; Dexter op. cit., page 85.

11

Towards the End of May

West Indies, 1960

PETER MAY with a bat in his hand combined grace and elegance, but shorn of cricketing trimmings he had the strained look of a suave bureaucrat. His face was 'fine-drawn, rather unemphatic', while on the cricket field he was 'taut as a wire … never still',[207] his hands twitching at his shirt collar, or clasping together perhaps, or gnawing at the base of his thumb. He looked precisely as you would expect a man with a 1950s preparatory school, Charterhouse and Cambridge background, but it takes a stretch of imagination to see him as a sportsman, certainly not the footballing university blue that he was. Nonetheless, there was no doubting his greatness as a batter.

May's cricket in the summer of 1959 was troubled, however, cut short by serious illness. He played only seven County Championship matches, not playing until the end of May because of his marriage to Virginia Gilligan and then succumbing to illness in mid-July. Instead of leading England in the fourth Test against India at Old Trafford he was soon to be in a hospital bed

---

207 *Peter May and Richie Benaud* by Michael Davie in *The Observer on Cricket*, page 44.

at the Central Middlesex, being operated on for an ischiorectal abscess, a painful and unpleasant internal condition far removed from the sylvan open-air pleasures of the cricket field. There would be no cricket for the England captain until December on the West Indian tour. In truth there were signs that captaincy, certainly on foreign tours, had affected his form with the bat. Under Hutton's captaincy in the 1953/54 tour in the Caribbean, May had averaged 46, but on the subsequent tours when he had the responsibilities of captaincy he had averaged 39 and 40.5 (in Australia) and 15.3 (in South Africa). After the first two Tests of the 1959/60 series he had only scored 29 runs in three innings.[208]

But in February there seemed to be other, more visible issues of concern. Ted Dexter, for example, was exercised by the pragmatism of May's approach to captaincy. From the beginning of the tour, he wrote, the skipper 'had warned us that some of the cricket we were going to play might be slow going … [and the plan was to] … simply match their rate and not an over more'. The future England captain, a devotee of bravura, did not approve.[209] There were rumblings too about players' wives joining the tour – this was a recurring issue. Few cricketers could afford to have their wives with them on tour. Dexter was conscious that his own hitherto disappointing performance was blamed on his wife Susan's presence and the avuncular Jim Swanton harrumphed about the presence of 'a covey of relations … two wives, one father and mother, two fathers-in-law, a mother-in-law and a fiancée'.[210]

With the third Test on the near horizon, May's uncertain health and the distractions presented by wives and others were for

---

208 May's overall Test average was 46.77.

209 Dexter, op. cit., page 86.

210 Swanton, op. cit., page 134.

the moment minor concerns. There were more obvious cricketing issues: May's form with the bat was mediocre, while others in the party were yet to convince.[211] Swanton was uneasy about the 'inability of Greenhough to find consistency of length or direction' with his leg spin, while Ross noted that Cowdrey 'was moping unduly about his comparative failure as an opener'.[212] Soon after winning the second Test, the MCC squad and the accompanying press flew on to Jamaica, Alan Ross sitting in the Viscount directly behind Fred Trueman and Brian Statham, who 'like exhausted warriors, slept the sleep of the just'.[213] Once on the island the players were to play a two-day, low-key game against Jamaica Colts before a more serious affair against a strong Jamaican XI where Peter May would find form at last, making 124.

The England management was at pains to establish good relations with the press, holding a conference every Sunday morning. It was intended to help with pieces written for English newspapers the following day but it became 'a cross-examination by the local writers'. Nonetheless the England captain would, once the tour had ended, announce that he was 'extremely happy' with press relations. There was just one caveat to that judgement: '... the one notable exception of Mr EW Swanton... [who] is liable to interfere with the running of MCC tours'. May reported that this was 'most undesirable and at times most embarrassing to the captain and the vice-captain'. This should be made 'abundantly clear to Mr. Swanton'.[214]

---

211 May's scores on the tour to date were 38, 2, 69, 1, 24, 24, 25, 0 and 28 – an average of 23.4.

212 Swanton, op. cit., page 139; Ross, op. cit., page 147.

213 Ross, op. cit., page 127.

214 MCC Archive, 1959/60 tour file, captain's report, dated April 1960.

Those early days in Jamaica provided a stark reminder of the difference between the cricketing lives of players and members of the press. The Jamaican tourist board flew the cricket writers to Montego Bay for some gentle, well-lubricated tourism, while the players 'never got as far as Spanish Town or Port Antonio, let alone Montego Bay'.[215] Instead the cricketers lounged around the pool at the Courtly Manor Hotel, contemplated the scope for, and wisdom of, a round of golf, or wandered off for yet another net.

Alan Ross, by contrast, was staying with Ian Fleming at Goldeneye, the writer's house on the island's north coast. It was where Fleming wrote all the Bond novels. A Commander Ross figures amongst them. 'Man called Ross. His body is now very slowly sinking to the bottom of a pitch lake in eastern Trinidad.'[216] Goldeneye was not a place noted for its creature comforts – Noël Coward, a near neighbour, described it as 'Goldeneye, nose and throat', and it was noted for its cold showers, hard beds and unspectacular cooking. A second celebrated cricket writer – Henry Blofeld – has an unexpected connection with Fleming. The novelist was 'inspired by memories of Henry's formidable mother when naming his arch villain in the Bond novels.[217] It did not deter visitors to Goldeneye, however, amongst them the writers Evelyn Waugh, Graham Greene and Stephen Spender, as well as Cecil Beaton and the future prime minister, Anthony Eden.

Instead of the familiar rhythms of the cricketing day, the minor variations of green and white, Alan Ross was able to

---

215 Swanton, op. cit., page 132.

216 *The Man with the Golden Gun* by Ian Fleming, page 101.

217 *Travelling Reserve* by Ian Wooldridge, page 14.

savour the house's seclusion, the clear blue of the ocean and its coral reef, the swimming from a beach of the palest sand in the early mornings, followed by breakfasts of paw-paw and eggs. Later there was the comforting rattle of Fleming's typewriter slowly turning out the next Bond adventure, while Ross, freed of pressing deadlines for once, could watch the hummingbirds and butterflies, go fishing, take the boat out for a gentle row, or drive the 'life-and-death road' between Kingston and Montego Bay, its narrow corniche scarred with the aftermath of a moment's inattention or bravado: 'a car hanging over a bridge', an upturned lorry or 'a head-on crash at a bend'.[218]

The third Test, played at Sabina Park, Jamaica, began two weeks after England's win in Trinidad and was played in often steamy heat. England's bowlers would have welcomed their captain's continuing good fortune with the toss on the first morning. England duly batted on a pitch resembling polished marble; it 'glinted like a mirrored floor, its surface rock hard and grassless'.[219] The first day was a disappointment for England: slow progress and a steady fall of wickets (165/6). Jim Swanton was concerned, among other things, by Ken Barrington's tendency to duck beneath the short ball, feeling that just one blow 'could break a bone and put him out of action'.[220] The short-pitched onslaught by Wes Hall and the other West Indies quicks was perhaps less inflammatory than in the previous Test, but Hall, in particular, was lethally quick and full of menace.

The cramped press box had a fine view from a shortish boundary of Wes Hall running in to bowl 'in his youthful zest

---

218 Ross, op. cit., page 131.

219 Dexter, op. cit., page 87.

220 Swanton, op. cit., page 156.

… his tremendous approach and robust action producing such pace', as well as of the spectators perched on every available roof or tree around the ground.[221] During the first day's play part of a tin roof collapsed with a thunderous roar, dislodging those who were illicitly watching the game from that precarious vantage point and causing a number of injuries. The press box was so small that Ian Peebles was obliged to act 'as postmaster, caterer, and sole contact with the outside world' since 'no one could get in or out' once seated.[222] It housed about 20, although Ross thought there was only enough room for eight. The seats were hard and the box was 'so hot and airless that a pressure cooker could scarcely have been less inviting'.[223] The cricket was good enough, however, to keep the uncomfortable members of the press engaged. A pitched battle between high pace aimed at the ribs and stubborn, defiant batting. It took a stoic innings of 114 by the makeshift opener, Colin Cowdrey, and an unbeaten 30 from David Allen batting at ten, for England to reach a respectable 277 all out.

Through the second day and into the third, England's position seemed ever more fragile. The packed bowl at Sabina Park was swamped in a 'drugging' heat according to Ross, his poet's eye drawn to the drama's setting: 'Fans fluttered listlessly in the stands, the flags above the pavilion hung limp, the coconut palms seemed made of tin.'[224] By close on the third day, halfway through the game, the home side had reached an ominous 291/2, with a relentless Sobers leading the way with 142 not out.

---

221 Peebles, op. cit., page 199.

222 Peebles, op. cit., page 199.

223 Ross, op. cit., pages 177–8.

224 Ross, op. cit., page 157.

The game was transformed on the Saturday with England managing to limit the West Indies to a lead of 76 and following that up with an unbroken stand of 65 between Pullar and Cowdrey on a pitch beginning to show large cracks in the surface. After the rest day, runs from Pullar (66), Cowdrey (97) and Peter May (45) and a defiant stand between Statham and Allen, as useful for the time consumed as for runs scored, led to the home side being set to make 230 in 245 minutes to win the game and level the series. For a time this looked feasible, but the loss of Rohan Kanhai, bowled by Trueman for 57, was enough for the chase to be abandoned. The third Test was duly drawn on what proved to be 'a nerve-racking, harassing day', marred by the England captain refusing to allow a runner for the injured Kanhai. The incident provoked an immediate 'storm of booing and catcalls' and 'left a nasty taste' once stumps were drawn.[225]

The cut and thrust of Test cricket was soon briefly set aside for two games contested on batters' wickets, first in Antigua and then in British Guiana – both drawn – played against the backdrop of what Alan Ross termed 'a curious little drama'.[226] For those directly involved the 'curiosity' was something more: pained discussions in hotel rooms, recrimination, and a stand-off between the captain and the team's manager. For the game in Antigua, Colin Cowdrey replaced Peter May as captain in a game in which he, Subba Row and Dexter all scored hundreds. May returned in Bridgetown but the scorecard recorded that he did not bat ('P.B.H. May … absent ill').

---

225 Ross, op. cit., page 172.
226 Ross, op. cit., page 197.

May's illness was not the only matter of concern. There were mutterings about the captain's wife, Virginia, and her continuing presence on the tour. She had been due to return to England by sea but instead had decided to travel on to Georgetown, where the fourth Test was due to start on 9 March. The whispers about the England captain which had surfaced in Australia 'spending too much time with his fiancée and too little with the team' returned.[227] May, it seemed, was very keen that she should be there, while Walter Robins, taking his managerial responsibilities seriously, was opposed. The two men were at loggerheads: Robins set on putting what he saw as the team's needs above everything; May was nursing his illness and isolation and needing something more than Robins' irascible certainty.[228]

May would later reflect that playing in the game in British Guiana in early March had exacerbated his medical condition, claiming that 'it was this ordeal in the humidity of the Demerara River estuary that finished me'. At all events, May's internal abscess began bleeding, worrying him enough to reveal the secret to Colin Cowdrey and Brian Statham, who had seen the captain dressing the wound in the team changing rooms. The captain's medical crisis became the main focus of concern, outweighing the presence or otherwise of any wives, lovers or family, and it soon became evident that May would not be available for the fourth Test. In the event the skipper played no further part in the series and did not return to cricket until the summer of 1961, retiring from the game at the end of that season. He was only 32 and the West Indies trip of 1959/60 was his last overseas tour.

---

227 Ross, op. cit., page 197.

228 Ted Dexter in his autobiography *85 Not Out* on several occasions refers to Robins' irascibility.

The loss of May was a major blow, compounded by doubts about the fitness of a number of players: Trueman (a ricked back), Ken Barrington (bronchial asthma); and Colin Cowdrey (a heavy chill). The Sussex batter/wicketkeeper, Jim Parks, was called up as cover, but didn't oust Swetman from the chosen XI, much to Ross's Sussex-supporting disappointment. Cowdrey called 'tails' and the coin obeyed once again as if May was still at the helm.

The fourth Test proved disappointing, characterised by slow play on an increasingly benign pitch. Rain delayed the start and England plodded to 152/2 at the close of the first day. Cowdrey – avoiding 'every suspicion of risk' – top-scored in a below-par 295 all out, the irrepressible Wes Hall bursting through the English middle order, taking 6-90. Slowly, inevitably, the game died, the victim of some rain, a moribund pitch and an all-embracing caution, epitomised by a third day in which just 107 runs were scored. There were hundreds for Sobers (145), Subba Row (100) and Dexter (110), those scored by the Englishmen ensuring the game was drawn. Cowdrey's men batted resolutely, closing the door on any West Indian hope of victory.

The drawn fifth Test followed a similar pattern: the toss won by England (for the fifth time of five in the series); nearly two days of English batting and another Cowdrey hundred (119); more runs in a drawn cause for Sobers (92); two declarations; and all hope of West Indies securing the win that would have squared the series denied by Cowdrey prevaricating until Jim Parks had made a maiden Test century (101*) after lunch on the final day before declaring the innings closed. So it was that England achieved their first series win in the Caribbean, the 1-0 scoreline having the ring of a solid footballing away win –

Southampton's win at QPR, perhaps, on 26 March 1960, the second day of the fifth Test in Port of Spain.[229]

England's series win relied to a considerable extent on slow cricket – what some would term time-wasting tactics. These reflected an assumption that the crucial win in Trinidad could not readily be replicated. So, containment tactics held sway, evident in adroit field placing, slow over rates and 'overdone time-wasting … [and] bowling to a large extent outside the off stump'.[230] According to May, England had tried to average 15 or 16 overs per hour, but failed due to the 'oppressive heat, the number of drink intervals and also because of the long innings of Sobers which necessitated continued changing of the field'.[231]

In the recent tour of Australia (1958/59) the batting averages had been topped by Cowdrey, May and Graveney. In this tour the places of the latter two were usurped by the new wave – Ted Dexter and Ken Barrington. Spin bowling was largely irrelevant (Allen's nine wickets costing 46.3 each) where in Australia Jim Laker had taken 15 at 21.2. The new order was evident: Ted Dexter topped the Test batting averages with 526 runs at 68.75 and was third in the bowling averages. Dexter would later note that Alan Ross, 'hitherto no Dexter fan' and a man who did not rate him 'as a bowler while Trevor Bailey was still around' did acknowledge the Sussex all-rounder to be a 'potentially great batsman'.[232]

May's report on his players noted the courage of Pullar, Barrington and Cowdrey; the 'fighting' qualities of Subba

229 Both clubs were then playing in the old Third Division.

230 *Wisden* op. cit., page 805. *Wisden* noted with disapproval that over rates fell to under 14 an hour.

231 MCC Archive, 1959/60 tour file, captain's report, dated April 1960.

232 Dexter, op. cit., page 88.

Row and Illingworth; the 'splendid tourists' among the party – Andrew, Greenhough and Alan Moss for example; the fielding of David Allen and Dexter; and the spin bowling of Illingworth and Allen. There were critical comments too: Roy Swetman 'disappointed' the skipper who was not enamoured of his attitude ('finds it difficult to remain humble'); Pullar's fielding did not match his batting (it 'gives the impression that he doesn't enjoy that part of the game'); Dexter's bowling which 'lacks control and direction' and Greenhough's 'accuracy was rather suspect'. Walter Robins agreed in the main with May, but his report noted that Alan Moss was 'too critical of his fellow players and inclined to grouse when things were not going his way'; Statham was 'too easy-going' to be the ideal senior professional; and Fred Trueman, while being very popular, could be 'difficult and aggressive'.

So the tour came to an end, the players flying back to London, spared the trial of a slow banana boat home. Apart from the cricket what would linger in the memory perhaps were the tall palm trees swaying in the trade winds; the ocean and white sand; riot police in tin hats and shorts; the rudimentary overcrowded benches at the Test grounds; bamboo groves and winding roads; the bullring atmosphere at Sabina Park. On the field what stood out was the majesty of Sobers' batting, the fury of Wes Hall's pace and the dour, remorseless certainty of the English.

For the MCC tour party there was also the conundrum of tour management and leadership. The lordly Dexter might have baulked at what he saw as Walter Robins' irascible nature, but the equally regal *Wisden* deemed the management of the 1959/60 tour to be 'excellent', praising Robins' 'firmness, tact and enthusiasm'.[233] Robins was lauded for his safe pair of hands on the tour and the prevailing view was that he had fostered team spirit to such an extent that it was regarded as a happy tour. Nonetheless, May's relationship with the manager was tested by the events before the fourth Test. Ted Dexter would note that Robins' 'mantra throughout the tour had been that we were all lazy and good for nothing' while Cowdrey regretted that, after the tour, 'apart from a few formal greetings over the next few years he had little time for me'.[234] With Peter May's retirement from the game less than a year away, the issue of the England captaincy would preoccupy the man soon to become chairman of selectors, Ted Dexter's 'old bête noir', Walter Robins.[235]

For his part the manager, at the tour's end, played for MCC against a British Honduras XI in Belize. Wearing his Free Foresters cap, he opened the batting with Raman Subba Row and made a ponderous 14 before being caught and bowled.

---

233 *Wisden Cricketers' Almanack 1961,* page 812.

234 Dexter, op. cit., page 87; Cowdrey op. cit., page 103.

235 Dexter, op. cit., page 131.

12

On the Road

Rawalpindi to Colombo via Lahore and Delhi, 1961/62

ALAN ROSS was one of the coterie of cricket correspondents who, for various reasons, did not travel to India, Pakistan and Ceylon to cover the MCC tour of 1961/62. Calcutta born, he was seven years old when he was sent to England to attend prep school. In 1961, however, he assumed the editorship of the *London Magazine* and his literary focus was on that new role rather than the compilation of his idiosyncratic, elegant accounts of England cricket tours. It would not have escaped him that touring India and Pakistan was of a different order to other tours. In 1961/62 the two countries remained bitter political enemies, so much so that 'there were no Test matches between India and Pakistan from … 1960/61 until 1978-79'.[236] The 1960s would end in riot, bloodshed and the creation of an independent Bangladesh arising out of East Pakistan. An unfinished Test match between England and Pakistan in Karachi in March 1969 was, as we shall see, a landmark on that tumultuous journey.

---

236 *Wounded Tiger* by Peter Oborne, page 171.

To some writers and cricketers this was the tour to avoid. There was certainly no long queue of eager English cricket writers seeking entrance to the subcontinent's press boxes. As for the players, there was a tendency for them to withdraw from what were deemed to be 'less attractive destinations'. It would be gruelling, was the thinking, with much travelling, not always in the most comfortable transport; too much cricket (24 matches, including eight Tests to be played, five against India and three against Pakistan); too much time away from home (136 days), and there were many doubts about playing the game in sustained heat, as well as in the absence of Western comforts and food. Even 30 years later, when Keith Fletcher managed an MCC tour of India and Pakistan, 'corned beef sandwiches were … used as emergency back-up fodder'.[237]

The reluctance to tour began with the likely first-choice captain, Colin Cowdrey, declaring himself unavailable, saying that he felt the need to take a break from Test cricket, perhaps with the thought of the Ashes tour the following year. In the event the captaincy was given to Ted Dexter. Some of the selected squad were not of full Test match quality, with many 'untried and untested'. Dexter – one of only eight men who have captained England tour parties before the age of 27 – was scathing in describing the tour, the 'thousands of miles … in ancient, lumbering trains and buses rattling over rutted and potholed roads, staying in accommodation that Mowgli might have recognised'.[238] As well as the absent Cowdrey, there was no Trueman, Statham, May or Subba Row as altogether eight established cricketers turned down the invitation. It was in

237 Wilde, op. cit., page 191.
238 Wilde, op. cit., page 248.

effect an 'A' squad. Dexter was inclined to deplore 'this lack of commitment on the part of these senior players' but was 'determined to aim at positive cricket and won't be put off by fear of being beaten'.

The tourists' batting would rely heavily on Ken Barrington, Mike Smith, Peter Richardson, Geoff Pullar and Dexter himself; the principal spin bowling options were Tony Lock and David Allen; but there were two untried wicketkeepers, while the pace bowling – in the hands of David Smith (Gloucestershire), 'Butch' White (Hampshire) and Alan Brown (Kent) – looked to lack the pace and cutting edge of those who had chosen not to tour. As well as being disconcertingly short of high-class players, the tourists of 1961/62, like many others, 'never did accustom themselves to the different type of food, the all-too-many functions and the unusual living conditions' – so *Wisden* observed in its summary of the tour.[239]

The itinerary was both punishing and seemingly whimsical in its choice of venues, while the web of journeys required to ensure that 11 English cricketers would be in place and in whites when the day's play began was complex and tiring. When plans for the tour were drawn up and road-tested, who questioned its good sense and practicability? Dexter's men – as well as acclimatising to the subcontinent's distinctive climate and culture – were the victims of the quirky decision to open cricketing matters on 13 October in Rawalpindi, northern Pakistan; then travel 200 miles south to Lyallpur (now Faisalabad), with just one day between games to allow for travel, nets and rest; then play a Test against Pakistan in Lahore – a further 100 miles – before travelling well

239 *Wisden*, op. cit., page 869.

over a thousand more, south to Pune in India, to play Combined Universities. They would be required to return to Pakistan to conclude the tour – but not until 19 January 1962 – to play the second Test (at Dacca in East Pakistan). For the intervening two and a half months the English cricketers criss-crossed India from Ahmedabad to Madras. Despite the challenge of it all, Ted Dexter for one was 'enthralled' by 'the vivid colours, the odours and cacophony of the place'.[240]

Cricket tours of such length invariably test more than cricket and for some players there is additional pressure from playing infrequently. The malign consequence of that in the 1950s and 1960s was such that the selectors were keen to restrict the size of touring parties. The alternative was cricketers struggling with time on their hands, rather than a bat or ball, watching others in action. When MCC toured West Indies in 1959/60 while Dexter, Barrington, Mike Smith and Illingworth played in 12 or 13 games, others were often idle: Keith Andrew played in only four, while Tom Greenhough and Alan Moss turned out just six and eight times respectively. For obvious reasons the reserve wicketkeeper was the most likely to be an idle bystander, so the selectors felt it necessary to take into account not only ability with the gloves, but also their batting and whether they were of the 'right stuff' – a 'good tourist' in fact.

Nor was the strain confined to the players; for managers of touring parties the long weeks of responsibility and travel were anything but relaxing. Some coped with that better than others while some derived comfort from a glass or two of something restorative (or not). Indeed, 'some of the heaviest drinking has

240 Dexter, op. cit., page 101.

been done by those charged with running tours'. The manager of the 1961/62 tour, Tom Pearce, would, on those occasions when the game was being played in a 'dry' state, ensure that transport was laid on to drive the players over the border to the nearest available watering hole. Ken Barrington took a particularly jaundiced view of the expedition: 'Fifty miles there in this bleeding old bus, and fifty miles back, and we couldn't start the journey back till the manager had been carried on to the bus!'[241]

And so the touring Englishmen arrived in the Punjab garrison town of Rawalpindi, a few miles south of Pakistan's capital, Islamabad. Hot, humid and frequently thundery, this was a far cry from Lord's. The opposition for the first match of the tour was a President's XI and it began on 13 October 1961 and was played on a bowler-friendly pitch. MCC lost the toss – here Ted Dexter seemingly lacked Peter May's dexterity (the Sussex man would win it once only in the Test series). The President's XI batted first, making 208. MCC began well in reply, courtesy of Russell and Richardson reaching 69/0 by the close of the first day. However, an overnight thunderstorm rendered the wicket treacherous and the off-breaks of Javed Akhtar took full advantage: he ended the innings with 7-56 in 17 overs. After a stand between Mushtaq Mohammad (102*) and Zia Allah of 120 had rescued the home side from a troubled 36/5, MCC were set 207 to win, a challenge which proved out of reach and the game was drawn.

The first Test was now less than a week away: days which would be largely taken up with a three-day game and travelling.

241 Wilde, op. cit., page 405.

In Lyallpur Dexter won the toss, chose to bat and, for a while, might have regretted it, his side relying on Barrington's top score of 55 to reach 252. The pitch was mud-caked and starved of grass and offered considerable spin to the extent that the off-spinner Afaq Hussain took 6-89. Batting became more problematic as the game wore on with the home side struggling to 119 before MCC's second-innings 106. It was enough: needing 240 to win the home side fell short by 29 runs with David Allen taking seven wickets. The win was narrow but a timely boost before the serious business began in Lahore.

Lahore proved to be a bustling city, a beguiling mix of noise and vivid colour, its streets a teeming confusion. Arriving by air early in October, Ted Dexter would comment on its 'shocking poverty'.[242] The city had a turbulent history, violent too – it was less than 15 years since, in the time of India's partition and the creation of Pakistan, that the Hindu quarter of the city had been burned down with 'death trains' arriving from the east 'with blood dripping from the carriages on to the track.'[243] Elsewhere in the city was Lahore's Gymkhana cricket ground, 'A beautiful spot nestled in Lawrence Gardens ... [where] century-old sheesham trees, with their crooked bark, long leaves and pale flowers enclose a well-tended ground.'[244] The ground and 'its oriental-style pavilion' built in the 1880s is a reminder of the lost age of empire. Test matches in the early sixties were played elsewhere, at the Lahore stadium, not yet named for the then Libyan leader Colonel Gaddafi – that would follow ten years later.

---

242 Dexter, op. cit., page 101.

243 *All-India and Down Under* by Richard Knott, page 229.

244 *The Lost Homestead* by Marina Wheeler, page 251.

Staying at the 'less than luxurious Airport Hotel', the England captain, Ted Dexter, chose to treat the opposition management to a dinner, 'making sure their glasses were topped up' and keen to establish good relations, as well as pre-empting 'the recurring problem of local umpires at the matches displaying any national bias'.[245] Perhaps in the back of his mind was the furore that surrounded the unofficial tour of Pakistan in 1955/56 when the English players had 'kidnapped' an umpire, Idris Begh, the incident triggered by drink and resentment about what was seen by the visitors as biased umpiring. A number of the present squad – Barrington, Lock and Peter Richardson – had been on that tour.

The first Test began well for Pakistan: they won the toss and chose to bat first, their score reaching 254/3 at the end of the opening day. The two quick wickets taken by 'Butch' White – bowling only his 11th and 16th balls in Test cricket – augured well, but England struggled for wickets thereafter with Javed Burki making 138. Resuming next day, the score progressed to a promising 315/3 before Imtiaz Ahmed declared the innings closed at 387/9. Despite the pitch deteriorating into 'the customary concrete slab', a good stand between Smith and Barrington of 192 put the visitors into a strong position. Both Smith and Barrington were run out – Smith on 99 – and the England innings duly closed on 380. The pitch did not offer the comfort of the first innings: Pakistan were dismissed for only 200 with the wickets shared amongst Brown, Allen and Bob Barber (three wickets each). Ted Dexter took the wicket of the Pakistani captain. Set 208 in 250 minutes, an unbroken

245 Dexter, op. cit., page 102.

stand between Dexter (66*) and Barber (39*) ensured a victory by five wickets.

There was little time for any celebration, thanks to the treadmill designed by the tour planners. On 26 October, with the first Test won, the party was obliged to embark on the marathon trip to play against Combined Universities, which was comfortably drawn, the tourists' batting shored up partly by Geoff Pullar and the Middlesex pairing of Eric Russell and John Murray, but principally by a whimsical tour de force from Ken Barrington – 149 not out in 290 minutes. As an encore he went on to take two wickets. His bravura performance prompted a pitch invasion – not riotous for once, but rather a benign crowd bearing gifts, including a pair of sunglasses which he promptly donned and wore till the last ball of the game. The Surrey man was a prodigious batsman, a natural comic with a liking for wacky imitations (of Garry Sobers for one), and an idiosyncratic regimen for preserving his health in India, shunning the local food for a steady diet of egg and chips supplemented by a battery of medicines in order to keep illness at bay.

Two more draws followed, the first against West Zone in Ahmedabad, 400 miles to the north, at the beginning of November, a game notable for another resolute century from Geoff Pullar (104); then on the road again, over 300 miles south to Bombay where the home side, set 188 in 150 minutes, eventually fell behind the required rate and were obliged to defend resolutely to save the game. When Pai and Gupte, both on 0* at the close, walked off the field at 137/7, the English would have been pleased with their increasing control of the game, but more, perhaps, the fact that there was no cricket or travel the following day. Instead, the relative comfort of the same bed for the next six days, a gentle net and an opportunity to finalise plans for the first Test against India.

In the steamy heat of the Brabourne Stadium – named for a former governor of Bombay whose well-born pedigree included Wellington College, the Royal Artillery and the House of Commons – England's bowlers would have been glad to see their captain win the toss and choose to bat. The pitch proved benign and England's batters from the outset went about their business carefully. No wicket fell for almost three hours, Pullar and Richardson putting on 159. It soon became clear that on such a pitch a result would be very unlikely. Ken Barrington, suffering 'bouts of exhaustion and periodic booing' was the rock on which the formidable England total of 500/8 declared was set.[246] He was undefeated on 151 when Dexter declared the innings closed. Almost two days of the game were over when the Indian openers, Contractor and Jaisimha, embarked on the daunting assault on what was England's highest ever total in India. Before the close, Brown had forced Jaisimha to retire temporarily after being struck on the head.

Over the remaining days the game followed a predictable pattern, a victim of the placid pitch: the England spinners plugged away diligently, Lock and David Allen taking seven of the wickets to fall, bowling 84 overs between them, and the visitors began their second innings with a lead of 110. By the start of the final day England were 237 ahead with seven wickets still in hand, leaving Dexter with the problem of when to declare and what the ideal target should be. In the event he called his

---

246 Peel, op. cit., page 63.

men in at 184/5, with Barrington (52*) again undefeated and so India were set 295 to win at 72 runs an hour. It was a target that did not appeal to the home side and the game was duly drawn with five Indian wickets down and 115 runs still required. Towards the end England were sufficiently unexcited by the distant prospect of a win that Dexter asked his part-time bowlers, Barrington, Mike Smith and Richardson, to bowl. Four days of earnest batting on a toothless pitch guaranteed that the fifth day would lead nowhere, though no doubt Peter Richardson enjoyed his two Test wickets. He would only take one more in his 34 Test matches: at Dacca against Pakistan in January 1962.

A day's grace, 450 miles of travelling east, and then a moribund encounter with the President's XI in Hyderabad on a pitch as bland as the featherbed the tourists had just left behind. The two sides were captained by Sussex team-mates Ted Dexter and Mansoor 'Tiger' Pataudi, 'the son of the only man to have played Test cricket for both England and India'.[247] The Nawab of Pataudi was, like Lord Brabourne, an alumni of Wellington College. He was the first Indian to captain Oxford University but, while still at the university, had lost most of the sight in one eye in a car crash after the first day's play against Sussex at Hove on 1 July 1961. A sliver of windscreen glass had penetrated his right eye. Pataudi would go on to have an illustrious Test career for India. Asked when he thought he could play Test cricket for India despite his damaged eye, he replied, 'with a laconic shrug of the shoulder, "When I saw the England bowling line-up."'[248]

Despite his accident, five months later Pataudi would make 70 on the first day of the game in Hyderabad in a total of 281/5

---

247 Dexter, op. cit., page 104.

248 Dexter, op. cit., page 105.

declared. In reply MCC struggled to 261, having been in deep trouble at 72/5, only to be rescued by Smith and Barber. Pataudi duly declared for a second time, a sporting decision which gave both sides a realistic glimpse of victory. An innings of 84* by Peter Parfitt saw MCC win the game by four wickets off the first ball of the final over.

The win in Hyderabad was an outlier in a relentless sequence of drawn games. After a day's break from cricket – and a 900-mile journey north to Jaipur – the pattern resumed against Rajasthan with a soporific game on a matting wicket which did not appear to help the bowlers, although David Smith of Gloucestershire took 6-47. MCC began slowly but Barrington and Knight made 108 in 55 minutes and Dexter declared with his team 46 runs behind. There seemed little appetite for the home team to enliven the contest: instead of chasing the game, Rajasthan chuntered along at barely two runs an over and a draw duly followed. There was one more game before the second Test, against Central Zone in Nagpur. The result was no different, with runs for Parfitt (166*) and Russell (101) on another slow pitch.

England contested 12 days of Test cricket against India in the last month of 1961 – two completed Tests as well as the first two days of a decisive match which finished on 4 January 1962. Through the first months of the tour England's progress had been largely untroubled, if occasionally short on compelling action: ten games undefeated, but with only three wins, the remainder being drawn games of varying intensity. In December all that was to change, perhaps the crucial factor being the spin of the coin in the fleeting moments before play began each morning. Meanwhile, the travel-weary English progressed across the northern spread of the subcontinent, trying to adjust to yet another change of scene – from Kanpur to Delhi and on to Calcutta. Each call by the Indian captain, Nari Contractor, as the coin turned in the morning sunlight, was correct and each time the Indians batted with their confidence boosted by their captain's luck and the groundsmen's skill in curating a batter's pitch. In the three 'December Tests' India never made less than 380 in the first innings. The average first-innings score for India in those Tests was just under 438.

The second Test began in Kanpur on 1 December and its outcome was only briefly in doubt, courtesy of yet another slow, batter-friendly pitch. It began well enough for the tourists, with the first Indian wicket falling at 41. Barry Knight, playing instead of Alan Brown, who had been wicketless in Bombay (0-79 over the two innings), bowled the Indian captain for 17. It was Knight's first Test wicket, while Brown was never to play for England again. As the score steadily mounted, Dexter's field placing became increasingly defensive, restricting the Indian run rate. Durani, batting at number four, spent an hour without scoring, but there was no disguising the fact that the Indians were gradually playing themselves into a formidable position. They did not declare until the third morning, with the score at 467/8.

After a long time in the field, the English proved brittle, the first five batters falling to Gupte's leg spin, with the captain himself out for just 2. At one point the visitors were 128/7 and only a stand between Bob Barber (69*) and Tony Lock (49) eked the score to 244, still 223 runs adrift. Contractor asked the English to bat again and, for the first time in Test history, England were obliged to follow on against India.

Normal service was resumed in the Englishmen's second visit to the batting crease, with the bland wicket having the final say. Three English batters scored hundreds – Pullar, Barrington and Ted Dexter who was 126* at the close, with the game saved and the tour's collection of draws increased by one. The England captain saw no value to be gained by declaring on a wicket that merely offered the bowlers further punishment. The dour spirit of the game was perhaps reflected in the mood around the ground, manifested in the number of stoppages, caused sometimes by spectators with mirrors and scraps of tin attempting to disturb the batsmen by reflecting the sun into their eyes. Hurled stones, fights and fires added to the restive atmosphere. Not a riot this time, but a definite sense of disquiet.

At last, in mid-December, in winning a game against North Zone in Jullundur by nine wickets, MCC's bowlers succeeded for the first time on the tour in dismissing a side twice. So comfortable were the visitors that Ken Barrington played but was not required to bat. It meant that, after two months of touring, the MCC party remained unbeaten. Approaching the halfway point of their odyssey across the subcontinent, they travelled to Delhi for the third Test, conscious that, while the cricket was not always of the highest quality or drama, there was little to suggest that the series might be lost. The pressure of touring was unrelenting, however, though Ted Dexter was glad that 'the tour schedule was so crowded that it left little time for the players to dwell on wives and girlfriends back in England'. There was cricket, travel, more cricket and then the Saturday night drinks parties 'where our two fast bowlers would often get out of hand'.[249]

249 Dexter, op. cit., page 105.

The final two days of the Delhi Test were washed out. What preceded the rain was a ponderous display, so slow that, had the weather remained fine through to the end, there would still have been no result. Over the three days of play only 13 wickets fell and five of those were sacrificed in futile attempts to progress the contest. For India the Nawab of Pataudi was capped for the first time. He would make an underwhelming 13 after his captain had won the toss and batted on a good pitch. Despite Pataudi's disappointing contribution, India scored 466 in the best part of two days, with hundreds from Jaisimha (127) and Manjrekar (189*). England's reply was reassuringly solid – 256/3 with Ken Barrington once again an unbeaten centurion (113*) – but that was as far as it got: three days of painstaking cricket; then rain fell through the Delhi night and on into the morning, turning the pitch to mud.

The bad weather and the thousand-mile journey to the next venue meant some days without cricket. On 22 December MCC faced East Zone in Cuttack in one more 'pointless … [game] … without any hope of a result'.[250] The home side took seven laborious hours to make what MCC had managed in four, batting on into the third day – Christmas Eve – thereby removing all hope of a result. Christmas Day, however, was 'far from being a happy celebration with the family; it was spent travelling from Cuttack to Calcutta'.[251] Then, on Boxing Day, MCC began a game against a Services XI. Played on a pitch with some life for once, it provided the easiest win of the tour. MCC won the toss, scored quickly (178 runs between lunch and tea) before Butch White (5-42 in the first innings) and Barry Knight (4-7 in the

250 *Wisden*, op. cit., page 887.

251 Dexter, op. cit., page 105.

second) bowled the visitors to an innings win. The early finish was welcome with the fourth Test starting on 30 December at Eden Gardens, Calcutta.

The year's end was almost upon the tourists without them having been unduly discomforted over almost three months of cricket. But then, in Calcutta, India won a crucial toss on a wicket which took spin from the outset, with patches of rough causing problems, especially for left-handed batters. The pitch's idiosyncrasies injected more life into the cricket, increasing the likelihood of a definitive result. England made changes – Geoff Millman and Parfitt came into the side for their Test debuts, while Geoff Pullar dropped out suffering from dysentery with Russell deputising. It started well enough with India reduced to 194/5 at one stage, but with nine of the Indian XI making double figures, they recovered to a competitive 380 all out (Allen 5-67). England's progress was one of slow decline, 107/3 at the end of day two falling away to 212 all out.

From that point England were never less than impaled. India batted solidly second time around, making 252, setting a daunting target of 421 in a little over eight hours. Russell and Barrington went cheaply (England 27/2) only four Englishmen got into double figures (Richardson, Parfitt, Knight and Dexter); and wickets fell steadily to end in a disappointing 233 all out, 187 short of the target. Despite the good work of the England spinners – Allen and Lock taking 15 wickets in the match – the batting was largely undistinguished. The defeat was only the second Indian win against England, the loss made worse by its severity.

For the fifth Test, to be played in Madras, England dropped Russell, pushing Barber up the order to open with Richardson, and brought in Mike Smith to bolster the middle order. It made little difference. India won the toss and scored solidly on a wicket taking spin, with Pataudi making 103 in a total of 428. England once again contrived to surrrender the game in their first innings, losing their top four batters in short order. It did not get better: 209 all out, with Barrington's 48 the top score. Dexter scored just 5 in two innings. And so, in just over a fortnight either side of Christmas, the series had been conclusively lost.

By the time of this second Test defeat the tour was three months old, but far from over, with two more countries to visit and seven matches to play, including two Tests against Pakistan. The first of these – strangely the second of the series – was in Dacca in East Pakistan. This proved to be 'one of the strangest Test matches for many years.'[252] From before tea on the fourth day neither side showed any interest in winning the game, the resulting cricket proving 'excessively dull and pointless'. Ted Dexter had lost the toss (for the sixth time out of seven); the pitch proved slow and dead, resembling 'rolled plasticine',[253] with the ball hardly bouncing above a few inches. Pakistan scored only 175 on the first day and meandered to 393/7 before declaring. Forty-eight hours later, England were 333/1 (Pullar 165), but, after the rest day, fell away to 439. Thereafter, the game drifted towards a dreary end, its farcical nature exemplified by part-time bowlers, Peter Richardson and Geoff Pullar, bowling in tandem for more than an hour on the final morning.

If the cricket was torpid and dispiriting and time seemed to stand still as the inevitable draw was reached, what followed was a different kind of purgatory: a six-hour flight, Dacca to

252 *Wisden* op. cit., page 893.

253 Dexter, op. cit., page 108.

Bahawalpur, followed by 14 hours on a train, arriving in heavy rain. There was no play on the first day and fog on part of the third day and yet another draw was recorded. In Karachi in early February the third Test too was drawn, largely through the batting of Dexter (205) and Parfitt (111). The captain was gratified by the series being won: 'The only time, incredibly, that an England team has ever done so in Pakistan.'[254]

Tired cricketers would have yearned for home but there was still Ceylon to be visited for three more games of cricket before the players could pack away their kit. Ted Dexter in his autobiography *85 Not Out,* published in 2020, hints at the longing for home he could still feel many years afterwards. He liked the fact that in Ceylon 'playing golf at six thousand feet … the ball flew in the thin air'. That hints, perhaps, at golf mattering as much as the cricket by that stage of the tour. But, more tellingly, he remembered the homely comfort of the former tea planters' houses in Nuwara Eliya which 'looked like the Edwardian mock-Tudor villas of a Surrey town'.[255]

254 Dexter, op. cit., page 108.
255 Dexter, op. cit., page 108.

13

Watching Benaud Bowl

Australia, 1962/63

THE CRICKETING summer of 1962 in England had been little more than 'a bleak late spring',[256] but the Test series against Pakistan had been comfortably won (4-0) with Ted Dexter captaining the side in all but one of the games. He had also presided, however, over the first series defeat by India the previous winter. It was that disappointment perhaps which triggered a contest for the captaincy of the 1962/63 tour of Australia and New Zealand, the selectors also considering two other possibilities in Colin Cowdrey and the Rev. David Sheppard. The latter was a high quality batter, but not playing regularly as a result of his work as a parish priest. For his part, Cowdrey was regarded as a safe pair of hands, 'brisk and efficient' in Alan Ross's words, the 'most experienced, accessible and warm' of the three. Nonetheless, there was a 'magnetism' about Dexter which appealed, if he could only 'thaw out sufficiently as a human being'. With Dexter's temperament, Ross admitted, his appointment would be 'something of a gamble'.[257]

256 *Challenge Renewed* by John Clarke, page 11.
257 *Australia 63* by Alan Ross, pages 11-12.

The decision was to be announced at the Gentlemen versus Players fixture at Lord's in July where Sheppard scored a calm and assured hundred (Dexter made 55 and 1).[258] Sheppard's appointment was widely anticipated, but in the event Ted Dexter was given the job. Seemingly it was Gubby Allen who significantly influenced the decision, while Walter Robins, the chairman of selectors, had begun 'to blow increasingly hot and cold' on Sheppard.[259] Given events to come, it is interesting that some believed it was Sheppard's vocal opinions on apartheid in South Africa that persuaded the selectors to choose Dexter, rather than opt for a working clergyman with liberal views.

Despite the decision to stick with the present captain, there was change in the air – this was the early sixties after all, and cricket was not exempt from contemplating different ways of doing things. The English cricketing world was exercised about the over-defensiveness of its cricketers – the cricket on the recent India/Pakistan tour was a case in point – and the divide in status of its players, either amateur or professional. A committee was considering whether that divide should be abolished.

In the wider world, however, there were events far greater and more dangerous than run rates, over rates and players' status. A fortnight after the MCC touring party had arrived in Australia in October 1962 it was clear that 'the nuclear clock was ticking – and the whole world knew it'.[260] The Russian leader, Nikita Khrushchev, had threatened world peace and raised the prospect of a nuclear war. While the cricketing tourists were at sea in the

258 Played on 18 July 1962, this was the penultimate Gentlemen v Players encounter. The last in its traditional form was played on 8 September 1962 in Scarborough.

259 *Dexter v Benaud* by EM Wellings, page 4.

260 *Winds of Change* by Peter Hennessy, page 259.

latter part of the journey to Australia, there had been a 'surge of shipping out of the Barents and Black Seas' – Russian ships trending south with ballistic missiles set to be sited on Cuba, their nuclear warheads pointing at the United States.[261] Two days before MCC played a Western Australia Country XI in Kalgoorlie an American U2 aircraft photographed missile sites on Cuba. Over the next two weeks the Americans instituted a blockade, prepared to prevent the Russians from reaching Cuba. By the time MCC were in Perth struggling against a Combined XI the Russians had backed down.

Also in the offing was a potential upheaval in the nature of cricket. In November, while preparing for the first Test in Brisbane and with four amateurs in the side, 'Lord' Ted Dexter as the captain and Bernard Fitzalan-Howard the 16th Duke of Norfolk as manager – the Advisory County Cricket Committee 'had decided to recommend the abolition of amateur status'.[262] Predictably not everyone welcomed the change: EW Swanton, for example, thought it 'unnecessary but deplorable'.

Despite the committee's recommendation, there is no escaping the fact that the cricket establishment retained a firm hold on the game and so the men in contention for the role of tour manager to Australia and New Zealand were very much on the 'amateur' side of the cricketing divide. They included, for example, S.C. (Billy) Griffith (Dulwich College and Cambridge) and Walter Robins (Highgate and Cambridge). But the appointment of the 16th Duke of Norfolk to the role was very unexpected. He was after all the hereditary Earl Marshal

---

261 Hennessy, op. cit., page 251.

262 *Arlott, Swanton and the Soul of English Cricket* by Stephen Fay and David Kynaston, page 183.

of England, had organised the coronation of Queen Elizabeth II in 1953, and would oversee the funeral of Winston Churchill. He was known to be a cricket enthusiast, while his father had built the cricket ground at Arundel Castle. Billy Griffith had been the clear favourite for the tour manager's job but he had been recently appointed secretary to MCC and it was thought he needed to be in St John's Wood, not thousands of miles away, for six long months.

The Duke's name had been tentatively put forward, he slept on the decision and agreed. It was suggested that the manager's appointment arose from concern about the captain. 'Dexter … had the reputation of being a haughty, difficult young man who would instantly alienate the Australian press,' the *Daily Mail*'s Ian Wooldridge later wrote. In his account there was a discussion in a Lord's committee room during which someone observed that managing the team was relatively easy, but asked a more difficult question: who could manage Dexter? "I can," muttered the Duke.'[263] After telephone calls from Lord's to the Palace and to Norfolk's castle in Sussex, it was agreed.

The press was stunned, and edgy too, since its members knew that the manager's role traditionally meant dealing with urgent queries from London telegraphed to their correspondents abroad early or late in the day. 'Could one disturb the Earl Marshal of England in the early hours?'[264] Whatever the wisdom of the decision it was evident to some that the peer had soon made a difference: Lyn Wellings noted that there was 'no loafing in bed as on previous tours'.[265] The Duke would breakfast early and he

263 Wooldridge, op. cit., page 21.

264 Clarke, op. cit., page 20.

265 Wellings, op. cit., page 6.

expected the players to do the same. Wooldridge, describing him as 'a portly, florid aristocrat', recounted a telling story of the Duke, at a formal dinner, getting to his feet with the port bottle circulating and addressing the room: 'Gentlemen, I wish this to be an entirely informal tour. You will merely address me as "Sir".'[266] As the tour unfolded it became clear that the Duke saw himself as a sporting ambassador. He would, according to one playing member of the tour party, arrive in an Australian state, make a short speech there about the merits and benefits of the Commonwealth – but leave the hard work to Alec Bedser, the designated assistant manager.

The selectors opted for a touring party of 17. Seven members of the group that had criss-crossed India and Pakistan the year before were omitted – three batters (Richardson, Barber, Russell), three bowlers (Brown, Smith and White) and the Yorkshire wicketkeeper, Jimmy Binks. Some selections were straightforward: Cowdrey, Barrington, Sheppard, Pullar, Graveney and Parfitt (significantly all batters). Parfitt's fielding was a bonus and would compensate for 'the vintage locomotion of some of the others'.[267] There was a reassuring solidity to the batting overall suggesting that the Test side would bat down to at least number nine.

The bowling was more of a problem, relying heavily as it did on two quick bowlers in their early thirties (Brian Statham and Fred Trueman). The Worcestershire medium-pacer, Len Coldwell, was selected after a successful summer in England (152 wickets at 17.90), but there were doubts – Alan Ross judged

---

266 Ian Wooldridge (of the *Daily Mail*) in an article *'What Have We Here?'* in the *Benson and Hedges Test Series, The Clashes for the Ashes*.

267 Ross, op. cit., page 13.

him 'unsuited for export', his pace and qualities better suited to a green wicket in English late spring or early summer than the dry heat of Adelaide or Melbourne. Ross was equally unsure about the selections of David Larter (tall, young, raw) and Barry Knight (lacking pace). As for the tour party's spin attack, it lacked the quality of recent times. It included David Allen, he of a 'low trajectory and rhythmic torpor', plus Fred Titmus and Raymond Illingworth: three off-spinners then, but with no front-line bowler who turned the ball the other way.[268] So the English bowling attack had a 'thin and monotonous' look.[269]

The side would have been stronger with the inclusion of Johnny Wardle (now playing his cricket in the Lancashire League). The omission of veteran tourist Tony Lock was controversial. Surprisingly passed over, he promptly signed for Western Australia and would play against the tourists early in the tour. With no recognised leg-spin bowler and an over-reliance on off spin, the bowling would 'not look likely to keep Australian batsmen awake nights'.[270] Finally, there was a feeling that a factor in the overall selection was the demanding itinerary, with 11 of the games to be played away from the main conurbations. After all, it was not a side of lithe young men: the average age of the squad was 28.4, a further reason perhaps for the inclusion of a 17th player. Only five players were 26 or under: Allen, Knight, Larter, Parfitt and AC Smith.

---

268 David Allen had been considering retiring from the game when he was called up for the tour of West Indies in 1959/60. Jim Parks judged that Allen turned the ball more than Mortimore, Titmus or Illingworth. See *Wisden 2015*, obituary of David Allen.

269 Ross, op. cit., page 15.

270 Clarke, op. cit., page 22.

Only 16 members of the touring party met up at Lord's on the afternoon of 26 September 1962, dining later that evening in the Tavern. The 17th, Brian Statham, was absent as a result of his wife's illness – the fast bowler would fly direct to Australia later on his own, arriving in Perth on 8 October. Earlier there was some concern that his passport had expired on 6 September.[271] After a night in a Paddington hotel, the party travelled to London Airport the following morning, some of them looking the worse for wear after a night celebrating the start of a cricketing adventure 'as their fancies took them'.[272] The Duke of Norfolk was there to see them off, the occasion marked by a mood of 'false bonhomie' and much polite conversation. It was, as the times required, a formal gathering of MCC's heavyweight committee men, the cricketers' families noticeable by their absence. This was an age when cricketers' wives were kept at arm's length on cricket tours: only Ted Dexter, Colin Cowdrey and David Sheppard would have their wives with them on this trip, and then for only part of it. The London *Evening Standard*'s John Clarke was not alone in regretting their partial involvement 'if only because the prospect is so fearful of a day coming when all wives travel'.[273]

The travel arrangements themselves broke new ground with the traditional long cruise to the southern ocean severely cut back in favour of flying to Aden, via Rome and Cairo, before boarding the P&O flagship, the SS *Canberra* on her maiden voyage, for the second half of the journey. On the 1958/59 tour the party had travelled entirely by sea, leaving a week earlier. The arrangements

271 An indication perhaps of Statham's concern about his wife was that he had not confirmed he was intending to tour. MCC Archive, 1962/63 tour file, letter dated 15 August 1962.

272 Clarke, op. cit., page 24.

273 Clarke, op. cit., page 25.

for the 1962 journey meant the players were able to spend a week longer with their families but still arrive in the early days of October. The MCC party travelled first class by Comet airliner (Flight BA230), taking up so much room that some of the cricket writers on board were obliged to travel tourist class. A number of the pressmen, including Jim Swanton, elected to join the *Canberra* at Southampton or Naples. The press party 'was not as large as in recent years' with no provincial writers included. It included John Woodcock (*The Times*), EW Swanton (*Daily Telegraph*), Ian Wooldridge (*Daily Mail*), Crawford White (*Daily Express*), Charles Bray (*Daily Herald*), Brian Chapman (*Daily Mirror*), Ron Roberts (*Sunday Telegraph*), Leslie Smith (*Reuters*), Lyn Wellings (*Evening News*) and John Clarke (*Evening Standard*).[274]

The flight involved occasional delays spent in drab airport buildings, the heat enveloping, time slowly killed; there were games of bridge, for example, for Cowdrey, Graveney, Illingworth and Smith, and uncertainty about the political situation in Aden where they were obliged to wait for 36 hours in what felt like a distant, overheated rock a very long way from home.

The shift from airliner to the *Canberra* provided a stark contrast, the ship carrying over 2,000 passengers, while the touring party's habits altered to reflect the change, with physical training beginning on the very first day at sea. The English long-distance runner, Gordon Pirie, who was emigrating to New Zealand, offered to help with fitness routines, much to the disgust of some, including Fred Trueman who 'refused to do any running and even jokingly threatened to throw Gordon Pirie overboard'.[275] The Yorkshireman thought bowling a

274 MCC Archive, 1962/63 tour file, letter to Billy Griffith from Norman Preston.
275 Dexter, op. cit., page 117.

thousand overs a season for his county was enough running. At Colombo the Duke of Norfolk came on board, 'immaculate in light-coloured tropical suit and wearing his MCC touring tie.'[276] The Duke was accompanied by three of his daughters and laid down some markers: 'You may dance with my daughters, you may take them out and wine them and dine them, but that is all you may do.'[277]

The final days aboard ship were troubled by a heavy swell, the result of a typhoon more than a thousand miles to the east. It meant that the trip from Colombo to Fremantle would be uncomfortable. Nonetheless the old courtesies prevailed, with Jim Swanton hosting 'a splendid little dinner party in a private room for the Duke' with the denizens of the English press invited.[278] Shortly before arriving at Fremantle on 9 October there was a gala dinner on board at which the MCC cricketers dressed up, without a thought for racial sensitivities, as a calypso band. There was a week before the first game of cricket.

Before that there were three days of nets and then a party consisting of the Duke of Norfolk and 14 others, 12 of them cricketers, set off in a DC3 flight to the gold mining town of Kalgoorlie some 375 miles from Perth. The flight took two hours and was marked by cloud and turbulence. The cricket by contrast had a festival quality over the two days, with a hundred from John Murray – perhaps the high point of his tour – and a ten-wicket win. It was indeed far from Lord's. Colin Cowdrey took it all in good part, writing to Billy Griffith back in St John's

---

276 Clarke, op. cit., page 29.

277 Dexter, op. cit., page 117. Dexter notes that 22 years later Colin Cowdrey married one of the Duke's daughters.

278 Clarke, op. cit., page 34.

Wood that 'Kalgoorlie provided a lot of laughs, not least in the cowboy hotel'.[279] The facilities were enough for John Woodcock to remonstrate loudly with Swanton that he hadn't made a formal complaint. There were only two lavatories in the hotel, two basins and a single electric razor point. Evidently the Duke found himself fifth in the razor queue.

The real business began in Perth with two games that would reveal the nature of what lay ahead. Peter May's men four years before had drawn both the equivalent games buoyed by the runs of May himself, Cowdrey and Tom Graveney. This time the outcomes were more clear-cut and unsettling: a ten-wicket win followed by an equally overwhelming defeat (by a Combined XI notable for its formidable top four and Tony Lock keen to make a point). Against Western Australia, in a manner that recalled other such debacles, only a rearguard stand between Titmus and Smith rescued the visitors from the ignominy of 161/7 on an admittedly lively pitch. It was like 'dreadfully old times'.[280] Alan Ross thought the early batting displayed 'the kind of paralysis MCC are prone to abroad'.[281] Lock, playing against his countrymen, took 4-68: Ted Dexter later would observe that 'there was not another spinner in Australia as effective as he was'.[282] Two hours later, however, after Brian Statham and David Larter had made good use of the pacy wicket, the situation had been resolved satisfactorily – Western Australia all out for just 77 (Larter 4-25) – and from that point MCC controlled the game, winning at a canter.

---

279 MCC Archive, 1962/63 tour file, letter from Colin Cowdrey to Billy Griffith dated 1 November 1962.

280 Clarke, op. cit., page 45.

281 Ross, op. cit., page 17.

282 *Tony Lock: Aggressive Master of Spin* by Alan Hill, page 161.

Two days later the attention turned from cricket to golf when a combined MCC and press team played a Governor's team at the Royal Perth club, with the *Times*'s John Woodcock partnering the Duke of Norfolk. Despite doubts about his aristocratic pedigree, the manager proved to be surprisingly open. Ian Wooldridge noted that 'he had much more time for the sheepshearers of the outback, far less for Melbourne's pushy social hostesses'. His preferred golfing partner, it seems, was Fred Trueman.[283]

It must have all seemed pleasantly bucolic – English cricketers lording it on a greenish wicket and then a round of golf along the Swan River estuary. How different was the resumption of cricket, with the Combined XI winning the toss, putting the visitors in and, on a lively pitch, bowling them out for just 157. Worryingly it was an 'inability to cope with the rising ball outside the off stump' that caused most of the problems.[284] At one point MCC had sunk to a miserable 14/4 with Cowdrey, Dexter, Graveney and Barrington all gone. MCC never secured any control in the game thereafter, despite five wickets for David Allen (5-76) and a stand between Sheppard (92) and Dexter (60). The game ended with the Combined XI knocking off the required 111 'with contemptuous ease'.[285]

There were clearly problems with the batting: Cowdrey bagged a pair in the second game and Tom Graveney's three innings – 14, 1 and 2 – were both causes for concern. Graveney was troubled by a bad back and, at one point, asked assistant manager Alec Bedser if he had ever had fibrositis. The ex-Surrey

283 Wooldridge, op. cit., page 20.

284 *Wisden*, op. cit., page 812.

285 Ross, op. cit., page 18.

and England man's reply was succinct: 'Only for about 28 years.'[286] There were evidently other problems, partly cricketing but also of news management. On 14 October the *News of the World* had run a story by Frank Butler headlined 'Trust GP, the Thin Man of Athletics, to upset the MCC's fat cricketers'. The long-distance runner had talked to members of the Australian press describing the English cricketers as 'unfit and paunchy'.[287]

Perth had not gone well. Glad to be on the move, Colin Cowdrey wrote to Billy Griffith describing the very cold winds and 'the curious wicket' which he felt had lost some of its pace. He was encouraged that David Allen was bowling 'magnificently (in the Laker mould)', but all things being considered he was glad to be on the way to Adelaide. 'You can imagine my delight at leaving Perth. I was beginning to think I would never score another run.'[288] Some of the press, notably Lyn Wellings, were already sensing trouble. Wellings fretted over 'the evidence that the team [had begun] to relax its purpose'. After the thrashing by the Combined XI the *Evening News*'s man noted unsettling evidence that some of the players 'seemed to have celebrated defeat in such a manner that they could hardly keep awake'.[289] There were players hiding behind dark glasses and others struggling with tiredness. To be fair, it was eight o'clock in the morning and there was a four-and-a-half-hour flight ahead.

There was still a month before the first Test started in Brisbane on 30 November 1962. Before then there were six matches to play, taking in four of Australia's major cities –

286 Clarke, op. cit., page 39.

287 MCC Archive, 1962/63 tour file, article dated 14 October 1962.

288 MCC Archive, 1962/63 tour file.

289 Wellings, op. cit., page 6.

Adelaide, Melbourne, Sydney and finally Brisbane – plus two more remote outposts. First in Adelaide, Colin Cowdrey's drear run of poor form continued. Captaining the side in Dexter's absence, he promptly lost the toss and on the first day watched the home side – strengthened by the inclusion of Garry Sobers – bat steadily through the day. The great West Indian all-rounder was a familiar face from MCC's tour of West Indies in 1959/60 when he had scored three big hundreds – and Fred Trueman had dismissed him no less than four times. In Adelaide he made 42 and 99 for his South Australian employers. Colin Cowdrey registered yet another duck when MCC's turn at the crease came, but the tourists, boosted by hundreds from Ken Barrington (104) and Fred Titmus (137*), were able to declare at a formidable 508/9. That sober accumulation of runs, as well as rain on the last day, made a draw the most likely outcome, but it proved a close-run thing, with MCC requiring just 16 more runs in the nine remaining minutes to win, when the umpires decided that the rain was wet enough to merit an abrupt ending. Cowdrey, finding some form at last, made a ponderous 32*, opening the innings and batting through in MCC's score of 95/1.

Despite the draw there was muttering amongst some members of the press over clear signs that, for this group of players, the 'cricket did not count as much as it should'.[290] Some disapproved of Ted Dexter's absenting himself in order to play golf once the team had arrived in Adelaide and later choosing to go to the races. Wellings, for one, questioned the players' predilection for time spent on the golf links, worrying about their respective swings rather than their individual batting, bowling

290 Wellings, op. cit., page 7.

and fielding, the last of which had proved below standard against South Australia. Lyn Wellings and the *Guardian*'s Denys Rowbotham were both critical, although others amongst the cricket writers did not agree. Of those, Wellings noted, 'the most pompous among them sent us to Coventry'.[291] Meanwhile, Peter Parfitt and John Woodcock went 'duck shooting with a lanky, friendly farmer'.[292]

The captain, however, had his admirers. Jim Swanton, for his part, approved of the England skipper's distinctive qualities, his 'youth and colour and personality', although he baulked at his 'chewing at the crease … a recent habit this, that somehow does not accord with his public image'.[293] There is no doubt that Ted Dexter viewed the Test series as a most serious enterprise, even at a time when the world's peace stood in the balance. This was a moment in history when it seemed that 'a detonator to a nuclear war' was armed and ready to fire. On the very day when MCC were winning in Perth, across the globe President Kennedy was addressing the American people 'to tell them about the threat they were under'. With the benefit of hindsight and retaining his undiminished patrician *sang froid,* Dexter wrote, in his later years, that once the threat had diminished, he and his men could get on with the 'far more pressing task of beating the Australians at cricket'.[294]

The relative comfort of air travel was replaced by a 13-hour train journey to Melbourne on board the silvered carriages of *The Overland*, a sleeper service on which, disconcertingly,

291 Wellings, op. cit., page 7.

292 Clarke, op. cit., page 70.

293 Swanton, op. cit., page 120 and Kynaston and Ricketts, page 69.

294 Dexter, op. cit., page 118.

passengers travelled 'feet first, as in coffins', rather than the more conventional 'crossways to the train's direction'.[295] Cricketers and writers stood for a while in the corridors drinking beer before being tucked up in bed. The pitch at the MCG was benign and the opposition bowling underpowered to the extent that the tourists batted without pity or problem, eventually declaring at 633/7. Barrington made a double century (219*), while Dexter and Knight both scored hundreds. Swanton believed that he had never seen 'the ball driven harder than it was by Dexter on this November morning in Melbourne'.[296] As for Barrington, according to the Australian wicketkeeper Wally Grout, 'he seemed to walk out to bat with a Union Jack trailing behind him'.[297]

The batting extravaganza was deceptive, both in the short term – the wicket was equally placid when the Australian XI batted (they made 451) – and more widely with regard to the visitors' overall preparedness for the Test in Brisbane, now just two weeks away. There were troubles aplenty. The visitors' spin bowling in Melbourne looked innocuous (Allen and Titmus took just three wickets between them for 208 runs in 64 overs); Trueman's fibrositis had meant he was scarcely match fit; Coldwell was unfit; Larter had lost his rhythm; and Barry Knight's pace seemed underpowered for Test cricket in Australia; so too Dexter's. Brian Statham was as 'ever-reliable but no longer quite so whippy'.[298] Alan Ross worried that the English attack lacked the pace, variety and intensity to bowl the opposition out twice.

295 Clarke, op. cit., page 62.

296 Swanton, op. cit., page 121.

297 Knott, op. cit., page 69.

298 Ross, op. cit., page 23.

As if to drive home the size of the challenge ahead, MCC were soundly beaten in Sydney by New South Wales – their bowlers battered by Bobby Simpson and Norman O'Neill and their batters perplexed and embarrassed by Richie Benaud whose 7-18 in 18 overs helped dismiss MCC for a feeble 104. Benaud was exploiting 'the old English anxiety against leg spin'.[299] There was some encouragement from a strong showing against Queensland at Brisbane, but the overall signs for the tourists were less than encouraging. Certainly Dexter believed that he had 'a side quite capable of taking enough matches off the Australians to bring back the little brown vase'. Nevertheless, the Gabba in Brisbane was not an easy place to begin the series. 'It was high summer … and hot as hell.'[300] England's record at Brisbane gave little cause for hope: they had not won there since 1936, with four successive post-war defeats.

Alan Ross spent the evening before the first Test in the Rainbow bar where the barman 'was pirouetting from end to end of his command like a ballet dancer', while a sexy-looking singer 'breathed huskily into her microphone'. Later he slipped out to buy some Chinese food from a place around the corner. The players might have been fretting about the days to come, but the cricket writer was content to watch the coloured lights flickering on the river, while 'frangipani exhaled their musk alongside the poinsettias'.[301] The night was warm; the days to come would be infinitely hotter.

---

299 Kynaston and Ricketts, op. cit., page 51. They are quoting John Woodcock and the comment was made about the 1961 tour of England by Australia.

300 Dexter, op. cit., page 119.

301 Ross, op. cit., page 23.

The last morning of November – the first day of the Test series – was sunless, cloud holding sway while the batting strip resembled a camel's hide in colour. The England batting line-up looked stronger than the bowling attack with wicketkeeper/batter AC Smith winning his first cap and batting at number six, the all-rounder Barry Knight at nine. Australia's correct call at the toss and decision to bat was ominous enough for the press box sweepstake to predict the day's outcome as anything from an optimistic 270/7 to a chilling 350/2. The prevailing view was that the first hour's play would be crucial. The Australian opener, Bill Lawry, 'hunched over his bat like a kangaroo', was soon caught behind off Fred Trueman.[302] Australia's underwhelming lunch score of 97/3 cheered the English pressmen; so too the 'rock melons, paw paws, pineapples and bananas' provided by the Queensland Cricket Association as a side dish.[303]

Through the afternoon England's initial advantage steadily slipped away. Trueman had been both accurate and hostile, but as the cloud disappeared and the heat grew, it was clear that others could not provide the same degree of fiery aggression. Barry Knight's medium pace, 'slower by dozens of miles per hour, stirred regrets for the absence of Trevor Bailey'.[304] Australia's Brian Booth (112) dominated the rest of the day which ended at 321/7. There was a feeling that the home side had been 'let off the hook'.[305]

Before the start of the second day there was a brief flurry of rain. That and the low cloud might have encouraged the England

302 Ross, op. cit., page 24.
303 Clarke, op. cit., page 93.
304 Ross, op. cit., page 25.
305 Clarke, op. cit., page 95.

bowlers, but Mackay and Benaud held firm until Barry Knight took three quick wickets to close the Australian innings at 404. When England batted, the comparison between the sides was soon evident: Benaud spun the ball several inches from the very start of his spell, while the England batting was anaemic and diffident. That changed with the arrival of Dexter, who appeared to relish the challenge of leg spin from both ends. Nonetheless it was Australia's captain, Richie Benaud, whose 6-115 was the main factor in earning his side a slender lead of 15 runs.

On the fourth day Ted Dexter's policy was one of containment, hindered somewhat by the evident frailty of his side's out-cricket – the lack of a 'a back-of-the-hand spinner' was very apparent to Alan Ross; so too the visitors' fielding which 'alternated between brilliance and ineptness'.[306] Australia batted on into the fifth day, Benaud delaying his declaration (at 362/4) until after 11.30 and this with thunderstorms in the offing. England needed 378 to win, presenting both sides with a major challenge in the time left. Benaud's caution, delaying the declaration for fear of Dexter's explosive power, was justified by the England captain's imperious innings of 99. So it was that England left Brisbane level in the series for once and with three weeks before the struggle would resume over New Year in Melbourne.

There was a sense of déjà vu about the start of the Melbourne Test. Benaud won the toss once again and, unsurprisingly, decided to bat. First thing, there had been rain threatening, while the recent weather had been unpredictable for a while. Alan Ross, driving the thousand miles or so south from Brisbane, had slithered 'over red gravel roads, the intersecting creeks and

306 Ross, op. cit., page 37.

gullies nearly all flooded'. His car's wipers had hissed constantly while the grey skies dripped.[307] But when Fred Trueman opened the bowling on 29 December the sky was a promising blue. The lunch score of 91/1 was a marked improvement by Australia on the first morning in Brisbane, but soon the momentum changed, England taking three quick wickets, two to the seemingly innocuous pace of Len Coldwell. The breakthrough prompted Dexter into setting an attacking field and the day ended with Australia 263/7. 'A better fielding side,' Ross wrote, 'would have had Australia all out.'[308] What followed were three days where the initiative swung to and fro before England secured their first win in Australia since Adelaide in early 1955, this time by seven wickets.[309] The win leant heavily on the batting of Cowdrey, Dexter and Sheppard and Trueman's 5-62 in the second innings.

Melbourne was a high point for the England side, but 'the killing schedule of this tour' precluded anything more than token celebrations.[310] By the following morning MCC were already batting on the island of Tasmania against a Combined XI at Launceston. Moreover, at this point on the tour there were mutterings of discontent – when Dexter's 'pretty wife' had arrived, as one pressman described her, and when the players had been required to travel by coach to Bendigo for a game in mid-December. Then affairs on the field started to go wrong. England's tenuous grasp on the Ashes was soon removed when the Australians won at Sydney on 'a grey-brown strip, like a

307 Ross, op. cit., page 50.

308 Ross, op. cit., page 77.

309 Of that victorious England XI in Adelaide only Colin Cowdrey and Brian Statham were playing in this win at the MCG.

310 Clarke, op. cit., page 152.

carpet worn almost beyond use'.[311] England had won the toss and batted – but the conditions were such that they might well have been tempted to insert the home side. It proved to be a close game resolved only when Alan Davidson's left-arm pace wrecked the England second innings, taking 5-25 in a limp total of 104.

With the sides now level the battle transferred to Adelaide soon after. This was the moment when the tour was beginning to lose any sense of real drama to be replaced by a grey torpor. It was 'stalemate' in Adelaide, the result of 'a fear by either side of losing'.[312]

The teams returned to Sydney for the final match with the series level at one Test each. Hopes of a classic decider were soon dispelled, a good proportion of the blame being attached to the pitch. It was grim fare, 'dull and lifeless' and ending in a draw. Soon afterwards the Duke of Norfolk wrote: 'This type of approach is considered by the modern cricketer as the only way to success … I find it inexplicable.'[313] The soporific Friday 'will remain a day we must never repeat'. The prime culprit was the pitch, deemed not of Test standard. 'It would have been a much better game at Arundel,' was the Duke of Norfolk's dismissive comment, fondly remembering the bucolic cricket ground attached to his family seat. For his part, Ted Dexter described it as a 'fiasco', adding that, 'It hadn't been mowed for weeks, leaving the turf on the outfield so long and lush not a single ball had reached the boundary when we batted on the first day.'[314] The statistics for the match reveal the true extent of the

311 Clarke, op. cit., page 162.

312 *Wisden*, op. cit., page 826.

313 MCC Archive, 1962/63 tour file, letter to Billy Griffith, dated 4 February 1963 and sent from the Hotel Windsor, Melbourne.

314 Dexter, op. cit., page 127.

problem: Barrington's 101 in the first innings took 320 minutes and included only four boundaries; the Australian Peter Burge's 103 lasted 332 minutes – it was painful, the game ending with 'Burge and Lawry, like entombed miners tapping listlessly for help' seeing the game through to what passed for an ending. 'No one was listening any longer,' Ross wrote, once the game was dead.[315] A week on, the view was that 'we should have regained the Ashes'.[316] That they did not was down to an inadequate pitch, but also the way 'the modern cricketer' chose to play the game.

The series, hailed at the outset as a great showdown between the cavalier Dexter and the urbane and relentless Benaud, left a profound sense of disappointment in its wake. 'I am,' John Clarke wrote two days after the final day's play, 'more despondent about the future of big cricket than I have ever been.'[317] The drawn series mean that Benaud had never lost any of his six series against England, but there was much regret and disappointment in the air. Later the England management took issue with the schedule (too many up-country games); the lack of air-conditioning in hotels; the presence of some players' wives; and the overlong nature of both the tour itself and Test match days. The Duke of Norfolk was particularly critical of seemingly intractable problems: 'who to open the batting ... and how we can make these people hold their catches'.[318]

There were troubling injuries too (Pullar's knee, Trueman's back) and issues of players' conduct: late-night rowdiness at a hotel; one or two players, for example, were 'intent on sampling

315 Ross, op. cit., page 177.

316 MCC Archive, 1962/63 tour file, written comment by the Duke of Norfolk, dated 2 February 1963.

317 Clarke, op. cit., page 164.

318 MCC Archive, 1962/63 tour file.

Australian hospitality to the full'. Ted Dexter, for example, described Barry Knight as a 'bit of a playboy', while other players were judged not to be 'team men', and 'selfish to a fault off the field'. Few in the squad emerged with enhanced reputations – perhaps Barrington and Titmus – but the overall sense was of chances missed and performances that disappointed. Brian Statham was judged 'best when he really had a go', but now lacked the energy to do this on every occasion; David Larter proved 'disastrous' when he tried to swing the ball (for his part, Larter found Dexter 'a remote and unhelpful captain');[319] David Allen bowled well, but should eschew experiment; Graveney and Pullar both had problems arising from their front foot method while Sheppard's 'fielding let him down'. There were other failings too, equally damning and several players' bonuses were cut. Fred Trueman had been there before.

After some five months the tourists were understandably tired, but there was more touring to come, including three Tests – all won convincingly – in New Zealand. There the 'playboy' Barry Knight, brought back into the side having been omitted since Brisbane, took nine wickets at 16.88 each and scored 208 runs at 69.3, and Colin Cowdrey averaged 146. When the tour finally ended the players went their separate ways, the majority flying back to London, arriving on 21 March. The Duke of Norfolk and Colin Cowdrey flew back on a Qantas flight the following day; Peter Parfitt stayed in Colombo, David Sheppard in Sydney; the physio Sam Cowan set off to travel across the United States and Ted Dexter was bound for South Africa to play two games for the International Cavaliers. He got back

319 See The Cricket Statistician, spring 2022: a review by David Miller of *Bowling Fast – The Highs and Lows* by Richard Sayer.

to England at the end of March. A month later, on 1 May, he was back at work, captaining Sussex in an innings victory over Glamorgan and scoring 118.

As for Alan Ross, he flew Qantas to Hawaii intending to finalise his written account of the tour. It was perhaps symptomatic of an Ashes series that had never caught fire that he shunned his typewriter for the pleasures of Waikiki Beach, surf-riding, catamarans, daiquiris and 'soft-footed Polynesian girls with hibiscus in their hair.'[320] Ross returned to England via San Francisco, New York and Puerto Rico, but he left the writing of his book until he reached home, 'under the Sussex downs, less green than I have ever seen them'. *Australia 63* emerged from typewriter days in Clayton Manor, close to the downs and not too far from the sea and Hove's cricket ground. It would be his last chronicle of England touring.

---

320 Ross, op. cit., page 183.

14

A Short Tour in India

Bangalore to Amritsar, 1964

AS THE summer of 1963 unfolded, English cricketers, or some of them, began to wonder what the winter to come might hold: cricketing employment or job-seeking, the heat of India perhaps, or some unknown, less intriguing exile. Thirty-six of them would be formally asked by MCC about their availability for the short tour to India due to depart at the end of December. It is hard to gauge what emotions might have been stirred by MCC's initial enquiry but, the human spirit being what it is, some would have been less enthusiastic than others. Weighed against the gratification of being considered good enough and the prospect of being selected in the final group, was an awareness of the harsh realities of the touring life – the absence from the comforts of home and family; worries about the quality of the chosen squad and its chemistry and how one might fit in; the attitude towards you of both captain and management; the food, weather, the prospects of illness and/or injury far from home; the vagaries of playing form; and whether or not your technique and skills were suited to the pitches and climate on the far side of the world.

The 36 initial enquiries produced a touring party of just 15, a selection partly noteworthy for those who were not included.[321] Of the players involved in the summer series against the West Indies, ten were missing from the party that eventually travelled to India on 31 December: Dexter, Brian Close, Cowdrey, Trueman, Lock, Statham, Derek Shackleton, Richardson, David Allen and Keith Andrew. That would have been the core of a hard-headed, experienced team. In the event, Colin Cowdrey's broken left arm sustained at Lord's against West Indies in June prevented him going out with the main party to India. He was replaced as captain by MJK (Mike) Smith of Warwickshire. Others who might have been selected but weren't included Geoff Boycott (second in the 1963 averages with 1,628 runs at 45.2) and Ken Palmer of Somerset (third in the bowling list, with 139 wickets at 16.07). Of those chosen there were certainly some fired by the prospect of touring. Ken Barrington, for example, contemplated it with great enthusiasm, partly for financial reasons and also because 'he remembered the previous tour with glee'.[322]

Of those who declared themselves unavailable, Bob Barber and Tom Graveney cited 'family reasons'; Brian Close and Brian Statham 'business reasons'; Tony Lock was 'under contract to Western Australia'; while in the case of Ted Dexter 'no reason was given'.[323] There was some criticism of MCC for its approach to the tour: Trevor Bailey, for example, wrote to Billy Griffith about the issue: 'I find the decision to send a fully representative side to India this winter most bewildering.' Set against that,

321 The 15 players in the original selection were Cowdrey, Smith (MJK), Barrington, Binks, Bolus, Edrich, Jeff Jones, Knight, Larter, Mortimore, Parks, Price, Sharpe, Titmus and Wilson.

322 Peel, op. cit., page 79.

323 MCC Archive, 1964 tour file, note dated 18 August 1963.

the tour captain Mike Smith received a heartwarming picture and poem welcoming the team to India from a Miss Sundari Rukmangadan of Bangalore.

Preparations for the tour included dental check-ups for all players; information about areas of India where total prohibition of liquor was in force; reassurance that dinner jackets would not be needed on this occasion and, for the 'required' overnight stay prior to the flight at the Great Western Royal Hotel, Paddington, MCC would pay the bill 'except for drinks, tobacco, cigarettes and other incidentals'.

The tour was by way of being an experiment. Much shorter than traditional tours, it comprised only ten games – of which five were Test matches – and meant that the outward journey could be delayed until the end of December – Christmas at home, then, but no New Year's Eve wassailing.[324] More time was saved by flying direct, rather than travelling by sea, an option henceforth consigned to history. There were, however, some doubts expressed about the arrangements. Lyn Wellings would later declare (in the 1965 *Wisden*) there had been 'too much travelling at times, which cut into sleeping hours'. In retrospect too it was thought-provoking that on those previous occasions when the party was fewer than 16 in number, what followed were urgent demands for reinforcements from home. That was true of the West Indies tours of both 1947/48 and 1959/60 as well as the 1963-64 tour of India. After the 1954/55 tour of Australia and New Zealand, the manager, Geoffrey Howard, had reported that a party of 18 players was too many, citing undue costs and the problem of keeping everyone fit. Sixteen cricketers was enough,

324 It was less than half the length of the previous tour to India, Pakistan and Ceylon two years before: 60 days as opposed to 136.

Howard believed. Lessons had been learned, though not always with total success: with the cricket coffins, the liniment and bandages, were considerable stores of European food – 'MCC [had] arranged for their team – and the attending writers – to take tinned food from England.'

Before the tour party travelled to the subcontinent advice had been thorough and, some might say, alarming. Each sentence began 'DON'T' and covered, for example, drinking water (not from taps) and alcohol (avoid 'locally distilled spirits'); street vendors (avoid buying soft drinks and fruit); what not to eat (salads, milk 'unless you are sure that it has been recently boiled'); the need for sunglasses, 'prickly heat powder' for groins after a bath; and the need to ensure enough salt intake. The 11th commandment was 'DON'T fail to put on clean shirts and underclothes every day or so; abandon jock straps.'

On diet, it made little difference: as early as the first Test there were a number of stomach problems. The all-rounder Barry Knight later reported that he 'had heeded a British Army colonel's advice who advised us that if we drank Scotch, it would kill the bacteria and bugs in the food and water and get us through the tour'.[325] If food remained a challenge, there were improvements in travel with nothing quite to rival the experience of a decade before when on an overnight train to Bahawalpur, with the amateurs comfortably ensconced in first class, 'the professionals emerged from their [inferior] carriage coated in the red sand of the Sind desert and gasping for air'.[326]

---

325 *Beyond the Pavilion* by Barry Knight with Andrew Leeming, page 117. Knight kept fit enough to play in all five Tests.

326 Chalke, op. cit., page 28.

It would be a Test series of constipated run-scoring, emasculated fast bowlers, parsimonious spin bowling, two inexperienced Test captains, a predominant mood of shared caution, vast crowds and, in England's case, bad memories of some players' runs – specifically, those emerging from troubled guts. The problem was not confined to the players. Henry Blofeld recounts that, in the Connemara Hotel, Madras, Michael Melford arrived at breakfast 'looking as if his life expectancy might stretch to five minutes if he was lucky'.[327] Once the spate of stomach disorders took hold 'doctors were [unable] to give a definite diagnosis'. It was, to coin a phrase, a problem that ran through the entire tour.

Two of the ten matches were played before the first Test – one won and one drawn – and there were only ten days before the series itself began in Madras on 10 January 1964. India won the toss – as they would do in each Test – and batted slowly, well into the second day, thereby rendering a draw the most likely outcome. England's reply was even slower, partly explained by an outbreak of stomach trouble that removed Micky Stewart and Jim Parks from the action entirely and incapacitated Fred Titmus, fresh from his five-wicket haul in the first innings, and Barry Knight, whose Scotch whisky precautionary regime evidently needed more time to work. Brian Bolus and the ever-staunch Ken Barrington resisted to great effect on a wicket that became increasingly dusty. Perhaps the most revealing statistic of the game was that the Indian slow left-armer Nadkarni bowled 21 successive maiden overs – 131 balls without conceding a run. Lyn Wellings in his review of the tour laid much blame on the pitches – from Madras

327 Blofeld, op. cit., page 75.

through to Kanpur – calling them so bland that 'a competent craftsman could bat successfully with a broom handle'.[328]

The road from Madras to Bombay for the second Test took in Ahmedabad, well over a thousand miles to the west, for a game against West Zone. Its main event in what was another drawn game was the injury to Ken Barrington, who broke a finger trying to catch a sharp edge into the slips. It ruled him out for the rest of the series at a time when numbers were already depleted and the England middle order looked decidedly flakey.

John Woodcock of *The Times* never saw Barrington more crestfallen than he appeared at Ahmedabad. He overheard the Surrey man ruing 'all those Test match runs going a-begging'.[329] What compounded the blow was that the injury happened when the draw was certain and the game had entered 'the formal and pointless stage'.[330] In the aftermath there was a flurry of communication with Lord's from the manager, David Clark, soon after which Billy Griffith contacted Colin Cowdrey to remind him who the nominated replacements were, only to discover that both were far away, coaching in South Africa. In what Cowdrey later described as 'a moment of rash loyalty', the Kent man volunteered to fly out to fill the yawning gap in the England middle order.[331] He had not touched a cricket bat for more than six months. It was, Mike Smith later reported, a 'remarkable achievement' to play in a Test match 'at 24 hours' notice … and with less than a week to acclimatise'.[332]

---

328 *Wisden Cricketers' Almanack* 1965, page 800.

329 Peel, op. cit., page 79.

330 *Wisden,* op. cit. page 810.

331 Cowdrey, op. cit., page 151.

332 MCC Archive, 1964 tour file, captain's report.

Peter Parfitt was a second replacement, but both men arrived too late for the second Test where the England batting line-up had an unconventional, quirky look, missing all but two of their recognised batters. Edrich, Sharpe and Mortimore were too unwell to play; Micky Stewart relapsed over the tea interval and both wicketkeepers played *faute de mieux*. So dire was the situation that David Clark evidently approached the *Guardian*'s correspondent, Henry Blofeld, pointing out that with only ten fit players the obvious stand-in was either the manager – or Blofeld. 'You and I are the last two to have played first-class cricket,' Clark said, and, as Blofeld was the younger man, he should prepare himself for the morrow. David Clark's most recent game 'had been playing in a fathers-and-sons game in Oxford the previous year'.[333] In the event Micky Stewart played, getting 'out of bed [to] take his place at short leg when England lost the toss'.[334] He had returned to his hospital bed by lunchtime.

Rarely can a drawn game be regarded as a triumph but, in such dire circumstances and with India seemingly unwilling to press home the advantage, the second Test was a rare high point for England in the tour. Titmus once again excelled as both batter and bowler and the visitors ended the game at a serene and untroubled 206/3 with Brian Bolus and Jimmy Binks providing a resolute spine to the innings. It was, though, far from exhilarating, the English scoring at only 1.5 runs per over as time petered out. At one point the persistent Nadkarni bowled ten consecutive maiden overs. An unduly imperial *Wisden*,

333 *England – The Biography* by Simon Wilde, page 326. Clark played his 75th and last game for Kent at Canterbury in August 1951 while Henry Blofeld played his final first-class match at Fenners for the Free Foresters in June 1960. His best score was 138 for Cambridge against MCC in the previous July.

334 *The Joy of Touring* by Henry Blofeld, *Wisden* 1975, page 122.

perhaps in Wellings' waspish voice, decried the 'spineless Indian performance', while lauding the England side's 'out-cricket … [whose] fire distinguishes the best Celtic rugger pack'.[335]

A telegram from Billy Griffith and David Clark to 'CARR MCC LORDS' summarised the state of the sickbeds: 'All invalids much better. Sharp discharged. Edrich Mortimore two or three days. STEWART TEMPERATURE NORMAL REMAINING HOSPITAL FOR COMPLETE CURE AND CONVALESCENCE 7 TO TEN DAYS THEN REPATRIATION. No cause for worry.'[336]

The schedule had the players playing back-to-back Tests with just two non-cricketing days between them. Moreover, the venues were on opposite sides of the subcontinent: the Brabourne Stadium, Bombay all the way to Eden Gardens, Calcutta, a distance of some 1,100 miles. England were strengthened and cheered by the arrival of Parfitt and Cowdrey – who was back in India for the first time since childhood. On arrival it was clear that the situation was troubling with the squad reduced to just five fit men. There was, Cowdrey laconically noted, 'no plan for a team selection meeting … If you could get on the field you played.'[337] He felt decidedly rusty, his bat a stranger to him, but he was able to have two lengthy sessions in the nets, grateful to 'a long queue of Indian bowlers' all too willing to test the Englishman's eye and touch. From the Bombay Test onwards each member of the team was provided with Entero-Vioform, a drug used to treat sickness and diarrhoea.

---

335 *Wisden*, op. cit., page 811.

336 MCC Archive, 1964 tour file, telegram to Donald Carr at Lord's from Billy Griffith and David Clark.

337 Cowdrey, op. cit., page 152.

India batted first once again, but the outcome was the lowest of the three first innings to date (241), thanks in part to a quicker pitch on the first day and an impressive spell of pace bowling by John Price (5-73). The England batters struggled in reply, the innings only rendered competitive by a century from Colin Cowdrey (107), but it was slow going with the total of 267 scored at the soporific rate of only 1.8 an over. The slow pace of it all was not eased by the umpires' 'amazing decision' to take the players off the field for two and a half hours when 'one millimetre of rain fell on the third day.'[338]

At the heart of the ponderous cricket were the slow, easy-paced wickets. Cowdrey described them as resembling 'a brown, grey marble slab which had lost its shine' and where 'you could feel each delivery double-declutch on pitching'.[339] Bowlers were handicapped too by the lack of bounce. For batters the result was great difficulty in timing shots. Predictably perhaps the match ended unsatisfactorily in what *Wisden* judged a 'pointless' final day: India's second innings did not start until the fourth afternoon, leaving no time for any kind of satisfying denouement.

The Test series reached its finale at Kanpur, the game beginning on 15 February 1964. Its immediate predecessor in Delhi the week before had seen no respite from the prevailing torpor: 1,258 runs scored (at 2.5 runs per over) but on that 'defunct strip of turf' there was no hope of a result.[340] Colin Cowdrey scored another hundred despite being off the field with dysentery for one session; the Indian captain made an unbeaten double century (203*), but any drama was confined to the hail of

338 *Wisden*, op. cit. page 812.

339 *The Cricketer*, April 1964.

340 *Wisden*, op. cit., page 815.

stones pelted at the fielders just before the lunch interval, together with a threatened strike 'tongue in cheek' by the England players, much put out by the absence of any water in the dressing room for the third successive day.[341]

The series had begun to resemble a dour goalless draw between two battle-hardened but punchless football teams in the dreary corners of the Championship. But the final Test at the Modi Stadium in Kanpur would prove different, at least at its very start and for a brief while thereafter. The pitch, however, was curated to the same dull, 'drugged' specification as its four predecessors and the outcome was a match where the game seemed to have an unshakeable trajectory, with the players increasingly subdued and numbed by the surface. Where it differed was at the coin toss on the first morning and Pataudi's decision after the coin came down in his favour. It was quite clear that the pitch would be blameless – unutterably bland – but Pataudi did the unthinkable and asked the English to bat first, 'a decision so unpredictable that not even Pataudi could give a rational explanation'.[342] It was quixotic, only defensible by the need, after so much routine cricket, to 'try something different'.

There were difficulties off the pitch at Kanpur too where the manager noted problems over food. Clark was unsure whether any resentment was caused by the fact that 'we used our own food or because I had to complain of the lunch provided'. He was concerned that lunch on the first day 'was exactly what we had asked should not be provided i.e. very oily fish followed by fried

341 Pataudi's 203* was, at that time, the highest ever score by an Indian against England.

342 *A History of Indian Cricket* by Mihir Bose, page 232.

chicken.' Subsequently he visited the kitchen, which proved to be 'very dirty and extremely primitive'.[343]

Pataudi's gamble didn't work. England duly made 559/8 before declaring, occupying the crease for most of the first two days. The pitch proved to be a 'dead, bounceless slab of rolled clay', according to Michael Melford.[344] The wackiness of Pataudi's decision was reinforced by India's inadequate reply of 266 (Titmus 6-77), made at a lethargic 1.5 runs per over. So it was that the series stuttered to the most inconclusive of endings: after 25 days of cricket there was to be no winner. As if to emphasise the unsatisfactory outcome, the second Indian innings at Kanpur saw England use ten bowlers, some of them merely 'occasional trundlers'.[345]

The series had largely been an unedifying spectacle marred by outbreaks of crowd discontent, with fielders pelted with fruit, bricks and, at Kanpur, metal bolts fired from crossbows. The tour still had one game left, a three-day match against North Zone at Amritsar starting two days after the final Test – drawn of course. By 28 February the touring party was homeward bound. While the cricket had often disappointed, some players emerged with credit, notably Fred Titmus (27 wickets in the series at 27.66) and Colin Cowdrey, who averaged 103 with the bat. Mike Smith's end-of-tour report noted the positive contribution of other players, Micky Stewart, John Price and John Mortimore among them, while drawing attention to some doubts, including Jimmy Binks' wicketkeeping and David Larter's bowling, which the captain described as 'disappointing'. The Northamptonshire

343 MCC Archive, 1964 tour file, captain's report.

344 *Was It Worth While? The Cricketer*, April 1964.

345 *Wisden*, op. cit., page 816.

quick bowler 'needed a lot of encouragement'. Ken Barrington, once again, was a 'splendid tourist' and the 'most popular player'. He was 'irreplaceable after his broken finger'.[346]

Other successes included the concept of the short tour of eight or nine weeks, as opposed to the traditional much longer version, as well as the effective management partnership of captain Mike Smith and manager David Clark. A report of the tour highlighted a number of issues: the difficulty of maintaining 'privacy and free time'; the pressure of official functions; the variable nature of accommodation – 'at Brabourne Stadium … one room was offered without even windows'; the need for air-conditioning; the fact that at Delhi 'the water was turned off for the whole Test match'; crowd disturbances, notably at Kanpur where 'players were apprehensive of their wellbeing'; and the disadvantage of a short tour which results in the ill or injured not having enough time to recover. At a subsequent Lord's meeting 'it was agreed that the arrangement of a three-day game at Amritsar' – 492 miles from Kanpur – 'after the last Test had been pointless'.[347] Mike Smith also noted that Indian seam bowling was not strong enough to merit sending 'specialist opening bats' to India, but 'it is essential that the best bowlers available are sent'.[348]

The series would not be remembered for the cricket. Instead the players and press would recall for many years the heat and the pitches – '48 degrees Celsius and the flattest wicket I have ever bowled on' (Barry Knight) – and, in Henry Blofeld's case, the furious contretemps involving the Maharajkumar of

---

346 MCC Archive, 1964 tour file, captain's report.

347 MCC Archive, minutes of the sub-committee to consider Managers' Reports, 15 May 1964.

348 MCC Archive, 1964 tour file, captain's report.

Vizianagaram, an erstwhile owner of the ground in Delhi, and Lyn Wellings which culminated when 'Wellings picked up his typewriter, swirled it round and threw it at Vizzi's ample midriff.'[349] Michael Melford, writing to Billy Griffith, described the Maharajah of Baroda complaining about 'sensational cricket writing'. Melford added that 'it got Wellings' ulcer working a treat'. He was disappointed that 'Jim [Swanton] wasn't speaking immediately after Baroda ... If he had ... Wellings would have been certain to blow him out the loudest raspberry ever heard East of Suez.'[350] That episode was perhaps the most dramatic moment of the tour.

---

349 Blofeld, op. cit., page 76.
350 MCC Archive, 1964 tour file.

15

The Long Goodbye

South Africa, 1964–65

TED DEXTER travelled to South Africa sometime after the rest of the touring party since he was flirting with the prospect of a career in politics. 1964 was an election year and the Sussex and England man was standing as a Conservative candidate in the constituency of Cardiff South East. Coincidentally the party flew out of London on Thursday, 15 October, election day. Dexter duly lost by nearly 8,000 votes, beaten by James Callaghan, who in time would become a Labour prime minister. When Dexter joined up with the MCC squad he assumed the role of Mike Smith's vice-captain. It was the end of October before he played, batting first wicket down against a South African Colts XI: he made a solid start, scoring 44 and 50.

Dexter's dalliance with politics somehow chimed with the spirit of the times where sport and politics had a tendency to collide and where cricket correspondents might veer into issues beyond the game itself. The *Guardian*'s Frank Keating had touched on the changes in the air when describing Dexter's explosive innings of 70 in the second Test against the West Indies at Lord's in June 1963: 'The magisterially defiant cameo represented the last sneering fling of Empire.'[351] The autumn of 1964 was fraught with political uncertainty. More specifically, 15 October 1964 saw Harold Wilson win a narrow victory for Labour in the general election; Nikita Khrushchev lose power in Russia; the Chinese detonate their first atomic bomb; while in Tokyo the Olympic Games were underway – with South Africa banned from participating. Rhodesia was also in the middle of a political crisis. The cricket commentator Charles Fortune had his own strong views about which his readers and listeners were left in little doubt: 'The new Labour government in England was subjecting Rhodesians to a barrage of wordy intimidations.'[352] England's cricketers were regularly warned about the dangers of other countries' political sensitivities – Fred Trueman had taken umbrage about a minister's advice a decade before – but the critical need for caution was greater in these more uncertain times. Wicketkeeper John Murray reported that the touring party 'were well briefed before we left to lay off talking politics in Africa'. That was all very well, it seems, but Murray added, 'Gee, nobody talks anything but politics to us.'[353]

The tour party was a blend of the tried and tested – Barrington, Titmus, Allen, Parks – and innocents abroad – Boycott, Brearley, Robin Hobbs. The batting, without Cowdrey, looked fragile, while the pace bowling was worthy enough, but lacked high pace.[354] There were, however, two experienced off-spinners, while Hobbs augmented Barrington's occasional leg spin. Some members of the press muttered about the batters who

---

351 *A Northern Wind* by David Kynaston, page 193.

352 *MCC in South Africa* by Charles Fortune, page 15.

353 Fortune, op. cit., page 15.

354 The other squad members were: Barber, Parfitt, Cartwright, Thomson, Brown and Price.

had been omitted, notably Tom Graveney, and the inclusion of the uncapped Mike Brearley. The flip side of Dexter's election defeat was the fillip it gave the England middle order, his useful medium-pace bowling and the overall panache he brought to the game.

The party travelled in two aircraft – MCC's anxious nod at the ghost of the Munich air crash – one travelling via Salisbury; the other, which included the captain and the manager, Donald Carr, via Nairobi. The tourists checked in at the Victoria Hotel in a hot and humid Bulawayo, the hotel's name a reminder of another kind of tourists' baggage. Charles Fortune flying in from Cape Town was struck by how 'well knit' the team already seemed. A short while later when he arrived Ted Dexter was less impressed with the status quo, observing that Geoffrey Boycott was already 'being well and truly boycotted by the other younger pros' who found him 'self-centred and obnoxious', while they avoided bowling to Mike Brearley in the nets because he was 'so inept, we don't want to make him look worse'.[355] Such talk does not suggest a shared, trusting enterprise. When Brearley dropped a slip catch against a Matabeleland Invitation XI in the first game of the tour, no doubt there were shaken heads and hands on hips from some of the side. The fielding lapse also gave the 'first symptom of an infection soon to become chronic'.[356] Once again Englishmen abroad were not reliable catchers of a cricket ball.

It was early December before the start of the first Test in Durban, some seven weeks after the tour had begun. Mike

355 Dexter, op. cit., page 165. Brearley did not play a Test in this series and his debut at Test level was not until 1976.

356 Fortune, op. cit., page 13.

Smith won what would prove to be a decisive toss and England began batting on a slow wicket, their scoring rate hindered by an even slower outfield. There was heavy cloud and England, with Boycott and Bob Barber at the crease, meandered to 79/0 at lunch. It was two and a quarter hours before Boycott's first boundary and, once Barber fell to Trevor Goddard, the Yorkshireman tended to monopolise the strike when Dexter joined him. Progress was slow: tea at 178/2, and 260/4 at the day's end. There was no acceleration on the second morning – just the grinding out of 61 more runs in the session – but a partnership of 206 between Ken Barrington and Jim Parks took the visitors to a solid 485/5 declared, their frame of mind boosted by the signs of turn in the wicket as the second day wore on. Parks and Barrington – known as 'The Colonel' or 'The Run Machine' to his team-mates – had set a new record sixth-wicket partnership against South Africa. The English strategy was based on ruthlessly wearing the South Africans down over almost two days in the field. The loss of three quick wickets for only 20 before the close was the result.

There was morning mist before breakfast on the third day sufficiently dense that 'the big cargo vessels lying just off shore could not be seen'. Rain seemed likely but never fell and England's spinners, Titmus and Allen, dominated, the latter taking 5-41 in a South African total of 155. Adrift by 330 runs, the home side were asked to bat again and by the end of the third day were 125/3. England finished their work on an archetypal Durban day of exhausting weather: 'No wind nor cloud but heat and humidity enough for an orchid house.'[357] Titmus wheeled

357 Fortune, op. cit., pages 69 and 72–3.

away in the airless heat for 45.5 overs taking 5-66, the second foray at the crease by the South Africans little better than the first. England won by an innings and 104 runs (with a day to spare). Then, because Donald Carr was a man who 'did things in style', there was champagne – for both sides – back at the Eden Roc hotel. England's win 'ended a run of 12 Test matches without success'.[358]

The prize for an early finish was a day of easy leisure in Durban before moving in stages north towards Johannesburg, initially by road to Pietermaritzburg – 'about fifty miles and uphill all the way' – and then by train.[359] Spared a stint of fielding in African heat, England's cricketers metamorphosed temporarily into water-skiers, wrote their Christmas cards or recorded seasonal messages to loved ones at home.

The Johannesburg Test was played over Christmas, beginning on 23 December, with no play on the festive day itself. Mike Smith won the toss on a hot, cloudless morning, the air stirred by a westerly breeze, and his team batted their way to safety, the innings finally ending at 531, just before the close of play on Christmas Eve. England's batting was buoyed by hundreds from Ted Dexter (172) and Ken Barrington (121). Dexter's innings was flawless, 'a moment for posterity to cherish', while he stood at the crease 'omnipotent and petulant – commanding and complaining'.[360] As for Barrington, he reached his hundred with a thunderous six. The weather changed on the second day,

358 *Wisden Cricketers' Almanack 1966,* page 804. The twelve previous Tests had seen four draws and a defeat against Australia in England (1964); five draws against India (away) and two defeats by West Indies in England in 1963. Played 12; Won – 0, Drawn – 9, Lost – 3. The last win was achieved against West Indies at Edgbaston by 217 runs (Fred Trueman took 12 wickets in the match).

359 Fortune, op. cit., page 76.

360 Fortune, op. cit., pages 83–4.

Christmas Eve, with heavy cloud rolling in and the rest day was wet and decidedly chilly.

There was a strong sense of déjà vu when South Africa batted on Boxing Day, Titmus and Allen proving almost as demanding to face as they had been in the first Test. The home side doubled their first-innings score in Durban, reaching 317 (compared to 155), but they still could not avoid being asked to bat again to save the game. For four days the English called the tune, but a fine century from the Rhodesian Colin Bland, using his feet against the English spinners, earned a draw, helped by the rain that fell after the tea interval.

***

Imagine the disciplined sacrifice involved in eschewing the New Year's Eve celebrations, 11 English cricketers in Cape Town, far from Lord's and home, and due to play in the third Test beginning on the first day of the New Year. Rain was in the air on that first day of 1965 and it meant a delayed start before the visitors' quintessentially English opening attack of John Price and Ian Thomson began their line and length work. On a placid wicket South Africa steadfastly batted their way to 501/7 before declaring, the game rendered safe enough, but with too much time lost – almost two days were over before Geoff Boycott and Bob Barber opened the England reply. The consensus was that it was too easy for a batter to survive on such a sleep-inducing pitch, the result was what *Wisden* reported as 'unenterprising cricket'.[361] Criticism of the run rates was not confined to the home team. England's rookie opening bat Geoffrey Boycott, for

361 *Wisden 1966*, page 808.

example, was 'reducing even the strokes he has' (and thereby) 'threatening to become a bore'.[362] The slow pace and dour mentality in which the game was being played was not the main issue, however. Rather the drama came from the umpires and the different interpretations of the game's protocols. It would precipitate a furore second only to the unforgotten 'Bodyline' series in Australia three decades before.

Before coming to Cape Town there had been a feeling amongst the touring English that they were getting a raw deal from the South African umpires. In the third Test discontent spilled over into trouble on the issue of whether a batsman should 'walk' after being deemed 'not out' by the umpire, but knowing he was in fact 'out'. At Cape Town two related incidents prompted uproar. First, when the South African opening batter, Eddie Barlow, was judged 'not out', although the England players were convinced that he had edged a catch to Parfitt in the slips off Fred Titmus. Barlow stayed at the wicket, unmoved; Titmus 'gave Barlow a verbal volley for standing his ground … Barlow gave as good as he got.'[363] Barlow went on to score 138. While the England captain, Mike Smith, hesitantly applauded the South African's hundred, the other England players 'were so piqued at the Barlow incident that they did not'.[364] Later there were apologies, the incident important enough to merit a press conference at 9.30 on the second morning.

There was more to come: when Barrington was on 48 there was a loud appeal for a catch behind off Peter Pollock. The umpire stayed motionless and after a lengthy pause, Barrington

362 *South African Diary 4* by John Woodcock in *The Cricketer,* March 1965.

363 Wilde, op. cit., page 391.

364 *Wisden 1966*, page 808.

'walked', spurning the prospect of another hundred, but evidently determined to make a point, or perhaps heeding his conscience. The *Daily Mail*'s Ian Wooldridge took the view that the Surrey batter had 'retired unhurt in the cause of re-establishing a principle', while his sports editor at the *Mail* was more bullish, seeing the incident as exemplifying English moral superiority: 'We chaps know how to play the game – even if you don't'.[365]

The Test was drawn. According to Charles Fortune it was 'a strange, amorphous, tarnished and unsettling match.' One man didn't 'walk' and made 138; another did and never progressed beyond 48; there were 'unforgettable antics' by the English fielders; Smith and Dexter batted as if 'chained'; and the unlikely pairing of Boycott and Barrington took six wickets between them, with the Yorkshire opening batter bowling 20 overs in the South African second innings.[366]

Onwards then from Cape Town, via East London and Bloemfontein, to Johannesburg for the penultimate Test starting on 22 January. The game began with one of those quixotic moments beloved by single-minded captains – Hutton in Brisbane (1954) and Pataudi in Kanpur (1964) – when, having won the toss, they perversely opt to bowl first. Mike Smith, along with Dexter, Barrington and the manager, Donald Carr, had studied the pitch with evident interest for a long time before choosing to do what had not been done by an England captain in South Africa since Percy Chapman in Durban 34 years previously. David Allen – 14 wickets in the three previous Tests at 27 runs each – was dropped in favour of the medium-pacer Tom Cartwright,

365 Peel, op. cit., page 91.

366 Fortune, op. cit., page 108.

suggesting that the wicket might seam.[367] Press box and players were nonplussed: the *Guardian* suggesting that perhaps 'Smith mistook the perspiration on his spectacles for dew on the ground,' while Bob Barber, who might have fancied a bat that morning, referred ironically 'to Mike Smith's green-tinted spectacles'. Soon after Price and Thomson had signally failed to unsettle the South African openers, Goddard and Barlow, Fred Titmus turned to Barrington fielding in the gully, shook his head and said, 'Admit it Kenny, you're wrong.' The undefeated South African opening batters lunched serenely at a comfortable 118/0 while hot and sweaty English bowlers looked askance at the team's maker of decisions and contemplated the long afternoon to come.[368]

The home side played the better cricket for much of that Test and, with rain having reduced the possible hours for play (three and a half hours were lost in the first two days), Goddard was able to declare at the end of the second day at a robust 390/6. The game drifted towards an inevitable draw, the resistance of the England batters, notably Parfitt (122*) and Barber (61) in the first innings and Boycott (76*) in the second proving invaluable. The South African captain pre-empted a further uproar about umpiring standards: Van de Merwe had 'run out' Mike Smith when the England captain, assuming the ball was dead, had wandered nonchalantly out of his crease. The umpire promptly gave him out; Goddard had the presence of mind and decency to call his opposite number back and peace was restored. The relative comfort in which the England players regarded their

367 It would be only the 29-year-old Cartwright's third Test; he would play for England only twice more. In Johannesburg his aggregate bowling figures were 2-196.

368 Peel, op. cit., page 92.

situation in the Test was illustrated perhaps when Bob Barber called the 12th man, Mike Brearley, on to the field 'ostensibly for some dry gloves.' That subterfuge hid the fact that Brearley and Barber were presently embroiled in a chess match and the batter's summons, according to Brearley, was 'to inform me that his next move was Queen's pawn to QB4.'[369] At all events the cricket at Johannesburg soon reached stalemate, while England now had only to avoid defeat at Port Elizabeth to win a series for the first time since the tour of West Indies four years before.

The fifth Test was played at Port Elizabeth from 12–17 February. South Africa won the toss and elected to bat on a true, batter-friendly pitch. The South Africans amassed 502 runs in the first two days, with Graham Pollock making 137 against a much-weakened English attack. Barber, Price and Cartwright were all injured and England were obliged to call up Somerset's Ken Palmer, who had been spending the winter coaching in Johannesburg. He and Ian Thomson opened the bowling, bowled 82 overs between them in the first innings and shared just two wickets.[370] Geoff Boycott came on as first change and bowled 26 overs in all. The England approach was plodding, the over rate for those days singularly dreary. Mike Brearley, watching as 12th man from the pavilion, was 'appalled and embarrassed' when his team-mates bowled just 29 overs in a two-hour session.[371] The England batting was as flimsy as their bowling, with the wicketkeeper John Murray and the off-spinner Fred Titmus batting high up the order at two and three. It was

369 *The Art of Captaincy* by Mike Brearley, page 191.

370 Ken Palmer's one wicket was South Africa's number seven batter Van der Merwe, the only Test wicket of his career.

371 Brearley, op. cit., page 188. His response reflects badly on current over rates.

the young Boycott (117) and the resolute old stager Barrington whose batting helped save the game and earn the draw, with the English batting line-up holding out in their first innings until tea on the fourth day. Rain closed in at the end with England's resilience ensuring the series win.

England's success over the previous three months had relied heavily on their batting (Barrington averaged 101.6 in the Tests) while Titmus and Allen between them took 35 wickets, more or less half of those that fell. Boycott's emergence as a rock-like opening bat was also a cause for English optimism, but there were shadows lurking, threats from a world beyond cricket. During the Port Elizabeth Test the *Daily Mail*'s Ian Wooldridge watched with mounting disgust as black South Africans were denied entry to the ground and then were set upon and beaten by police. Wooldridge had been drafting his report on the state of the game for transmission to London and, because the telephone lines were down, was obliged 'to read it at the top of his voice in the presence of about thirty hard-faced members of the republic's *broederbond*'.[372] Instead of an anodyne account of Geoffrey Boycott's single-minded batting that day, Wooldridge chose to speak out to the world – and those stone-faced men in the chilling atmosphere inside the room – with a more serious account of the state of play: 'The wretchedly evil face of apartheid was displayed here today,' he began. It was a brave stance that predated the troubles to come when MCC's cricket tour of South Africa was cancelled because of the 'D'Oliveira affair'. In the autumn of 1968 D'Oliveira's selection by England would be deemed unacceptable to the South African government, an

372 Frank Keating in *The Guardian*, 5 March 2007.

impasse that resulted in the tour's cancellation and the 30-year gap before MCC toured there again.

Coincidentally, a few days after the Port Elizabeth Test ended, Basil D'Oliveira was playing for a touring Worcestershire XI against Rhodesia in Bulawayo. D'Oliveira scored 73 and 19 in a game in which Tom Graveney also played. The following year, on 16 June 1966 at Lord's, he would make his Test debut for England, a selection which would have considerable implications for the history of the game, attitudes to apartheid and world politics, as well as placing an England XI in physical danger, as we shall see, 5,000 miles away in Karachi, West Pakistan in March 1969. In that notorious Test match were the familiar touring faces of Tom Graveney, Colin Cowdrey – and Basil D'Oliveira.

16

Under Smith Down Under

Australia, 1965/66

JIM SWANTON witnessed eight England cricket tours of Australia and was greatly exercised by the fact that England scored their runs more slowly than their Australian hosts on every tour but one. The exception was that of 1965/66, under the captaincy of MJK Smith.[373] The appointment of the MCC Secretary Billy Griffith as team manager signalled a clear intention that things needed to change, that England would henceforth play the 'right sort of cricket.' Griffith 'was vested with unprecedented authority' to ensure that this happened, with a parallel drawn to English football where Alf Ramsey had been given similar authority.[374]

The selection committee – of three former batters, Doug Insole, Peter May and Don Kenyon, and a solitary bowler, Alec Bedser – met on 15 August 1965. Insole chaired the committee despite his limited experience of touring (only once, to South Africa) and his unexceptional Test batting average (27.20). The

---

373 The scoring rate in 1965/66 was 45 runs per hundred balls compared to Australia's figure of 43. See *Swanton in Australia* by EW Swanton, page 132.

374 *Lord's 1946–1970* by Diana Rait Kerr and Ian Peebles, page 239.

chosen squad numbered 16, the batting included Ken Barrington who in the summer had been dropped for slow scoring (decidedly *not* 'the right sort of cricket), Colin Cowdrey and Geoffrey Boycott. As for the bowling, the spin option of Titmus and Allen was proven, but the pace attack looked raw, relatively untried and potentially injury-prone.[375] There was no Ted Dexter, who had chosen, at the age of 30, to forgo Test cricket in favour of his business, media and other sporting interests (golf and horse racing).

He was destined to return briefly and with limited success for two Tests in 1968. Also absent was the 35-year-old Brian Statham, whose final Test had been at the Oval against South Africa some ten days after the selectors had convened their meeting at Lord's.

The tour began with a going-away gathering at Lord's including a dinner at the Tavern, followed by a night in a hotel, before flying to Ceylon the next afternoon. They would not return for some five months. The players flew economy class, disconcerted by its cramped, overcrowded discomfort and later a number of players were afflicted with minor illnesses, stomach disorders and colds, which were seen as a direct result of the long, uncomfortable flight. There were also stops en route at Frankfurt, Damascus, Abadan and Bombay. The traditional stopover in Ceylon was in unwelcoming weather, while the greeting on arrival in Australia was less than warm, 'a chorus of indifference', with a widely accepted view that it was 'the worst English party ever to arrive in this country'. No Hutton, Compton, Tyson or Laker. Instead, *The Australian* reported that

375 The full squad was Smith, Allen, Barber, Barrington, Boycott, Brown, Cowdrey, Edrich, Higgs, IJ Jones, Larter, Murray, Parfitt, Parks, Russell and Titmus.

those selected had 'all the prestige of a team that was picked by prodding a pin into the telephone directory'.[376]

There were encouraging signs, however – both of quality and of the wished-for positive approach from the travelling Englishmen – in an early game against Western Australia in Perth at the end of October. There were hundreds from Bob Barber and Jim Parks, three declarations and a narrow win for MCC (by nine runs) and 12 wickets shared between Jeff Jones and David Larter in the course of the match. At one point Mike Smith had asked Billy Griffith when he thought he should declare. 'Now', said the manager. The winning margin was tight enough for the captain to watch events unfold with great unease. When it was all over, Smith remarked, with one of his 'dead-pan looks, "That's the last time I take the ruddy manager's advice on a declaration."'[377]

Sickness had dogged the touring side from the outset and Colin Cowdrey, a key figure in the England middle order, was declared unfit for the first Test in Brisbane beginning on 10 December. Moreover, on the trip out Geoffrey Boycott had been ill enough to be left behind in bed in Singapore and on arrival he was disconcerted to see that, in his absence, Edrich and Eric Russell seemed to have the openers' places for the first Test. 'They are scoring my runs,' he moaned.[378] The Yorkshireman's stomach trouble and sciatica prevented him playing until the middle of November.

---

376 *The Professional Amateur: The Cricketing Life of Bob Barber* by Colin Shindler, page 178.

377 Swanton, op. cit., page 132.

378 Shindler, op. cit., page 180.

Before the first day's play of the Brisbane Test there had been a long team meeting over what the batting order should be. It was felt that Boycott should be protected, given his lack of match fitness, not least because his bowling would be required. In the event, because Russell had damaged a finger on his right hand when fielding and would not bat, Boycott opened with Barber. The game was rain-affected with only two and a half hours on the first day and all of the second washed out. Australia batted first, their initial progress very slow – 79 runs in the first 36 overs – and the mood matched it, sombre, grey clouds and 'beyond the walls of the Gabba ancient shunting engines, belching black smoke'.[379] Remorselessly, Australia batted on into the fourth day of the game – Doug Walters making a maiden Test hundred (155) – shunning the idea of a declaration at the end of day three. It was 'baleful batting' for much of the innings while against the English spinners 'batsmen used their bats like trenching tools or sexton's spades'.[380] The spirit of the game was not improved when England batted, although Parks and Barrington both made valuable contributions to the England reply of 280. With a deficit of 163, however, the visitors were asked to bat again and by the close, on a day of 'meaningless' cricket, the game had subsided into a largely cheerless draw. It was troubling that, despite the good intentions of brighter cricket, the overriding mood was one of dour struggle. It seemed that the 'arrogance and style and swagger' displayed in the early games of the tour, when the tourists played as MCC, were abandoned when playing Test cricket as England.

379 Clarke, op. cit., page 83.
380 Clarke, op. cit., page 84.

The second Test was two weeks away, to be played in Melbourne over the New Year, with the England party troubled by illness, injury and indifferent form: Brown and David Larter were unfit; so too Ken Higgs, who had felt queasy as far back as the flight to Australia.[381] Peter Parfitt was struggling with his form with the bat while Bob Barber had lumbago. The English new ball attack was in the unlikely hands of left-arm paceman Jeff Jones – playing only his second Test match – and the medium pace of Barry Knight, who had recently arrived from England and who 'less than a month before had been minding his own [men's boutique] business in Colchester'.[382] A Test match in Melbourne was a far cry from the world of the width of lapels and inside leg measurements and Knight had only one game – against South Australia in Adelaide – to acclimatise before the Test.

In Melbourne Australia won the toss and batted, slowly enough to provoke some minor discontent in the crowd, particularly when Bill Lawry and Bob Cowper were together on the first afternoon. After David Allen had removed both openers, the makeshift pairing of Knight (4-84) and Jones (3-92) steadily worked their way through the solid Australian batting. In their total of 358 only one batter, Peter Burge, failed to reach double figures. By the second afternoon the England openers, Boycott and Barber, were at the crease and scoring quickly. Boycott's urgency was unexpected, the London *Evening Standard*'s John Clarke commenting that he 'never thought to see him in the role of ringleader of a riot in a Test match'.[383] Things became less riotous subsequently, but a succession of England batters drove

381 David Larter made two tours of Australia without playing a Test match there.

382 Clarke, op. cit., page 114.

383 Clarke, op. cit., page 114.

home the advantage, Edrich (109) and Cowdrey (104) leading a convincing reply. The final score of 558 put them 200 runs ahead on first innings, but with time slipping away.[384] For a brief while, when the home side were 176/4 on the final day, there was a suspicion that England had enough momentum to win the game, but two errors by the English wicketkeeper, a catch and a stumping (off Bob Barber's leg spin) were spurned – crucially as Peter Burge and Doug Walters earned the draw in what had been a fine Test match.

The Tests at Sydney and Adelaide, starting on 7 and 28 January respectively, saw the two teams' fortunes swing wildly, from euphoric victory to grim defeat, the consequence being a series still in the balance for the final Test at Melbourne in mid-February. The pitch at Sydney on 7 January was grassy and the expectation was that the ball would turn increasingly as the game wore on: the winning of the toss would be critical and Smith, rather than Booth, standing in as skipper for the unwell Bobby Simpson, did what lucky captains should do and called correctly. Geoff Boycott and Bob Barber, watched by his father from the famous Hill – he had arrived in Sydney early that morning – walked out to bat. Prior to play Bob had spent part of the morning 'splashing about in the hotel pool with his two-year-old daughter' before driving to the airport to collect his father.[385] That day Jack Barber saw his son and Boycott put on 234 for the first wicket. Bob Barber's innings of 185, his

384 The England innings had lasted from 31 December 1965 to the morning of 3 January 1966 because of the rest day on 2 January. In passing it's noteworthy that cricket took precedence over celebrating the New Year, with play on both New Year's Eve and New Year's Day.

385 Chalke, op. cit., page 32.

first Test century, was an 'innings of magnificent aggression'.[386] The openers' flamboyant opening was followed by a much more sedate hundred (103) from John Edrich. It seemed that England had virtually rendered the game safe with the first day not yet concluded. At 4.50pm, England were 308/1; just over half an hour later, the score was 317/5.

Despite the efforts of Neil Hawke (7-105), England's total of 488 on a pitch showing signs of wear, was seemingly unassailable, the lead boosted by a last-wicket stand of 55 between David Allen and Jeff Jones. It was soon evident that England's bowling attack was substantially stronger than at Melbourne: David Brown, returning after a muscle injury, took 5-63 and was backed up by a commendably varied attack of Jones, Boycott and three spinners, Barber, Titmus and Allen. The latter, noted John Clarke, 'has so often seemed more expendable [to selectors] than he does to critics'.[387] Australia fell away to 221 in the first innings and then, even more disastrously, 174 when following on, with both Allen and Titmus taking four wickets. The game was won by an innings and 93 runs, putting England one up in the series. It was the first time since Laker's Test at Manchester 1956 that they had won by an innings against Australia. Better still it was won by positive tactics, brave batting and flair. The spirit of adventure conceived in the staid surroundings of a Lord's meeting room had held firm for five days and made the return of the Ashes a realistic proposition.

It didn't last. For the tourists, Adelaide at the end of January proved to be the flip side of the coin – although Mike Smith won both pre-match tosses. England had followed the famous victory

---

386 *Wisden*, op. cit., page 835.

387 Clarke, op. cit., page 178.

in Sydney with two soft weeks of travel and excursion – 'holiday cricket' – in New South Wales and then Tasmania for two games. Australia by contrast returned to the fray energised, focused and with four significant changes, bringing back Simpson and including Tom Veivers, Ian Chappell and the Victoria batter Keith Stackpole, who would make his Test debut. England also ran into an in-form Graham McKenzie, who took the early wickets of Bob Barber (0) and John Edrich (5), while Boycott fell to Neil Hawke for 22. At Sydney the three of them had contributed 350 runs. This time the English batting faded away like morning mist (all out for 241), while not one Australian wicket fell until they had reached 244.

By the end of the second day the home side were in firm control. The extent of English disappointment was evident at the Sunday press conference when the correspondents' questions met stoney management taciturnity: 'The main ingredient was silence.'[388] The situation would get worse, with Bobby Simpson making 225 in an Australian total of 516 before the English top three batters, so dominant a fortnight before, were now, with their work done and their pads and batting gloves discarded in a dispirited dressing room, contemplating the inevitable. Moreover, the brio and adventure on show at Sydney was long gone, replaced by exactly the kind of plodding defensiveness that those back at Lord's – and indeed Billy Griffith and Mike Smith – had wanted to dispel. What had seemed likely on the afternoon of the first day when England were 150/5, became cold fact on the penultimate day: an innings defeat, an outcome made worse by its manner, with Barrington's defiant 102 taking six hours, with

388 Clarke, op. cit., page 150.

only four boundaries, while Cowdrey's 35 over two and a half hours was similarly sluggish. The series was levelled, leaving the outcome of the Ashes dependent on the final Test at Melbourne, due to start in ten days' time.

The scene was set for the defining showdown with the England camp significantly less buoyant after the acute disappointment of Adelaide. The group had shifted its base from a motel on the outskirts of Melbourne to the more central Windsor Hotel, perhaps a more congenial setting for a team that was clearly out of sorts. There was, according to one observer, a 'malaise' affecting the England players that 'defied diagnosis'.[389] Billy Griffith issued 'another call to arms', reiterating the diktat from Lord's about the need for positive cricket, an appeal that did not go down well with everyone – it was, it seems, 'much to Boycott's contempt'.[390]

On the first morning, 11 February, Mike Smith won the toss and England chose to bat. Soon things began to unravel. In the early skirmishes, Boycott opted to run a quick single, Barber initially refused it and eventually was left stranded halfway down the wicket to be run out for 17. The incident was 'sheer cricketing lunacy' according to Jack Fingleton. A hundred from Ken Barrington (115) – his fastest of the series – promised better things and at 485/9 (declared) by midway through the second day, there was still the prospect of a positive result. Well over an inch of rain fell on the night of the second day's play and the Australian first innings was similarly cheerless, at least from the visitors' point of view. There was a plodding century from

389 Clarke, op. cit., page 156.

390 Shindler, op. cit., page 189.

Bill Lawry, 'an avid, but tedious, accumulator of runs',[391] and a marathon 307 by Bob Cowper, whose dismissal closed the Australian innings at 543/8 declared. He batted for more than 12 hours. England contributed to the tedium by their time-wasting tactics, at one point bowling just 96 balls in an hour. *Wisden* described the resulting drawn game as a 'sour ending' to a tour which otherwise had been 'generally appetising'.

The run of stalemates continued through the final New Zealand leg of the tour – three drawn Test matches – and England returned to the UK once again without the Ashes. Lyn Wellings was charged with writing the *Wisden* account of the tour for the 1967 edition.[392] He welcomed the signs of more 'aggressive enterprise' from the tourists; praised Bob Barber for the 'superlative achievement of the whole tour'; and warmed to Smith's ability to 'take the players along with him'. He was less convinced by the captain's undue caution and his 'negative out-cricket'. Predictably in curmudgeonly mood, he blamed the arrival of Smith's wife and two small children for the decline in Smith's form. Arriving just before Christmas, Wellings saw them as 'a crippling additional burden'. It was a view held by others including some of the England players. The *Guardian*'s Frank Keating would note the different attitudes towards the wives of 'members of cricket's patrician class' accompanying tours, as opposed to the 'professional' cricketer. If the latter's wife was given the same treatment it would, Keating wrote, 'have caused mass suicide (by apoplexy) of the committee in the Long Room'.[393]

---

391 *Wisden,* op. cit., page 841.

392 *Wisden*, op. cit., page 812 *passim.*

393 Wilde, op. cit., page 346.

What was inescapable was the captain's disappointing form with the bat: he averaged 17.83 in the series with a top score of only 41. It was Barrington, Titmus, Cowdrey and Parks who topped the batting averages. Colin Cowdrey believed that once again a tour 'saw us failing to make the best of ourselves'.[394] The Kent man would assume the captaincy again that summer after the first Test against the West Indies when Smith's contribution was just 11 runs in his two innings. Six years later, in his late thirties, Mike Smith would play three more Tests without ever getting past 34 runs and being dismissed four times by the aggressive pace of Dennis Lillee. Mike Smith's tactical acumen was questioned after the 1965/66 tour – about his reliance on seam bowling and apparent distrust of leg spin, for example. But Ian Woolridge of the *Daily Mail* observed the true worth of the man: despite Captain Smith turning up for a press conference in slippers, a crumpled shirt and scruffy trousers, he knew that 'this was a captain whose players would follow him into outer space'.[395]

394 Cowdrey, op. cit., page 167.

395 *MJK Smith – No Ordinary Man* by Douglas Miller, page 101.

17

A Close Call

West Indies, 1968

THE DRAMA of MCC's tour of the West Indies in 1968 began months before at Edgbaston in a County Championship match between Warwickshire and Yorkshire. It proved to be 'a match with tremendous repercussions' and its events on 18 August 1967, the final day's play, were bitterly acrimonious.[396] Yorkshire's captain, the 36-year-old Brian Close, was a highly successful county captain and had assumed the captaincy of England for the last Test of 1966 after the home series against the West Indies had been lost. Close was a hard, uncompromising Yorkshireman, a professional like Len Hutton and born in Rawdon, a 20-minute walk from the latter's birthplace. He was charismatic, brave and a man who led from the front. A grammar schoolboy from a working-class background, he was emphatically not someone who would have captained his country in a previous age.

On the final day of Yorkshire's game in Birmingham, Close orchestrated his team's slow play – they bowled just two overs in 15 minutes – as Warwickshire closed in on a win in a game that

396 *Wisden*, page 617.

Yorkshire could not afford to lose. One over of Fred Trueman's contained two no-balls and three bouncers, all eating up precious time. At one point 'the Yorkshiremen ran off during a shower', leaving the two batters and the umpires standing in the rain.[397] It was a very public incident, so much so that the novelist Penelope Fitzgerald commented on it in a letter to her daughter Tina: 'The crowd actually attacked the Yorkshire team with umbrellas because they played so slowly – the bowler actually stopped to dry the ball between each over.'[398]

As for Close, he had heard on good authority that the cricketing establishment was 'looking for ways to remove him'.[399] He had been warned by a member of the press. 'For God's sake, Brian, keep your nose clean because they are just waiting at Lord's for a chance to prevent you leading the side in the West Indies.'[400] For a member of that establishment, Henry Blofeld, the issue was clear-cut: Close was 'sacked for wantonly wasting time'.[401] Swanton's view was that Close was 'unpredictable' – there were 'few more damning words in the Swantonian lexicon'.[402]

The selectors convened a meeting the day after the Edgbaston match was over and at that stage took the view that Close should stay as captain, but discussions continued in the corridors and offices at MCC's headquarters and the mood began to change. It may be that the shift was partly influenced by a letter received from an 'Old West Indies Cricketer' several weeks

397 *Birmingham Daily Post* 19 August 1967.

398 *So I Have Thought of You: The Letters of Penelope Fitzgerald* ed. Terence Dooley, page 49.

399 Wilde, op. cit., page 98.

400 *I Don't Bruise Easily* by Brian Close, page 121.

401 Blofeld, op. cit., page 84.

402 Kynaston and Ricketts, op. cit., page 77.

before. That letter argued for an end to appointing '3rd or 4th class types of men to lead … cricket teams both at home and away'. The letter ended with: 'Why not go back to your old policy appointing university graduates as captains?'[403] The typed letter has a handwritten note and initials, presumably those of Donald Carr, MCC's assistant secretary, endorsing its sentiments. What is certain is that MCC was greatly concerned that the captaincy of Brian Close (Aireborough Grammar School) might prompt 'a most unfavourable public reaction … in the West Indies'. To the backdrop of this mounting controversy, Close led the England team to an eight-wicket victory. Opening the batting with him, in Boycott's absence through illness, was the next England captain, Colin Cowdrey (Tonbridge and Oxford University), on whom would now fall the responsibility for leading the forthcoming tour of the Caribbean.

A fortnight later Yorkshire, with Brian Close at the helm, overwhelmed Gloucestershire at Harrogate to win the County Championship. The home side's captain failed to score but will have savoured the moment, with some thought given to how the winter's cricketing tour might unfold. He would be there to see it, not as a central figure, but covering it for the *Daily Mail*. It would not be long before he was analysing the successes and failures of the men that he had been expecting to lead. Meanwhile Colin Cowdrey, as winter set in, was running a two-day camp at Crystal Palace in November for nets and overall strategy as well as easing the damage caused by Close's sudden and unsettling departure.

Over the closing months of 1967, the 16 selected players signed their agreements, sent their passports to Lord's, were

---

403 MCC Archive, 1968 tour file and also *England: the Biography*, page 329.

vaccinated for smallpox and yellow fever, had medical and dental checks, were measured for their kit, informed of the limitations on baggage (100lb) and given the training schedule. The tour was of relatively short duration (three months). Of the 16 selections, nine had been on the tour to Australia in 1965/66: Cowdrey, Titmus, Barrington, Boycott, Brown, Edrich, Higgs, Jones and Parks. The remaining seven were: Alan Knott (wicketkeeper), two spinners (Robin Hobbs and Pat Pocock), two batters (Tom Graveney and Colin Milburn), a batting all-rounder (Basil D'Oliveira) and a quick bowler (John Snow). According to Brian Close the group lacked a top-class all-rounder and a left-arm spin bowler.

After the home series against West Indies in the summer of 1966, Doug Insole had written to Billy Griffith with thoughts on what might usefully be brought to the attention of the West Indies Cricket Board of Control. The 'atmosphere between the teams on and off the field … was not as pleasant as it might have been'. Insole's view was that the cause was the inclusion of a 'thrower' in the West Indies XI and the situation was exacerbated by the fact that 'the player in question barely addressed a civil word to anybody outside the West Indies party throughout the entire tour'. Insole stressed that his letter was 'private' rather than 'official', but it was clear that a series only 18 months later and with the alleged 'thrower' still playing was likely to be contentious.

The MCC party flew to Barbados from London Airport on the morning of 27 December 1967 and was greeted by the West Indian captain, Garry Sobers, soon after the plane had touched down. Cowdrey travelled in hope despite what had gone before, both on the pitch and in the shady corridor conversations at HQ. Asked before the flight about his team's chances in the Test series, he weighed them at 50/50. What was inescapable, however, was that when the teams had met in England a year earlier the visitors had dominated, winning the series 3-1, with two of the victories being by an innings. Ironically it was only when Brian Close assumed the captaincy at the Oval, with England 3-0 down in the series, that the English managed to win the final Test. Close's immediate predecessors were MJK Smith and Colin Cowdrey. The latter's reappointment after the summary dismissal of Close was seen by some as quixotic, the events of late August being, to one member of the press, 'the nastiest public wrangle since the days of Douglas Jardine; it was the very worst kind of publicity'.[404]

A consequence perhaps of the furore was the extent and longevity of press interest; there were 21 reporters sent out from London to cover the 1968 series. It would be 'watched by three times as many English correspondents as West Indies had ever seen before'.[405] One of the most respected and experienced was Alan Ross, whose cricket writing days were now numbered. He and Henry Blofeld would slope off occasionally on boat trips up the Demerara River to explore what lay beyond. Blofeld was on the tour after being asked by Jim Swanton to be 'his dogsbody … although he didn't quite put it like that'.[406] While he was at the outset of his press career, by contrast Alan Ross had become 'a victim of changing times. His days as a touring correspondent ended in the West Indies in 1967/68 amid rumours that he went off the beaten track once too often for the liking of his editor.'[407]

---

404 *In the Main* by JS Barker, page 17.

405 Barker, op. cit., pages 18–19.

406 Blofeld, op. cit., page 83.

407 Wilde, op. cit., page 319.

There was more to the keen editorial interest in what would happen post-Close: there was evident and newsworthy antipathy between the two teams. When West Indies won by an innings and 55 runs at Headingley, the gap between the two sides was clearly considerable, so too that between the skippers. Sobers made 174 in the first and only innings and took 8-80 in the match, while Cowdrey made just 17 and 12. The England skipper went to the visitors' dressing room after the game where it seems he was not just '*ignored* by the jubilant West Indians. It was worse than that – he was patronised.'[408]

There were three weeks before the first Test at Port of Spain and preparations for the series were not helped by unsatisfactory practice facilities. Brian Close, in his unusual role as cricket correspondent, fretted that poor – 'barely adequate' – nets 'give bowlers a false impression of their ability [and] create unnecessary problems for batsmen'.[409] Moreover, the early games in Barbados were anything but gentle warm-ups. In particular the contest against the President's XI ending on 6 January felt more like a highly competitive Test trial thanks to the number of highly promising West Indians keen to press their claims. MCC were indebted to Boycott (135), Cowdrey (139) and Ken Barrington's somewhat rusty leg breaks (5-99) for leaving Bridgetown with a draw.[410] Even so, MCC travelled on 'sorely tried and thoroughly chastened'.[411] It was a salutary reminder that tours in the Caribbean were invariably something of a battle. As if to reinforce the point, exchanging Barbados for Trinidad saw little

---

408 Barker, op. cit., page 20.

409 *The MCC Tour of West Indies, 1968* by Brian Close, page 29.

410 Barrington had only taken 16 wickets for Surrey in the whole of the 1967 season.

411 Barker, op. cit., page 35.

change in MCC's level of preparedness – the bowling looked undercooked, while the batting was arguably worse, Kent's Alan Knott top-scoring with 39 not out, batting at number nine in a below-par first innings of 207 all out.

Selection for the first Test was in the hands of the three-man selection committee: Cowdrey, the vice-captain Fred Titmus and the manager, Les Ames. Unlike Billy Griffith, who had been a high-profile confidant and influencer to Mike Smith in Australia, Ames took the view that 'on the field the skipper is the gaffer'.[412] The selection process was not straightforward with the post-viral John Snow – whose fast bowling 'featured very highly' in the captain's plan of campaign – unable to 'muster enough energy to bowl long spells under a hot sun'.[413] Other issues were whether John Edrich or Colin Milburn should open; Parks or Knott behind the stumps; Hobbs or Pocock to bowl some spin?[414] In each case the selectorial triumvirate opted for the former, not always with the understanding or happy acceptance of those omitted. Alan Knott for one was disappointed after batting well in his two games, not least because 'no one had said anything' to him.[415] Afterwards he was told that the selectors thought the inclusion of Jim Parks would strengthen the batting. A disconsolate Knott sought solace by sloping off for a swim and a few glasses of Bacardi and coke.

The first day of the first Test: Friday, 19 January 1968. The venue: Port of Spain, Trinidad where the ground is in 'vibrant mood', the weather hot and sultry. The pitch has a 'curious

412 Barker, op. cit., page 18.

413 Cowdrey, op. cit., page 178.

414 Also omitted from the England XI were two pace bowlers, Ken Higgs and John Snow.

415 *It's Knott Cricket* by Alan Knott, page 29.

brown-matt appearance' while above 'one of the prettiest grounds in the world' has the grand backdrop of 'tree-covered mountain slopes'.[416] Colin Cowdrey gets the first decision right, winning the toss. As the West Indian opening bowlers, Wes Hall and Charlie Griffith warm up to begin the onslaught, there is 'an eerie hush' in the visitors' dressing room.[417] Geoffrey Boycott duly hits four boundaries in the first two overs to set the tone and England's batting begins to prosper.

Cowdrey had drawn on his previous experience of Caribbean tours when he suggested that his players would need three weeks to acclimatise – the heat, the light, the intensity of it all – and his judgement proved correct. The transformation from the ill-prepared cricketers of the opening 21 days to the highly competitive unit that more than held its own in the first Test was a testimony to the captain's intuition and leadership. Through the series he was to prove the better of the two captains, 'more assured, more shrewd and more inspiring' than Garry Sobers.[418] It helped that England's skipper won the toss on the first day in Trinidad. Over the next few months, it would also prove an advantage that his fast bowlers were the more potent of the two sets of pacemen.

On that opening day in Port of Spain the work of the early batters for England was to prove invaluable, not least the opening stand of 80 between Boycott and Edrich, with the former scoring 25 off the first 24 balls. That was followed by a resolute stand between Barrington and Cowdrey which saw a barrage of

---

416 It was Henry Blofeld who noted the vibrant mood (op. cit., page 84), JS Barker who commented on the pitch (op. cit., page 37), and John Snow who was enthused by the ground's beauty, see *Cricket Rebel*, page 51.

417 Peel, op. cit., page 127.

418 Barker, op. cit., page 37.

bouncers, notably from Charlie Griffith with whom Barrington had history. The Surrey batter had made no secret of his view that Griffith's bowling action was flawed – that he 'chucked' rather than bowled the ball legitimately. Barrington had once suggested that he might refuse to play against the West Indian quick man. That first auspicious day ended with England 244/2, Griffith wicketless, the new ball weathered and already the pitch beginning to take some turn.

Cowdrey's batting was often delicate and invariably composed. The 'old man of the party' at 40, Tom Graveney, came in to join him, batting at number five, and soon surpassed the excellent Cowdrey with 'a glorious exhibition of cultured batting'. Brian Close remembered those occasions when he and Graveney would 'joke as to which of us holds the record of most comebacks in Test cricket'.[419] Graveney's innings was a tour de force. Henry Blofeld believed it was 'perhaps the best hundred I have ever seen'.[420] By the end of the second day, despite temperatures approaching 100°, England had batted themselves into an invincible position. After a rest day of 'golfing, fishing, sailing and, as Trinidadians call it, fêting', they went on to reach 568 by the close of the innings on the third day.[421]

For a brief while before tea on the fourth day the persistent David Brown took three wickets in four overs to open up the possibility of an England win. Then the rain fell for some 90 minutes, flooding part of the outfield, and without the unfit John Snow, Cowdrey lacked the firepower to finish off the West Indian resistance. In the end, Wes Hall and captain Sobers held

---

419 Close, op. cit., page 20.

420 *Wisden*, op. cit., page 824 and Blofeld, op. cit., page 85.

421 Barker, op. cit., page 41.

the English at bay; Hall had been wicketless in the mammoth England total, but his unbeaten 26* alongside Sobers (33*) earned the draw in what had been a memorable Test match.

Watching the series unfold at least one cricket correspondent – Henry Blofeld – saw unmistakable signs of decay in what had once been a great West Indian team. It was, he wrote, becoming 'scuppered by old age'.[422] Its two legendary fast bowlers, Wes Hall and Charlie Griffith, were now both the wrong side of 30. The average age of the West Indian XI chosen for the second Test at Kingston, Jamaica, was 29.1, with six men over the age of 30. Perhaps Blofeld had turned a blind eye to England's overall greater age profile: the visitors' XI averaged 32. Six of its batters, from Cowdrey at number three to Titmus at nine, were all well over 30. Perhaps the telling difference, however, was the relative youth of the England pace attack – Brown was 25; John Snow and Jeff Jones both 26.

Alan Ross described Sabina Park, Kingston as 'a steeply enclosed cockpit of a ground' and at times it had a distinctly intense and claustrophobic mood, its sense of pent-up energy enhanced by the spectators hanging off the lighting pylons and clinging to the surrounding trees.[423] The sense of drama was enhanced by the 13-month drought in Jamaica breaking dramatically a day or so before the Test was due to begin on 8 February. The Test wicket had been well-watered as part of the preparation for the game but had been left unprotected against the weather. It left the two captains reflecting on the conundrum as to how the pitch might play given the rain. Cowdrey, who won the toss, was philosophical about his

422 Blofeld, op. cit., page 84.
423 Wilde, op. cit., page 272.

decision to bat first. 'Well, for better or worse, we'll bat,' he said with a rueful smile.[424] He need not have worried – England lost only two wickets on the first day: John Edrich (96) was resolute and stubborn while Colin Cowdrey (101) batted with great concentration. Wes Hall took four wickets but England's total of 376 seemed a competitive one; it looked infinitely better once the West Indies batting had slumped to 143 all out in their first innings in just 49 overs, hustled out by the England pace attack, with Snow (7-49) proving devastating. 'Brown was the quickest of the English bowlers, Jones the most unpleasant, Snow the most accurate.'[425]

West Indies duly followed on, with Sobers making an undefeated 113, but any optimism triggered by the recovery was soon to be lost by events in the middle of the fourth afternoon. Basil Butcher's dismissal, given out caught low down by Jim Parks off Basil D'Oliveira, lit the touchpaper. The first sign of the trouble to come, according to the England captain, was 'a bottle, swirling high up in the sunlight'.[426] That soon turned into a full-scale riot, a hail of bottles from behind the wire fence, screaming fans, steel-helmeted riot police running at the rioters wielding sticks and a thick pall of tear gas drifting across the ground, much of which found its way into the dressing rooms. The England players gravitated towards the middle of the pitch, away from the barrage of bottles and then Cowdrey moved back towards the screaming fans pleading with them to calm down. 'We must get on with the cricket,' the England captain implored, his words lost in the mayhem and having little, if any, effect.

424 Barker, op. cit., page 63.
425 Barker, op. cit., page 68.
426 Cowdrey, op. cit., page 179.

Eventually the English XI left the field and later used their sun hats to collect the broken fragments of glass.

It was a pivotal moment in a game marked by a fiery, cracked pitch, some 'strange umpiring' – noted by *Wisden* – cracked heads and broken glass, gas-induced tears and English cricketers gasping for breath in the dressing room. Eventually there was a feverish conclusion to the Test match. 'The whole episode knocked the stuffing out of us,' Cowdrey wrote much later, while Brian Close believed that, but for the riot, England would have won. Instead, and with the game extended to a sixth day to compensate for the time lost to the riot, England almost contrived to lose in a feverish final innings which ended with them chasing 159 to win. They were 68/8 when the umpires called time, the struggle against the spin of Sobers and Gibbs proving agonising to watch for the English in the ground. Two Tests down and neither side with a visible advantage.

There were just over two weeks before the third Test, time enough for two heavyweight, bullish batting performances in Antigua against the Leeward Islands (Boycott top-scoring with 165) and Barbados (Boycott again, 243). Both games were drawn. Fred Titmus captained the side in Antigua but didn't bat and only bowled a brief spell in the second innings. It was his last involvement in the tour. Two days before the Bridgetown Test there was a grim accident out of the blue at Sandy Lane Beach on the island of Barbados. Titmus, Cowdrey, Robin Hobbs and others, were offshore, clinging to the side of a small motorboat.[427] England's off-spinner was near the middle of the boat, unaware

427 Also there, according to Brian Close, were John Woodcock of *The Times*; Denis Compton (*Daily Express*) and Brian Johnston working for the BBC. See Close op. cit., pages 99–100.

that unusually the propeller was placed centrally. One minute all thought is of sun, sea and the drift of the tide; the next moment, after England's principal spin bowler had idly let his legs drift to the surface, there was a howl of pain as the propeller sliced into his left foot.

His team-mates hauled him out of the water, aghast at the bloody mess, and with Cowdrey, for one, 'as close to personal panic' as he had ever been.[428] Taken to hospital, Titmus was operated on by a Canadian surgeon, who amputated four toes, but not the left foot as was initially feared. Asked if Titmus might ever play again, the surgeon, drawing on his experience of operations back in Canada, was optimistic, claiming that 'the ice-hockey boys are usually playing again in four or five weeks'.[429] There was no doubt, however, that the tour was over for Titmus and he flew back home on 7 March.[430] He would be replaced by Tony Lock – not Brian Close, whose name was broached by some. Lock would fly in from Western Australia, but not in time for the next Test match.

After the drama on the beach, the Bridgetown Test was anything but. Instead, a drawn game on a flat pitch, with rain on the first day which in itself slowed the game's progress. West Indies batted cautiously – at 2.4 runs per over – with John Snow (5-86) the main threat.[431] It was the third day before England batted and then Edrich (146) and Boycott (90) helped England to a substantial first-innings lead. The visitors were still batting

428 Cowdrey, op. cit., page 183.

429 Cowdrey, op. cit., page 185.

430 Fred Titmus returned to cricket, but made only four more Test appearances, all in Australia during the 1974/75 tour. His final Test match was at Adelaide in January 1975.

431 Steve Camacho scored just 33 in the truncated day's play.

at the end of the fourth day. There was a fleeting moment at 109/3 when Parks claimed a catch off Jeff Jones, suggesting that England might sneak a win, but umpire Jordan turned down a confident appeal. The powerful Clive Lloyd went on to make 113 not out, the West Indies scoring at the fastest rate in the series thus far. After it was all over it was clear that Titmus's injury had been a blow. His replacement Pat Pocock, whom Close had thought before the tour 'hasn't yet reached international standard', had struggled, taking just two wickets for 132.[432] Despite the series remaining tied, Brian Close for one was uneasy about what lay ahead: Lloyd's hundred and the sight of the West Indies 'caning' England's bowlers, he saw as 'an ominous sign for the rest of the series'.[433]

For the fourth Test, to be played at Port of Spain beginning on 14 March, England included Tony Lock, while West Indies dropped Wes Hall and were also without Charlie Griffith for the final three days of the game after he had suffered a leg injury. Brian Close's premonition of trouble seemed to be borne out by the opening two days which West Indies dominated. Eventually, on the third day, Sobers declared the innings closed at 526/7, a total which seemed to suggest safety for the home team. Three of England's bowlers conceded over a hundred runs each.[434]

The balance of the game began to change as a result of brilliant batting from Boycott and Cowdrey (148). Then when it seemed that things might fall apart, Alan Knott, in only his third Test and playing instead of Parks, scored an invaluable and unbeaten 69. Nonetheless England's first innings ended at 414, 112 runs behind.

---

432 Close, op. cit., page 23.

433 Close, op. cit., page 118.

434 Lock 1-129, Jones 2-108 and Brown 3-107. John Snow was wicketless.

Basil Butcher's leg breaks had taken 5-34, impressive enough to tempt the West Indian captain to declare at a sporting 92/2, leaving England to score 215 to win in just 165 minutes. With Boycott (80*) and Cowdrey again batting well and timing the run chase to perfection, the game was won by seven wickets and with just three minutes to spare. Later that night the island's Pelican Inn was open till late, raucous with celebration. The Pelican was an English-type pub where 'every Englishman (except Swanton) came to celebrate and sing around the piano. They ran out of beer!'[435] Garry Sobers, meanwhile, 'shared his loneliness with a calypso singer in a Trinidad nightclub' and back at the hotel his shocked and outgunned players 'hid their disappointment'.[436]

The English cricket season of 1968 was a matter of only a few weeks away when Cowdrey and Sobers walked on to the pitch in Georgetown, Guyana for the final preliminaries of the series. By now the MCC party had been on tour for three months and remained unbeaten. Avoiding defeat in the final Test would mean a series victory; winning the toss was Cowdrey's first objective. In each of the Tests thus far whichever of the captains guessed correctly as to how the coin would fall meant batting first – and in each case registering an impressive total, never less than 349 and averaging just under 455. Were it not for the anomaly of the Port of Spain Test, where West Indies somehow managed to lose after scoring 526 in the first innings, the rule of thumb would be that winning the toss meant avoiding defeat. However, Cowdrey lost the toss for the third time in a row and soon John Snow and Jeff Jones were running in to bowl to Seymour Nurse and Steve Camacho.

---

435 MCC Archive, letter to Billy Griffith at Lord's dated 21 March 1968.

436 Close, op. cit., page 135.

Georgetown was a place 'accustomed to riots and demonstrations', troubled by political unrest, and the two teams drove from the airport 'with sirens screaming' behind a policeman 'at the head of the procession [who] enjoyed himself at speeds approaching 60 miles an hour, mainly on the wrong side of the road'.[437] The city is only a few degrees north of the equator and it is hot, both in its weather and, in the late 1960s, with its simmering political sensitivities. On the first day of the final Test, 28 March 1968, the wicket looked to be a good one, with the outfield appearing to be quick despite a shower of rain overnight. The West Indies total of 414 owed much to the batting of Rohan Kanhai (150) and Garry Sobers (152). It wasn't until the closing stages of the second day that the England innings began. That proved heavily reliant once again on Boycott (116) and Cowdrey (59), together with Tony Lock whose 89, batting at nine in the order, was vital as England's reply wavered. He and Pat Pocock put on 109 with the latter batting for 82 minutes before registering his first run. In the event, West Indies had secured a narrow but useful lead of 43 on first innings.

The match was to be played over six days, thereby placing England under greater pressure to avoid defeat. West Indies set a target of 308 while England were obliged to bat throughout the day to save the game. Lance Gibbs reduced them to 41/5, a sorry plight with Edrich, Graveney, Barrington and D'Oliveira scoring only eight runs between them. A stand between Knott and Cowdrey of 127 stopped the collapse and then, at the very end, it was the unlikely pairing of Alan Knott (73*) and last man Jeff Jones which held firm. This 'was one of two occasions

437 Close, op. cit., page 137.

when England's last-wicket pair have held out in the final Test of a series'.[438] When Jones took guard against Lance Gibbs, Knott muttered to the Welshman about how 'A Welcome in the Hillsides' would be heard back home if he could keep his wicket intact.[439] According to Colin Cowdrey, Knott and Jones even sang the opening lines of the song 'to lighten the atmosphere in the torrent of noise'.[440] The draw ensured that the tour was undefeated and the series won. Georgetown marked the occasion by a resumption of riot, with Tony Lock hit on the head by a stone and Cowdrey penned in the pavilion awaiting a police escort to the hotel.

There had been some vital and telling contributions to England's win: Alan Knott topped the Test batting averages, scoring 149 runs without being dismissed in his three innings; Cowdrey averaged 66.75 and Geoff Boycott 66.14. The three England pace bowlers, Snow, Brown and Jones, took 55 wickets between them, with Snow taking 10-142 in the final Test and 27 over the series as a whole. By comparison, Wes Hall and Charlie Griffith took just 19.

There were disappointments among the English party. Colin Milburn, for example, was not included in any of the five Tests; Tom Graveney's glorious 118 at Port of Spain was approaching half of his total runs in five Tests; while Jim Parks' disappointing scores in the first three Tests were not enough to keep Alan Knott out of the side for the tour's denouement. Finally there was Basil D'Oliveira, whose tour had been underwhelming and whose future would be so contentious. According to Brian Close,

---

438 Wilde, op. cit., page 454.

439 Knott, op. cit., page 34.

440 Cowdrey, op. cit., page 192.

he was 'the one real disappointment' of the tour.'[441] He batted too low down in the order, had a habit of dropping catches, while his bowling was notable only for its lack of success – three wickets only in the five Tests at 97.66 each. Feeling the pressure of his situation as a mixed race South African unable to play for his country and trying at a relatively late stage in his cricketing career (he was 36) to establish himself as an England cricketer, he underperformed on the pitch and 'off the field he enjoyed the good life. He was not often seen at the breakfast table at the team hotel.'[442] Later in that summer of 1968 Basil D'Oliveira would find himself at the centre of events that would have serious implications for English cricket.

---

441 Close, op. cit., page 155.

442 *Basil D'Oliveira: Cricket and Conspiracy: the Untold Story* by Peter Oborne, page 130.

18

Riot and Heat

Lord's, Cape Town and Pakistan, 1968

1968 WAS a year of riot across the world. There were serious disturbances in Paris at the Sorbonne in May, at the Democratic Convention in Chicago in August, at Grosvenor Square in London, in Spain, Mexico and elsewhere. Martin Luther King was shot in April, the war in Vietnam refused to die and race was increasingly an issue in the United Kingdom. In April the right-wing Conservative and shadow minister, Enoch Powell, delivered his notorious 'rivers of blood' speech. Cricket was not immune to the winds of change. The controversy over the 'D'Oliveira affair' would result in a vote of no confidence in the MCC committee and much bitter, long-standing argument.

The summer of 1968 was stormy meteorologically too. Jack Fingleton, the ex-cricketing cricket writer, had travelled to England to write a book about that year's Australian tour. He soon abandoned the idea, however, disillusioned by the dire English weather. 'It was,' he wrote, 'the worst summer of weather I had known since 1938.'[443] Then, as if to upstage both the rainswept

---

443 *Watery Reflections from Australia* by Jack Fingleton, in *Wisden Cricketers' Almanack 1969*, page 80.

gloom and the drama of an Ashes series, the cricket authorities at Lord's presided over a set of events which had ramifications beyond the game itself and would reach the seats of power in London, Cape Town and Islamabad. Basil D'Oliveira was at the heart of it all, although it was not of his making. Rather the starting point was what Henry Blofeld described as 'the dreadful mess the England tour selectors – Insole, Bedser, Kenyon and May' – had made of selecting players for the upcoming tour of South Africa.[444] The biggest mess was the exclusion – then the inclusion – of the Cape coloured, adopted Englishman, D'Oliveira.

The Australian series in England had been notable for its indifferent overall quality. Only one Australian (Bill Lawry with 135 at the Oval) made a century during the course of it, while England, after losing the first Test, never managed to win a Test until the very last day of the series. D'Oliveira, despite his underwhelming tour of the West Indies, was selected for the first Test at Old Trafford where he scored 9 and 87 not out, batting at number seven. His bowling had been useful and economical. Nonetheless he was dropped afterwards and remained out of the side until the fifth Test when he was recalled after the batter Roger Prideaux suddenly withdrew with a bronchial infection the day before the game. Both Barry Knight and Tom Cartwright, who had been alternatives as medium-pace bowlers, were judged unfit. So the selectors turned at the last moment to D'Oliveira, despite the perversity of the decision and the political implications. He batted at six and made 158, crucial runs to put England on the way to a 226-run victory. The

444 Blofeld, op. cit., page 87.

consequences of D'Oliveira's innings were clear enough and one of the first to comment on the situation was the umpire Charlie Elliot when D'Oliveira had reached fifty. 'You've put the cat amongst the pigeons now.'[445] By the end of the innings the cat had wreaked havoc.

D'Oliveira's hundred at the Oval was his third for his adopted country in what was his 16th international appearance. He had a healthy batting average, while his bowling was useful. True, there were question marks about his limited contribution to the recent series in the West Indies as well as his vigorous social life in the Caribbean. But the expectation was that he would be amongst the party chosen for the winter's tour to South Africa.

On the final day of the Oval Test, 27 August, Doug Insole fronted a press conference to announce the tour party. He announced the captain and vice-captain – Colin Cowdrey and Tom Graveney – before naming the rest of the squad in alphabetical order: Barrington, Boycott, Brown, Cartwright, Cottam, Edrich, Fletcher, Knott, Murray, Pocock, Prideaux, Snow, Underwood, together with either Jeff Jones or an alternative if he was unable to prove his fitness. It was only after Insole had intoned Alan Knott's name that the implications fully struck home – there had been no mention of D'Oliveira. There were immediate gasps and pandemonium thereafter, as well as anger. Alan Ross in *The Observer* the following Sunday wrote that, 'The rejection of D'Oliveira, whatever the ostensible reasons, will now come as a soothing breeze to the sweating but complacent apostles and fellow travellers of apartheid.'[446] He was not alone:

---

445 *The Cricketer Anthology of the Ashes* page 133.

446 *The Observer*, 1 September 1968.

Henry Blofeld found the omission 'incredible' and believed that the cricket authorities had 'sold out to the South African government and its policies of apartheid'.[447] Basil D'Oliveira himself heard the news at New Road in Worcester on 28 August soon after scoring 128 against Sussex. In the Worcester dressing room a transistor radio was on and Brian Johnston read out the selected names. Tom Graveney, when his team-mate's name was omitted, swore 'violently in fury and disbelief' while D'Oliveira 'put his head in his hands and wept'.[448]

As far back as 5 January 1968, Billy Griffith had written to his counterpart at the South African Cricket Association to confirm that 'the selection of the touring party would be a matter for the MCC selection sub-committee alone, and not subject to any external criteria'.[449] He received no reply. In due course the shadow foreign secretary, Alec Douglas-Home, raised the issue with John Vorster, the prime minister of South Africa. Later he made clear that MCC would be well advised not to press for a reply. Other unofficial enquiries as to who would be welcome were more forthright, along the lines of 'Anyone else. D'Oliveira – no.' At all events, the omission of D'Oliveira provoked a considerable outcry in the press.

John Arlott thought MCC 'had never made a sadder, more dramatic, or potentially more damaging decision', while Swanton, setting aside the politics, voiced his regret at the non-selection in cricketing terms. Ted Dexter declared that D'Oliveira 'has always been my first choice to bat number six for England' while raising the issue as to why, if the selection was to prove so

447 Blofeld, op. cit., page 88.

448 Oborne, op. cit., page 204.

449 *When Cricket and Politics Collided* by Richard Thorn, pages 40–1.

contentious, was he brought back into the fold for the Oval Test against Australia?[450]

There matters seemed to rest – until 16 September when Tom Cartwright failed a fitness test on his troublesome shoulder, the result of which was to force him out of the tour and leave a gap in the party. Promptly his replacement was announced – Basil D'Oliveira – a decision not entirely logical given the fact that Cartwright was a bowler first and foremost while D'Oliveira was, in Doug Insole's words 'regarded as a batsman only', his bowling not penetrating enough on overseas wickets. Two days before Cartwright had been fit enough to play for Warwickshire against a Gillette Invitation XI and bowl his allocated ten overs, taking 1-35 and dismissing Colin Cowdrey.[451]

Given the nature of the protagonists and their shared intensity of feeling it is unsurprising that this was not the end of the affair. MCC's driving force was the preservation of the game's traditions. While for the South African government what was at stake was the fundamental nature of its society, the maintenance of the ruthless separation between the white minority and those on the other side of the apartheid divide. South African policy was that 'no mixed sport' should be played, simple as that, a principle which Prime Minister Vorster had made clear in the House of Assembly in Cape Town as far back as 4 April 1967. Predictably its reaction to MCC's volte-face was simply to refuse D'Oliveira entry to the country of his birth.

450 Arlott's article was in *The Guardian* on 29 August 1968; EW Swanton's appeared in the *Daily Telegraph* the same day and Dexter in the *Sunday Mirror* – under the heading 'Dolly! Honest Bungling' on 1 September. Thorn, op. cit., page 46.

451 Cartwright had bowled 608.4 overs over the season, taking 71 wickets at 16.1 each. Peter Oborne, op. cit., page 222, noted the suggestion that Cartwright had felt 'uneasy about keeping D'Oliveira out of the side and that he used the injury as an excuse to withdraw'.

In so doing it insisted that 'he had only been picked because of anti-apartheid pressures in England'. The endgame was starkly predictable. The tour was summarily cancelled, the decision agreed at a meeting on 24 September. Thoughts turned to the nature of what might replace it, with a shortened tour of India and Pakistan the preferred option.

Then in November the India leg was cancelled for financial reasons with Ceylon (Sri Lanka as it now is) replacing it, a move not welcomed by the players. Those originally invited on the South African tour comprised the list for the hastily arranged alternative with the same pay despite the fact that the tour was shorter. The repercussions of the affair rumbled on, however, culminating in a Special General Meeting of MCC's membership – only the second in 200 years – held on 6 December 1968 at Church House, Westminster which, after hours of debate, concluded by rejecting a vote of no confidence in the powers that be. It was an 'acrimonious' meeting 'with much personal abuse aimed at (the Rev. David) Sheppard' who had proposed two resolutions, one critical of MCC's squad selection, the other calling for 'no further tours to take place till progress had been made towards non-racial cricket in South Africa'.[452] The future England captain Mike Brearley was involved in supporting Sheppard's stance and later talked of how the former prime minister – and cricketing traditionalist – Alec Douglas-Home, was 'glacial in conveying the message that we were naïve and childish'.[453] The meeting was packed with 1,000 or more members in the rotunda of the Assembly Hall and overflowing into the next room. The

452 Oborne, op. cit., page 227.

453 Mike Brearley: *'Basil D'Oliveira retained his dignity at the centre of the storm'* in the *Observer* , 6 December 1968.

resolutions were defeated but not by the commanding majority expected. It was evident that the issue was not going to go away.

Meanwhile, arrangements for the short tour of Pakistan were progressing. The expectation had been that the same group of players would travel, but in the event Geoff Boycott and Ken Barrington were unavailable – and were not replaced as batters, while Robin Hobbs was called in to strengthen the spin options.[454] It left just five mainstream batters in the party of 15 which left little scope for managing injuries or ill health so far from Lord's. Moreover, there were darker, more dangerous clouds gathering. On 7 November there had been serious unrest in Pakistan during which some 2,000 college students had rioted, one person had been killed, three buses burned, four policemen wounded and schools and colleges shut down. It seemed that 'MCC had unwittingly just agreed to tour a country which was beginning a slide into anarchy.'[455]

***

The particular challenges presented when playing cricket in Pakistan were not new to a good number of the 1969 tour party. Six of them had travelled there two years previously as members of an MCC under-25s team. Four were bowlers – Brown, Hobbs, Pocock and Underwood – while Keith Fletcher of Essex and the young wicketkeeper, Kent's Alan Knott, had also been included. The 1969 tour squad was managed by Les Ames – who had performed the same role for the under-25s in 1967 – and captained

454 Boycott wrote to the selectors explaining that the removal of his spleen in childhood rendered him susceptible to infection. Barrington had suffered a heart attack playing in Australia in mid-October.

455 Thorn op cit., page 54.

by Mike Brearley who, according to Alan Knott, was 'perfectly at home … [dressing] in their style, seemed to eat anything put in front of him, (and) mixed perfectly with everyone'.[456] Knott found the under-25s tour very arduous, while the report in *Wisden 1968* judged it only a 'qualified success', not least because of the heavy social programme, the challenge presented by a small squad and the amount of cricket to be played – seven first-class fixtures.[457] Keeping fit in the face of heat, the distances to be travelled, the stark contrast between a European diet and that in Pakistan, and the schedule were all significant challenges. Of the final 11 days of that tour, the England team was fielding for all but one day – after which the party was required to travel from Chittagong to Karachi 'across the face of the subcontinent' (a distance of over 2,500 miles) before attending yet another official engagement.

Heat and being far from home were not the only problems. In the second game the Warwickshire opener Neal Abberley cracked a finger from a beamer bowled at him, while in the same game Geoff Arnold was controversially run out 'backing up by the bowler Saeed Ahmed, the [Central] Zone's captain, without the preliminary custom of a warning'.[458] Later, at Dacca in mid-February, the umpires and the MCC captain disagreed about the amount of time play would be suspended for the pitch to dry out after a brief shower of rain. Brearley was convinced it was fit to play but the umpires disagreed, the discussion ending with a blunt refusal – 'We do not wish to discuss the matter further.' To Brearley's evident frustration, there was no play for two hours

456 Knott, op. cit., page 23.

457 *Wisden Cricketers' Almanack 1968*, page 889; the report written by Alex Bannister.

458 *Wisden*, op, cit., pages 892–3.

'until everything was bone dry; Pakistan saved the game'.[459] An understandable frustration led to an unseemly flurry of bouncers aimed at the last man in – these were the days when a certain courtesy was allowed to the batting tailenders.

On the plus side, David Brown bowled with enthusiasm and no little skill; Geoff Arnold, before the 'Mankading' incident, made a career-best 73; Knott made his maiden hundred at Peshawar, putting on 208 for the first wicket with Mike Brearley who went on to make 312 not out; Richard Hutton took a hat-trick and Robin Hobbs took 6-39 in an innings win at Peshawar.[460] But throughout there were signs that all was not well – the itinerary was 'unreasonable'; players became 'over-tired and jaded'; and slow wickets were 'mostly rolled mud on clay'. Alex Bannister even looked askance when 'a box containing the regulation-sized balls' went missing and when the home side seemed incapable of finding 'competent scorers', and individual batting scores failed to tally as a result. Underneath it all, perhaps, was the legacy of too many years of imperial self-regard and the legitimate resentment by those remembering all too clearly the days before partition.

---

459 Brearley, op. cit., page 139.

460 Vinoo Mankad 'was the first Test bowler to dismiss a batter at the non-striker's end for backing up too far'. See *Test Cricket – a History* by Tim Wigmore, page 67. Mankad's association with the act of 'Mankading' is inescapable, but Wigmore points out that Mankad is better remembered as an 'outstanding Test all-rounder'.

19

Corridors of Uncertainty

Pakistan, 1969

CEYLON – some golf, the beach, some warm-up games: it was, thought Michael Melford, 'one of the few places left in the world where they seem to like the British'.[461] In Pakistan, by contrast, 'an evil genie seemed to brood'. Once there, as Keith Fletcher wrote later, it was as if the players 'were being asked to bat with a gun at our heads'.[462] Ceylon, by contrast, was Tom Graveney unfurling a two-hour hundred at Colombo 'on a pitch as true as a billiard table', peppering the boundary with 13 fours and a couple of sixes. Beyond the boundary rope, however, there was the uncertain prospect of what lay ahead. Instead of the smooth unreeling of previous tours – venues, travel arrangements, accommodation – there was great uncertainty 'about where the Test matches should be staged, which up-country fixtures would be included, and where the players would stay.'[463] The riots in Pakistan meanwhile spread and became more intense before the East Pakistan phase of the tour was summarily called off.

---

461 *The Cricketer*, spring 1969: *This Tour of Sharp Contrasts* by Michael Melford.
462 *Captain's Innings* by Keith Fletcher, page 42.
463 Oborne, op. cit., page 196.

In the middle of the crisis was Les Ames, the tour manager, caught between the competing interests of the cricket authorities of two countries and their respective government officials. 'He received worthless assurances from Pakistan officials and misleading advice and information from British sources.'[464] Communications were in disarray and unreliable, a situation made worse by a cable strike in the UK. The players were unsettled by the fluidity of the situation – John Snow would later describe the tour as 'a shambles', seeing the MCC party as being 'used as a political pawn again – so soon after the South Africa affair'.[465]

The MCC party flew to Karachi on Sunday, 2 February, the day after the game against Ceylon at Colombo had ended in a high-scoring draw – 807 runs in the match for just 13 wickets and hundreds for Edrich (177) and Graveney (106) as well as Ceylon's Anura Tennekoon (101). There was great uncertainty amongst the party as to what might lie ahead. The city was under a dusk to dawn curfew and, instead of a city-centre hotel, the English party stayed within easy reach of the airport. It was becoming evident that the players were being exposed to what was an incendiary situation. Tom Graveney spoke for many when he declared that 'we had no right to be there playing cricket. Literally it was neither the time or the place for it.'[466]

The confusion spread as the amount of information declined. There were curt instructions for example to 'fly to Bahawalpur at 6am next day'; but the players were kept in the dark about 'conditions, both living and politics' and were 'rescheduled to …

---

464 Lyn Wellings in *Wisden Cricketers' Almanack, 1970,* page 914.

465 *Cricket Rebel* by John Snow, page 66.

466 Oborne, op. cit., page 196.

territories we knew nothing about'. At one point Ames, Graveney and Cowdrey flew to Rawalpindi to meet representatives of the Pakistan Board of Control, but with riots occurring all over Pakistan, nothing seemed certain, no decisions set in stone. On 3 February it seemed that the tour might be called off but soon it emerged that Dacca was to be reinstated as a Test venue. A revised programme was agreed – although the players and members of the accompanying press were unwilling parties to the deal – and the itinerary now included Bahawalpur and Lyallpur. As a result, Michael Melford and the rest endured 'a frightening 60-mile drive over a single track road' and again, after the game at Bahawalpur, there was another 60-mile drive, this time to Multan for an overnight stay before flying to Lyallpur, where play was scheduled to start early next morning. The MCC group arrived 90 minutes late, but Colin Cowdrey was not to be hurried, insisting that 'no English side ever started a game of cricket without first having a cup of tea'.[467]

The first Test was played at Lahore beginning on 21 February. The players were grateful for the fact that 'from the point of view of laundry, baths and various other refinements … the Inter-Continental Hotel … seemed like Shangri-La' compared to what they had experienced in their travels through Pakistan previously. The atmosphere in the city, however, was riotous: a week or so before the Test there had been some concern about the safety of British officials, while the Lahore office of the Oxford University Press had been 'badly destroyed by fire' on 13 February.[468] President Ayub Khan broadcast to the nation on the same day as the Test match was due to begin. He was

467 Oborne, op. cit., page 198.

468 The National Archives, file FCO 468.

also not beyond interfering in team selection, insisting that an influential student organiser, Aftab Gul, should be included in the Pakistan XI. Basil D'Oliveira met Gul at a reception two days before the match began and asked him if the Pakistan XI had been selected; 'No,' was the reply, 'but I know I'm playing. If I don't play, there's no Test match.'[469]

The first and last days of the Lahore Test were marked by student unrest. When Keith Fletcher went out to bat in only his second Test match he was 'accompanied by a number of student fans' and later, returning to the middle after the tea interval, he and Cowdrey 'were jostled by dozens of spectators' and, in Fletcher's case, 'almost dragged to the ground'.[470] Cowdrey's phlegmatic spirit was reflected in a fine hundred and later David Brown bowled with great fire and accuracy, while Keith Fletcher made a crucial 83 in the second innings. Pakistan, batting last, settled for the comfort of a draw after losing three wickets for 71.

Throughout the tour there were daily processions, demonstrations, and on one occasion, a general strike. During the stay in Lahore there were also renewed pressures to go to East Pakistan, despite the earlier decision not to travel there and the fact that the state of emergency had not been lifted. Nonetheless, four days later David Brown and John Snow were marking out their run-ups, preparing to bowl at the Pakistan openers at Dacca in East Pakistan. It was, at that time, an unsettling place to be. The state guest house had been set on fire and there was an 'alarming breakdown of law and order' especially at the city's

---

469 Oborne, op. cit., page 199. Gul duly made his Test debut in the Lahore Test, opening the batting and scoring 12 and 29. In six Tests he never scored more than his 33 at Lord's in June 1971.

470 Fletcher, op. cit., page 44.

Inter-Continental Hotel. Official papers at the time recorded that officials 'fully understand local concern over developments at the Inter-Continental Hotel where we presume MCC are staying'.[471] At the hotel there was concern about money being stolen and 'a mob of 300 or 400 workers in the staff canteen whose behaviour [resembled'] wild animals'. A pastry cook, it seems, was seen 'brandishing a knife at Bengali employees'.[472] At all times of the day or night, John Snow later wrote, 'we could hear gunfire – some of it only yards from the hotel'. Law and order was in the hands of students who had taken on responsibility for it from the police, who had withdrawn to camps on the fringes of the city.

The pitch at Dacca was by way of being a metaphor for the situation in which MCC found itself. Comprising 'hardened mud', it looked as if it would disintegrate early on and that concern was exacerbated by the 'general disillusion' felt by the players. It was 'impossible to play cricket of any purpose when … waiting for the first sound of rifle fire'.[473] Only 'resolute and disciplined' batting by Basil D'Oliveira saved the day. Later, with the first-innings scores broadly similar, Cottam and Underwood took three early wickets to hint at an England win, but solid batting from the Pakistan middle order earned the draw.

John Snow and the rest of the England party, now reinforced by the arrival of Colin Milburn hotfoot from a beach in Western Australia, were glad to leave Dacca, bound for Karachi in West Pakistan. 'All the way to the airport we kept looking back over our shoulders wondering if any attempt would be made to stop

---

471 The word 'presume' is telling.

472 The National Archives, file FCO 468.

473 Snow, op. cit., page 68.

our flight'.[474] There was little relief from the intensity of the overall situation: a 1,500-mile flight and only two days before the third Test began in Karachi. The strange atmosphere of the series was reflected in an internal memorandum written by an official, P.F. Walker, and dated 5 March: 'The continuing strength of the students in East Pakistan has been convincingly demonstrated by their successful control of the Dacca Test Match.'[475] The day after the Karachi Test began.

It proved to be climactic, the disturbances elsewhere echoed, with even greater intensity, by 'demonstrators who swarmed over the ground destroying everything in their path like an army of red ants on the march'.[476] Only one team got to bat in the match. Early on the third day England, at 502/7, were intent on batting on. Alan Knott was 96 not out, batting with David Brown, who had 25 to his name. Colin Milburn had opened the innings and made a barnstorming 139. Mushtaq had just bowled a googly and bamboozled Knott, the ball beating the bat, missing the stumps and fooling the wicketkeeper, Wasim Bari. David Brown had seen something much more troubling and shouted the length of the pitch to Knott: 'Come on. Let's get off.' They raced to the pavilion, quickly followed by the umpires and fielders. The mob had swarmed 'over the railings, hundreds of youths, some with red banners, advanced on the pitch as the players raced off, seized the stumps (trying optimistically to dig up the unmarked pitch with them) and wrecked the VIP stand. The object allegedly was to stop cricket being played during a strike in favour of teachers.

474 Snow, op. cit., page 68.
475 The National Archives, FCO 469.
476 Snow, op. cit., page 72.

Whatever it was, it ended the tour.'[477] Alan Knott would have to wait until 1971 to register his first Test hundred. Appropriately, perhaps, it was at Edgbaston in June – against Pakistan.

This was the breaking point beyond which the tour could not progress. Within a few hours the Englishmen were back at their hotel and by midnight flying out of Karachi. 'The flight home matched the tour,' John Snow thought. Nothing to eat or drink on the flight; a delay in Cairo (engine difficulties); more delays in Rome and Paris – and fog at London Airport. They had been away for some six weeks and in Pakistan for just over a month during which time the certainties of life were in short supply and players thought as much or more about the potential for a stray bullet as they did about line and length or corridors of uncertainty. So it was that, 'A naïve clique of bungling and incompetent MCC officials sanctioned by the British Foreign Office, made the extraordinary decision to send the England cricket team into a war zone.'[478]

---

477 Michael Melford in *The Cricketer,* May 1969.

478 Oborne, op. cit., page 196.

20

'And That, Gentlemen, Is Over'

THE MCC tours from the middle of the 1950s to the bleak day when two English batters were obliged to flee by incensed rioters racing across the field of play provide a window on a very different world. In those early days, with memories of the war only slowly fading and the concept of empire lingering, the divide between amateur and professional was still clear-cut; a cricketer could realistically contemplate a career as both cricketer and professional footballer; cricket tours were long and travel was by liner and then by rail, trundling for hours across distant lands.[479]

The period was not one marked by much English success: the Ashes, won in 1955, were lost comprehensively four years later and would not be recovered until 1970/71, in an unprecedented seven-Test series, under Ray Illingworth. Winning Tests away from home became markedly less common over the period 1954–69. The 1960s, in particular, a time when avoidance of defeat appeared to take an ever stronger hold on competing captains. Run rates slowed; so too over rates and draws became almost the norm. From 1955 to 1969 England drew more games than were

479 The 1953/54 tour party included six men with a footballing pedigree: Trevor Bailey, Denis Compton, Willy Watson, Fred Trueman, Brian Statham and Ken Suttle.

either won or lost: 68 Tests were played over that period of which only 17 were won and 37 drawn (54% of the total played).[480]

In 1971 England would regain the Ashes under the captaincy of Ray Illingworth. He, like Hutton a decade and a half before, benefited from being able to deploy a quick bowler capable of match-winning destruction: Frank Tyson in Hutton's side took 28 wickets at 20.82 each in 1954/55, while John Snow took 31 at 22.83. Success was short-lived with a 4-1 defeat in the series contested in 1974/75. The MCC tour party that year included Colin Cowdrey on his 11th tour. It would be his last, his Test career stretching back over nearly 21 years. He played his final Test at the MCG in February 1975 after a career which in terms of England tours far exceeded any other player.

The years from the tour of West Indies by MCC in 1954/55 to the premature conclusion of the Karachi Test in 1969 were marked by great uncertainty in the world beyond cricket, from the Suez crisis in 1956, the flirtation with nuclear annihilation over Cuba in 1962, to the collapse of empire manifested in the violent unrest in Pakistan and the serious political impasse over a 'coloured' cricketer which exercised government ministers in both London and Cape Town. The theatre critic Harold Hobson caught the mood of the time when he imagined the bizarre juxtaposition of Peter May on a 'sunny afternoon … making a century at Lord's against Middlesex … [while] old men are dozing in the Long Room, a hydrogen bomb may explode'.[481]

Change in cricket moved more slowly. England cricket captains and managers usually still had an Oxbridge background;

---

480 Of the 17 wins, 5 were against New Zealand, 5 against Australia, 4 against West Indies, and 3 against South Africa.

481 *Who Only Cricket Know* by David Woodhouse, page 14.

the longer form of the game was of greater significance for many people than limited-overs cricket; and the management of MCC's cricketing tourists still resembled perhaps a school trip where misdemeanours were noted and counted against you. Interestingly, a regard for Oxbridge status was not confined to England; both South Africa and West Indies appointed men with such a background over the period.

Of the press, Jim Swanton was regarded by some as a snob and showed some of its less attractive qualities. It wasn't so long ago that Gubby Allen had described fast bowlers Harold Larwood and Bill Voce as 'swollen-headed, gutless, uneducated miners'. When MCC tourists, for example, failed to acknowledge receipt of the club's token gift – an ashtray or cufflinks for the (rarer) non-smokers – to mark their completed tour, a mildly admonitory follow-up letter would be sent seeking a letter of gratitude. Management of tours varied from the lordly, through the avuncular to the heavy-handed. Resentments were keenly felt by, for example, Peter Richardson and Fred Trueman over comments and warnings made by manager Freddie Brown over their behaviour. Players who toed the line were accorded the label of 'splendid tourist', a phrase used in managers' and captains' reports about Ken Barrington, for example.

Both the length of tours and the travel arrangements changed over the period, with air travel becoming the principal means of traversing the considerable distances involved. Significantly many of the press, when the schedule allowed them, chose to drive or take the train. How better to see the land through which they were passing? Some felt that something was sacrificed when the 'team building' benefits of long sea cruises was lost. Those determining the itineraries for tours were caught between satisfying the preferences and/or demands of the cricketing Boards of Control in the countries to be visited – under pressure perhaps from the more remote corners of their territory to host the visiting English; the need to ensure the players were match-ready when it came to the Tests; and the mental wellbeing of the players, exiled in effect for approaching half a year.

Many members of the press were serial tourists too. Of those who feature in this book only Margaret Hughes and John Arlott, for different reasons, did not keep returning to the press boxes across the cricketing world. Most were from a generation for whom the notion of long periods away from home was not unusual – Swanton in a Japanese POW camp and Ross on the Baltic convoys, for example. Many had similar backgrounds: Wellings and Ross were both Oxford men, and almost all had played the game to a reasonable standard. Ex-players often found themselves drifting into writing about the game. On this writer's bookshelf, source material for what you are reading now are books by Alec Bedser (on the 1958/59 tour down under); Brian Close (West Indies 1968); Colin Cowdrey, Ted Dexter, Len Hutton, Barry Knight, Alan Knott, Ian Peebles, John Snow and Frank Tyson.

Not everyone was a natural tourist and there were a few cricketers who struggled to make an impression, either through illness or injury, or the mismatch between their qualities as a cricketer and the demands of the context in which they were required to perform, or because of an inability to adapt to the situation. While Frank Tyson was adroit enough to alter his bowling run-up, cutting it significantly shorter with no loss of pace and increased potency, others struggled to adapt, or make a lasting impact, perhaps through injury or limited opportunity. Others enjoyed the camaraderie or in Ted Dexter's case, for example, the golf and the tea planters' houses in Sri Lanka (Ceylon then) which reminded him of the plusher parts of suburban Surrey.

Throughout the tours of the fifties and sixties there were sensitivities about wives being – or not being – on tour. The majority of players were parted from those they loved and, when wives did arrive at some point on the tour's itinerary (not paid for by MCC), they were often caught up in controversy. Ted Dexter, for example, felt obliged to defend Susan Dexter's presence against press intrusion and disapproval. Jim Swanton, a confirmed bachelor it seemed before his marriage relatively late in life in 1958, was one of those who thoroughly disapproved of the distraction wives and relatives presented.

The cricket writers lived a parallel life to the tourists, close enough, for example, to help by bowling in the nets at times, but not restricted by the rules of cricketing tourism. There were also instances of friendships between writer and cricketer established through shared interests – Arlott and Tyson, for example, both had a love of books and literature. On Christmases away from home the players would celebrate the day together, often having to resume a Test match the following day, an obligation which must have tested their resolve when the bottles were being passed around. The press, by contrast, contrived to elicit an invitation from some old chum from the past to share the festivities in some pleasant dwelling with a golf course and a beach close by. Alan Ross was a good example of a newspaperman whose passion for cricket was equalled or surpassed by his love of language, poetry, landscape and travel. There was nothing better for him than a road trip in a Nash Rambler along some winding corniche overlooking a blue ocean, with a cricket match waiting down the road in a day or two. There was a definite sense that the pressmen were out to enjoy the opportunities presented by their working lives and the press box was for the most part a jovial environment, apart from the 'odd sourpuss' – probably Lyn Wellings whose pen, Ian Wooldridge held, was dipped in vitriol. Henry Blofeld thought that Wellings was 'the most difficult, bloody-minded and cantankerous inhabitant of the cricketing press box'. Evidently, he was never an easy man. He had played in the 1930 Oxford side with Ian Peebles and was judged to be 'possibly the best all-rounder'. However, he soon became '*persona non grata* ... and was dropped at the first opportunity'.[482]

There was, for a touring cricketer, nothing worse than being found to be surplus to requirements – hence the continuing debate about how many men to take on tour. Ian Peebles was one writer who knew from experience what this was like. There were inevitably errors of selection – players who toured who shouldn't have and others who were left behind. It was inevitable too that touring parties were affected to a greater or lesser degree by illness or injuries, the cases of asthma, bronchitis, tonsillitis, dysentery and shingles; the broken fingers, the damaged and dodgy knees, and the hamstring problems. When a cricket writer fell ill – as Ross did with appendicitis – the impact was only felt by an editor far away in London, not by a selection committee already baffled about the best balance of the team for the next Test.

Climate was often an issue for the players, despite the conscientious efforts to prepare them before travelling. Temperatures soared, sub-tropical rain swept in, hotels weren't air-conditioned so that players' sleep was troubled by heat as well

482 Blofeld, op. cit., page 72 and Peebles, op. cit., page 64.

as the prospect of the opposition's barrage of fast bowlers. That heat was also a factor in the disruption and rioting that marred several of the Test series. There were other factors, however – the torpid lethargy of some of the cricket which at times was painfully slow; perceived errors by umpires; perceived slights as a result of some misreading of an English captain's decision; and the underlying sensitivities arising from the political context in which the tour was being played.

Cricketers and cricket writers on tour shared a sense of outrage when the seamier side of the game intruded. With a neat sense of irony the former Australian Test cricketer – and later esteemed cricket writer – Jack Fingleton called his book about the 1958/59 tour *Four Chukkas to Australia.* The issue of 'chucking' or 'throwing', notably by several Australian quick bowlers, was a cloud over that series. Fingleton's book quotes the author on the back cover using the word 'chukka', thereby reviving memories of the word most used by English cricket writers on the 1958/59 MCC tour of Australia. 'And,' he continued, 'they were not always wrong!' Elsewhere, in the West Indies, there were strong feelings surrounding the persistent use of short-pitched bowling – a bouncer war – made worse by the fact that one of the men concerned, Charlie Griffith, was seen as having an illegal action, but was still a mainstay of his team's fast-bowling attack.

The most heated, riotous and dangerous events on a cricket field over the decade and a half covered by this book were in March 1969 at Karachi where cricketers were swept from the field by a heated mob bent on summarily terminating the game of cricket. For the players involved it was a terrifying experience. Later that night, as their aeroplane took the tourists away into the dark sky and away from the fires and the rioters stalking the streets, some of the escaping English cricketers would have reflected, as their heads lay back against the plane's headrests and they strained to see the last of Pakistan through the darkness, how was it that no one had seen fit to protect them sooner? Cricketers, they knew, should be seen clad in white on lush green grass, not escaping a riot on a hot night so far from home.

Afterword

THE ORIGINS of this book lie in its predecessor, *All-India and Down Under*, which chronicled and juxtaposed two cricket tours in the immediate post-war period. Reading and writing about the 1946 Indian tourists criss-crossing England and the travails of Hammond's men the following winter in Australia gave me a taste for cricketing odysseys – the trials and unexpected pleasures of playing cricket far from home – and indeed from Lord's. Reading accounts of tours in the 1950s I was struck by the extent to which landscape, travel, weather, illness and relationships, cricketers' backstories and personalities frequently enhanced the basic details of the game, what happens when bat meets ball on a Test match wicket. This book is about cricket, but also the world which surrounds it.

There were two other starting points. The first was reading Peter Oborne's history of Pakistan cricket – *Wounded Tiger* – and his highly commended account of the MCC tour of Pakistan in 1969. That of course is the end point of my book. He and I were both puzzled as to what possessed the cricket authorities to 'send the England cricket team into a war zone'.[483] He could find no files at the MCC Archive at Lord's to explain that – and

483 Oborne, op. cit., page 196.

nor have I. Having said that, you can see how events unfolded inexorably and understand all too well how one strand of crisis management leads inevitably to the next.

My second starting point was the work of Alan Ross, who figures large in this book – his poetry, his partial autobiographies and most notably his distinctive accounts of cricket tours to West Indies, Australia and South Africa. It is significant that his headstone in the Sussex churchyard where he is buried describes him, not as 'cricket correspondent' but 'Writer, poet and editor.'

Ending the book with that final dangerous riot in Karachi leaves untold what came next for the main protagonists – by which I mean the ones whose lives most intrigued me in the telling of the story. So first, the captains. Len Hutton died in 1990 having been a newspaper columnist and England selector, his status marked by a memorial service in York Minster; Peter May retired early from cricket having lost his love of the game and become an insurance broker as well as president of MCC in 1980/81. He died aged just 64 in 1994. Ted Dexter died aged 86 in 2021, having retired early from playing cricket and working instead as a journalist as well as pursuing his interests in golf, horse racing and business, and succeeding May as chairman of the England selectors; Mike Smith's Test career, seemingly over in 1966, had a brief, not very successful reprise six years later. Perhaps the most telling indictment of the touring life concerns Ken Barrington, the man who went into bat, it seems, trailing a Union Jack. He died while working as assistant manager on the 1981 tour of West Indies at the age of 50. His long career as a cricketing tourist had increasingly been associated with fatigue and stress.

Of the cricket correspondents, John Arlott worked as a broadcaster with the BBC until 1980, working at times with

Fred Trueman and Jim Laker among others. He died on the island of Alderney in 1991 aged 77. His last commentary was at Lord's in 1980 in the Centenary Test where he ended his broadcast with no hint of farewell, but with the words, '25 Boycott, 15 Gower and after Trevor Bailey, it will be Christopher Martin-Jenkins.'

Alan Ross took over the editorship of the *London Magazine* in 1961, fell in love with both horse racing and literary life and died in London in 2001. Clayton in Sussex was a spiritual home. At sea in the war he would dream of Sussex and its cricket; in peacetime he would buy the house in Clayton and play cricket for the village from 1972 to 1978 having, in his working life as a sportswriter, always been otherwise engaged on Saturdays. I liked too the breadth of his sporting interest – he was a Spurs fan, warmed by the moment when in Norway and trying to locate some football news on a 'complicated TV ... the magic words Tottenham Hotspur 2 Sunderland 0 spring out of nowhere'.[484] My own football allegiance is less regal (more League 2) but I know how Ross felt. Then there are his literary connections which deserve a book of their own. Watching Ted Dexter scoring a brilliant hundred at Hove with Ian Fleming, for example, or bumping into Philip Larkin at Leicester in 1956 when Keith Miller scored 281* and the visitors batted for two long days, reaching a massive 694/6. The meeting mattered enough to Larkin for him to write a letter on what was 'a nice sunny day', noting that he had not seen Ross for some 15 years. 'He now has a beard – flecked with grey, alas!'[485]

484 *Winter Sea* by Alan Ross, page 60.

485 *Selected Letters of Philip Larkin* ed. Anthony Thwaite, page 261. Letter to Judy Egerton, 14 May 1956.

Of the other cricket writers with a significant role in this book, Lyn Wellings died in 1992, his *Wisden* obituary recording his long-standing antipathy to one-day cricket, overseas stars playing for county sides, South Africa's isolation and the doings of the Test and County Cricket Board. Ian Peebles died in 1980 having worked in the wine trade as well as working as a journalist, while EW Swanton died of heart failure in 2000. Like Wellings he was a natural traditionalist, disapproving of the end of 'gentlemen cricketers' and, later in the 1970s, the intrusion of Kerry Packer's World Series Cricket into the game.

Finally some acknowledgements. To my wife Vanessa who has patiently put up with my enthusiasm for cricket and my sharing of anecdotes from the 1950s and 60s; to the National Archives; and to the MCC Archive at Lord's, in particular Alan Rees for whose help and interest I am most grateful. The archive is a wonderful resource, and I particularly remember the day when I read through a sequence of files sitting at a wide, highly polished table at the centre of which was a small plaque indicating that it had been gifted to the archive by Judy, the widow of the cricket broadcaster, Christopher Martin-Jenkins. It was where he wrote his books on cricket. I felt his presence and that of many others whose words and deeds fill this book.

I am very grateful to Pitch Publishing for commissioning this book and my thanks are due to Bruce Talbot for his thorough and sympathetic editing. I should like to place on record my thanks to the entire Pitch team for their encouragement, interest and support.

Appendix A

The Tours and Tests

Date	*Venue*	*Result*	*Key English Performances*
West Indies 1954			
15–21 Jan	Kingston	Lost, 140 runs	Watson 116, Statham 4–90
6–12 Feb	Bridgetown	Lost, 181 runs	Compton 93, Laker 4–81
24 Feb–2 Mar	Georgetown	Won, 9 wickets	Hutton 169, Statham 4–64
17–23 Mar	Port of Spain	Drawn	May 135, Bailey 2–20
30 Mar–3 Apr	Kingston	Won, 9 wickets	Hutton 205, Bailey 7–34
Australia and New Zealand 1954/55			
26 Nov–1 Dec	Brisbane	Lost, Innings and 154 runs	Bailey 88 and 3–140
17–22 Dec	Sydney	Won, 38 runs	May 104, Tyson 6–85
31 Dec–5 Jan	Melbourne	Won, 128 runs	Cowdrey 102, Tyson 7–27
28 Jan–2 Feb	Adelaide	Won, 5 wickets	Hutton 80, Appleyard 3–58 & 3–13
25 Feb–3 Mar	Sydney	Drawn	Graveney 111, Wardle 5–79
11–16 Mar	Dunedin	Won, 8 wickets	Cowdrey 42, Tyson 4–16
25–28 Mar	Auckland	Won, Innings and 20 runs	Hutton 53, Appleyard 4–7
South Africa 1956/57			
24–29 Dec	Johannesburg	Won, 131 runs	Richardson 117, Bailey 5–20
1–5 Jan	Cape Town	Won, 312 runs	Cowdrey 101, Wardle 7–36
25–30 Jan	Durban	Drawn	Insole 110*, Wardle 5–61
15–20 Feb	Johannesburg	Lost 17 runs	Insole 68, Bailey 3–54
1–5 Mar	Port Elizabeth	Lost 58 runs	Bailey 41, Tyson 6–40
Australia and New Zealand 1958/59			
5–10 Dec	Brisbane	Lost, 8 wickets	Bailey 68, Loader 4–56
31 Dec–5 Jan	Melbourne	Lost, 8 wickets	May 113, Statham 7–57
9–15 Jan	Sydney	Drawn	Cowdrey 100*, Laker 5–107

30 Jan–5 Feb	Adelaide	Lost, 10 wickets	Cowdrey 84, Trueman 4–90
13–18 Feb	Melbourne	Lost, 9 wickets	Richardson 68, Trueman 4–92
27 Feb–2 Mar	Christchurch	Won, Innings and 99 runs	Dexter 141, Lock 6–53
14–18 Mar	Auckland	Drawn	May 124*, Dexter 3–23

West Indies 1959/60

6–12 Jan	Bridgetown	Drawn	Dexter 136*, Trueman 4–93
28 Jan–3 Feb	Port of Spain	Won, 256 runs	Barrington 121, Trueman 5–35
17–23 Feb	Kingston	Drawn	Cowdrey 114, Trueman 4–54
9–15 Mar	Georgetown	Drawn	Dexter 110, Allen 3–75
25–31 Mar	Port of Spain	Drawn	Cowdrey 119, Illingworth 2–53

India 1961/62

11–16 Nov	Bombay	Drawn	Barrington 151*, Lock 4–74
1–6 Dec	Kanpur	Drawn	Barrington 172, Lock 3–93
13–18 Dec	Delhi	Drawn	Barrington 113*, Allen 4–87
30 Dec–4 Jan	Calcutta	Drawn	Dexter/Richardson both 62, Allen 5–67
10–15 Jan	Madras	Lost, 128 runs	Smith 73, Lock 6–65

Pakistan 1961/62

21–26 Oct	Lahore	Won, 5 wickets	Barrington 139, Brown 3–27
19–24 Jan	Dacca	Drawn	Pullar 165, Allen 5–30
2–7 Feb	Karachi	Drawn	Dexter 205, Knight 4–66

Australia and New Zealand, 1963/64

30 Nov–5 Dec	Brisbane	Drawn	Dexter 99, Knight 3–65
29 Dec–3 Jan	Melbourne	Won, 7 wickets	Cowdrey/ Sheppard 113, Trueman 5–62
11–15 Jan	Sydney	Lost, 8 wickets	Cowdrey 85, Titmus 7–79
25–30 Jan	Adelaide	Drawn	Barrington 132*, Trueman 4–60
15–20 Feb	Sydney	Drawn	Barrington 101, Titmus 5–103
23–27 Feb	Auckland	Won, Innings and 215 runs	Parfitt 131*, Larter 4–26

1–4 Mar	Wellington	Won, Innings and 47 runs	Cowdrey 128, Trueman 4–46

India 1963/64

10–15 Jan	Madras	Drawn	Bolus 88, Titmus 5–116
21–26 Jan	Bombay	Drawn	Titmus 84*, Price 3–66
29 Jan–3 Feb	Calcutta	Drawn	Cowdrey 107, Price 5–73
8–13 Feb	Delhi	Drawn	Cowdrey 151, Mortimore 3–74
15–20 Feb	Kanpur	Drawn	Knight 127, Titmus 6–73

South Africa 1964/65

4–8 Dec	Durban	Won, Innings and 104 runs	Barrington 148*, Allen 5–41
23–29 Dec	Johannesburg	Drawn	Dexter 172, Titmus 4–73
1–6 Jan	Cape Town	Drawn	Smith 121, Barrington 3–4
22–27 Jan	Johannesburg	Drawn	Parfitt 122*, Price 2–68
12–17 Feb	Port Elizabeth	Drawn	Boycott 117, Allen 3–80

Australia and New Zealand 1965/66

10–15 Dec	Brisbane	Drawn	Boycott 63*, Brown 3–71
30 Dec–4 Jan	Melbourne	Drawn	Edrich 109, Knight 4–84
7–11 Jan	Sydney	Won, Innings and 93 runs	Barber 185, Brown 5–63
28 Jan –1 Feb	Adelaide	Lost, Innings and 9 runs	Barrington 102, Jones 6–118
11–16 Feb	Melbourne	Drawn	Barrington 115, Jones 3–145
25 Feb–1 Mar	Christchurch	Drawn	Allen 88, Higgs 4–5
4–8 Mar	Dunedin	Drawn	Cowdrey 89*, Allen 4–46

West Indies 1967/68

19–24 Jan	Port of Spain	Drawn	Barrington 143, Brown 3–27
8–14 Feb	Kingston	Drawn	Cowdrey 101, Snow 7–49
29 Feb–5 Mar	Bridgetown	Drawn	Edrich 146, Snow 5–86
14–19 Mar	Port of Spain	Won, 7 wickets	Cowdrey 148, Brown 3–107
28 Mar–3 Apr	Georgetown	Drawn	Boycott 116, Snow 6–60

Pakistan 1968/69

21–24 Feb	Lahore	Drawn	Cowdrey 100, Cottam 4–50
28 Feb–3 Mar	Dacca	Drawn	D'Oliveira 114*, Underwood 5–94
6–8 Mar	Karachi	Drawn	Milburn 139

Bibliography

Allen, David Rayvern, *Jim – The Life of Jim Swanton* (Aurum, 2004)

Arlott, John, *Australian Test Journal* (Phoenix, 1955)

Arlott, John, *Basingstoke Boy* (Willow, 1990)

Arlott, John, *In Conversation with Mike Brearley* (Channel 4, 1986)

Arlott, Timothy, *John Arlott – a Memoir* (Andre Deutsch, 1994)

Barker, JS, *In the Main* (Pelham, 1968)

Bedser, Alec, *May's Men in Australia* (Stanley Paul, 1959)

Bedser, Alec, *Twin Ambitions* (Stanley Paul, 1986)

Berry, S (ed), *The Observer on Cricket* (Unwin Hyman, 1987)

Blofeld, Henry, *A Thirst for Life* (Hodder & Stoughton, 2000)

Bose, Mihir, *A History of Indian Cricket* (Andre Deutsch, 1990)

Bradman, Don, *Farewell to Cricket* (Hodder & Stoughton, 1950)

Brearley, Mike, *The Art of Captaincy* (Hodder & Stoughton, 1985)

Brearley, Mike, *Spirit of Cricket* (Constable, 2020)

Cardus, Neville, *Close of Play* (Collins, 1956)

Chalke, Stephen, *The Way it Was* (Fairfield, 2008)

Clarke, John, *Challenge Renewed* (Stanley Paul, 1963)

Clarke, John, *With England in Australia* (Stanley Paul, 1966)

Close, Brian, *I Don't Bruise Easily* (Macdonald & Jane's, 1978)

Close, Brian, *The MCC Tour of West Indies, 1968* (Stanley Paul, 1968)

Compton, Denis, *End of an Innings* (Oldbourne, 1958)

Cowdrey, Colin, *MCC – Autobiography of a Cricketer* (Hodder & Stoughton, 1976)

Dexter, Ted, *85 Not Out* (Quiller, 2020)

Dooley, Stephen (ed.), *So I Have Thought of You* (Fourth Estate, 2008)

Fay, Stephen and Kynaston, David, *Arlott, Swanton and the Soul of English Cricket* (Bloomsbury, 2018)

Fingleton, Jack, *Four Chukkas to Australia* (Heinemann, 1960)
Fletcher, Keith, *Captain's Innings* (Stanley Paul, 1983)
Fortune, Charles, *The MCC Tour of South Africa, 1956-57* (Harrap, 1957)
Fortune, Charles, *MCC in South Africa 1964/65* (Robert Hale, 1965)
Gilligan, Arthur, *The Urn Returns* (Rigby, 1955)
Gover, Alfred, *The Long Run* (Pelham, 1991)
Hamilton, Duncan, *Harold Larwood* (Quercus, 2009)
Hamilton, Duncan, *The Great Romantic* (Hodder & Stoughton, 2019)
Hennessy, Peter, *Winds of Change* (Allen Lane, 2019)
Hill, Alan, *Tony Lock* (The History Press, 2008)
Howat, Gerald, *Len Hutton – the Biography* (Heinemann Kingswood, 1988)
Hughes, Margaret, *The Long Hop* (Stanley Paul, 1955)
Hughes, Margaret, *All on a Summer's Day* (Stanley Paul, 1953)
Hutton, Len, *Just My Story* (Hutchinson, 1956)
Hutton, Len, *Fifty Years in Cricket* (Stanley Paul, 1984)
James, CLR, *Beyond a Boundary* (Hutchinson, 1963)
Kahn, Roger, *The Boys of Summer* (Harper & Row, 1972)
Kerr, Diana Rait & Peebles, Ian, *Lord's 1946–1970* (Pavilion, 1987)
Knight, Barry, *Beyond the Pavilion* (Amberley, 2022)
Knott, Alan, *It's Knott Cricket* (Macmillan, 1985)
Knott, Richard, *All-India and Down Under* (Pitch, 2023)
Knott, Richard, *Cricket – Wit, Wickets and Wisdom* (Running Press, 1996)
Kynaston, David, *A Northern Wind* (Bloomsbury, 2023)
Kynaston, David & Ricketts, Harry, *Richie Benaud's Blue Suede Shoes* (Bloomsbury, 2024)
Miller, Douglas, *Charles Palmer* (Fairfield, 2005)
Miller, Douglas, *MJK Smith – No Ordinary Man* (ACS Publications, 2013)
Murtagh, Andrew, *Touched by Greatness* (Pitch, 2014)
Oborne, Peter, *Basil D'Oliveira* (Little, Brown, 2024)
Oborne, Peter, *Wounded Tiger* (Simon & Schuster, 2014)
Peebles, Ian, *The Fight for the Ashes 1958-59* (Harrap, 1959)
Peebles, Ian, *The Ashes, 1954-55* (Hodder & Stoughton, 1955)

Peebles, Ian, *Spinner's Yarn* (William Collins & Sons, 1977)
Peel, Mark, *Gilly* (Pitch, 2023)
Peel, Mark, *England Expects* (Kingswood, 1992)
Ronayne, Michael, *A Guide to the Memorials of Cricket* (ACS Publications, 2017)
Ross, Alan, *Australia 55* (Michael Joseph, 1955)
Ross, Alan, *Cape Summer* (Hamish Hamilton, 1957)
Ross, Alan, *Through the Caribbean* (Hamish Hamilton, 1960)
Ross, Alan, *Australia 1963* (Eyre & Spottiswoode, 1963)
Ross, Alan, *Blindfold Games* (Collins Harvill, 1986)
Ross, Alan, *Coastwise Lights* (Collins Harvill, 1988)
Ross, Alan, *Poems* (The Harvill Press, 2005)
Ross, Alan, *Winter Sea* (The Harvill Press, 1997)
Sandford, Christopher, *Godfrey Evans* (Simon & Schuster, 1990)
Shindler, Colin, *Bob Barber – the Professional Amateur* (Max Books, 2015)
Shindler, Colin, *Barbed Wire and Cucumber Sandwiches* (Pitch, 2020)
Snow, John, *Cricket Rebel* (Hamlyn, 1976)
Sobers, Garry, *My Autobiography* (Headline, 2002)
Swanton, EW, *West Indian Adventure* (Museum, 1954)
Swanton, EW, *Report from South Africa* (Robert Hale, 1957)
Swanton, EW, *West Indies Revisited* (Heinemann, 1960)
Swanton, EW, *Swanton in Australia* (William Collins & Sons, 1975)
Swanton, EW, *Gubby Allen – Man of Cricket* (Hutchinson, 1985)
Swanton, EW, *Last Over* (Richard Cohen, 1996)
Thorn, Richard, *When Cricket and Politics Collided* (Matador, 2021)
Tyson, Frank, *In the Eye of the Typhoon* (Parrs Wood, 2004)
Tyson, Frank, *A Typhoon Called Tyson* (Heinemann, 1961)
Wardle, Johnny, *Happy Go Johnny* (Robert Hale, 1957)
Waters, Chris, *Fred Trueman* (Aurum, 2012)
Wellings, EM, *The Ashes Retained* (Evans, 1955)
Wellings, EM, *The Ashes Thrown Away* (Bailey Bros & Swinfen, 1959)
Wellings, EM, *Dexter v Benaud* (Bailey Bros & Swinfen, 1963)
Wheeler, Marina, *The Lost Homestead* (Hodder & Stoughton, 2020)
Wigmore, Tim, *Test Cricket – a History* (Quercus, 2025)
Wilde, Simon, *England – the Biography* (Simon & Schuster, 2018)

Wilde, Simon, *The Tour* (Simon & Schuster, 2023)
Woodhouse, David, *Who Only Cricket Know* (Fairfield, 2021)
Wooldridge, Ian, *Travelling Reserve* (William Collins, 1982)

In addition, Cricket Archive has been an invaluable online resource, including as it does past copies of *The Cricketer* magazine. The relevant editions of *Wisden Cricketers' Almanack* have also been indispensable.

Index

Abberley, Neal 255
Adcock, Neil 101
Adelaide 47, 49-52, 65-6, 72, 78-9, 90, 115, 122-3, 125, 176, 182-3, 189-90, 223-5, 227-242
Ahmedabad 157, 161, 199
Ahmed, Saeed 255
Akhtar, Javed 158
Alexander, Gerry 131, 137, 140
Allen, David 135, 151-2, 156, 159-60, 162, 168, 176, 181-2, 185, 192, 195, 208, 210, 212, 214, 217, 220, 223, 225
Allen, Gubby 14-15, 17, 87, 172, 266
Alston, Rex 88, 133, 141
Ames, Les 236, 254, 258-9
Amritsar 194, 204-5
Andrew, Keith 41, 59-60, 87, 112, 132-3, 152, 157, 195
Antigua 26, 148, 241
Apartheid 97, 172, 217-8, 250-3
Appleyard, Bob 41, 51, 68, 77, 87, 112
Archer, Ron 69
Arlott, John 8, 10, 59-60, 62-5, 68-9, 71, 79-81, 88, 108, 173, 251-2, 267-8, 273
Arnold, Geoff 255-6
Arundel 8, 174-90
Australia 7, 10-11,13-16, 20, 36-47, 49, 51-74, 76-81, 83-4, 87, 89-91, 103, 105, 109-121, 124-6, 128, 138, 143, 149, 151, 171-7, 180, 182-93, 195-6, 211, 213, 219-23, 225-8, 233, 236, 242, 248-9, 252, 254, 261, 265, 270, 272-3
Bahawalpur 86, 170, 197, 258-9
Bailey, Trevor 9,12,16, 26-7, 30, 35, 41, 54, 57, 61-2, 68-70, 73, 79, 92-4, 96, 99, 101, 104-6, 109, 114, 117-121, 124-8, 132, 151, 187, 195, 264, 274
Bannister, Alex 20, 22, 38, 255-6
Barbados 26-7, 29, 129, 132-4, 233, 235, 241
Barber, Bob 160-1, 164-5, 168, 175, 195, 208, 210, 212, 215-6, 220-8
Bari, Wasim 262
Barlow, Eddie 213, 215
Baroda, Maharajah 206
Barrington, Ken 10, 132-4, 136-9, 146, 150-1, 156-64, 166-9, 175, 181, 183, 185, 191-2, 195, 198-9, 205, 208, 210-1, 213-5, 217, 220, 222, 226-7, 229, 233, 235, 237-8, 245, 250, 254, 266, 273
Bedser, Alec 15, 29, 41, 45, 48, 56, 59-61, 68, 75, 81-2, 87, 111-3, 117, 124, 175, 181, 219, 249, 267
Bedser, Eric 39, 82, 111
Begh, Idris 160
Benaud, Richie 53, 69, 118, 121-2, 125-6, 128, 171, 186, 188, 191
Bermuda 19
Binks, Jimmy 175, 195, 200, 204
Bland, Colin 212
Blofeld, Henry 145, 198, 200, 205, 231, 234, 237-9, 249, 251, 269
Bolus, Brian 195, 198, 200
Bombay 111, 161-2, 165, 199, 201, 220
Booth, Brian 187, 224
Bowes, Bill 39, 42, 46, 55, 60, 64

Boycott, Geoffrey 195, 208-10, 212, 214-7, 220-7, 232-3, 235, 237, 241-6, 250, 254, 274
Brabourne Stadium 162-3, 201, 205
Bradman, Don 73-4, 115
Bray, Charles 55, 133, 178
Brearley, Mike 208-9, 216, 253, 255-6
Bridgetown 28-9, 132, 135, 138, 148, 235, 241-2
Brisbane 8, 52, 56-60, 62-3, 65-9, 71, 115-6, 120-1, 123, 173, 182-3, 185-6, 188-9, 192, 214, 221-2
British Guiana 18, 28, 30-1, 33, 132, 148-9
Brown, Alan 156, 160, 162, 165, 175
Brown, David 208, 220, 223, 225, 233, 238-240, 243, 246, 250, 254, 256, 260, 262
Brown, Freddie 14-5, 39, 45-6, 62, 64, 72, 88, 100, 103, 106-7, 112-3, 126-7, 266
Burge, Peter 191, 223-4
Burke, Perry 22, 25
Burki, Javed 160
Butcher, Basil 240, 244
Butcher, Roland 132
Butler, Frank 182
Cairo 177, 263
Calcutta 47, 154, 165, 167-8, 201, 277-8
Camacho, Steve 242, 244
Cambridge University 10, 84, 88, 96, 131, 141-2, 173, 200
SS *Canberra* 177-8
Cape Town 89-90, 99-102, 105-6, 108, 209, 212-4, 248-9, 252, 265
Cardus, Neville 39, 55
Carr, Donald 85-6, 96, 201, 209, 211, 214, 232
Cartwright, Tom 208, 214-6, 249-50, 252
Ceylon 42, 154, 170, 196, 220, 253, 257-8, 268
Chapman, Brian 119, 178
Chapman, Percy 214
Chappell, Greg 63
Chappell, Ian 226
'Chucking' 120, 127, 238, 270
Christchurch 82, 128
Christmas on tour 20, 71-4, 95, 97-9, 106, 133-4, 167, 169, 196, 211-2, 228, 268
Clark, David 199-201, 205
Clarke, John 177-8, 191
Clayton, Sussex 50, 83, 89-90, 193, 274
Climate 84, 110-1, 156, 194, 269
Close, Brian 195, 230-5, 238, 241-3, 246, 267
Coldwell, Len 175, 185, 189
Colombo 42-3, 111-2, 154, 179
Compton, Denis 16, 24, 26, 30-1, 34, 38, 41, 44, 50-1, 59-61, 75-6, 78-9, 81, 83-4, 99, 101-2, 109, 112, 220, 241, 264
Contractor, Nari 162, 165
Cottam, Bob 250, 261
Cowdrey, Colin 8, 10, 38, 41-4, 56, 59-60, 70, 76, 80, 83-5, 89, 91, 97-8, 102, 104, 108-10, 115, 117-8, 121, 123-4, 128, 131-2, 135, 137-8, 141, 144, 147-51, 153, 155, 171, 175, 177-83, 189, 192, 195, 199, 201-2, 204, 208, 218, 220-1, 224, 227, 229, 232-246, 250, 252, 259-60, 265, 267
Cowper, Bob 223, 228
Dacca 157, 163, 169, 255, 259-62
Daily Mail, The 38-9, 113, 174-5, 178, 214, 217, 229, 232
Daily Telegraph, The 10, 39, 178, 252
Davidson, Alan 69, 116, 125, 128, 190
Davie, Michael 110, 114
Delhi 154, 165-7, 202, 205-6
Dexter, Ted 114, 121-2, 125, 128, 132, 135-8, 140-1, 143, 146, 148-53, 155-74, 177, 179-81, 183-6, 188-92, 195, 207, 209-11, 214, 220, 251-2, 267-8, 273-4
Diet on tour 111, 161, 197, 255
D'Oliveira, Basil 108, 217-8, 233, 240, 245-53, 260-1
Douglas-Hume, Alec 73, 251, 253
Duckworth, George 72, 88

Durban 91, 103-7, 109, 165, 209-12, 214
Eagar, Desmond 113, 119
Edgbaston 211, 230-1, 263
Edrich, Bill 29, 41, 45, 51, 53, 55-9, 62, 68, 75-6, 79, 83, 86-7, 112
Edrich, John 200-1, 220-1, 224-6, 233, 236-7, 240, 242, 245, 250, 258
Evans, Godfrey 16, 21, 26, 28-9, 34-5, 41, 51, 56, 58-9, 68, 75, 83, 89, 98, 102, 109, 116, 121-2, 127-8
Evening Standard, The 14, 177-8, 223
Fielding, England's 30, 32, 45, 61, 152, 184, 188-9, 192, 209
Fingleton, Jack 117-8, 126, 227, 248, 270
Fleming, Ian 145-6
Fletcher, Keith 155, 250, 254, 257, 260
Food on tour 47, 100, 155-6, 161, 186, 194, 197, 203
Fortune, Charles 82, 88, 92, 95-6, 101, 104, 208-9, 214
Fremantle 38, 43, 46-7, 179
Gabba, The 57, 59-60, 186, 222
Georgetown 28, 30-1, 33, 149, 244-6
Gibbs, Lance 241, 245-6
Gilchrist, Roy 140
Gilligan, Victoria 119, 142
Goddard, Tom 48
Goddard, Trevor 98, 103, 210, 215
Gover, Alf 39, 67, 80
Graveney, Tom 10, 16, 33, 41, 51, 57, 68-70, 75, 80, 85-7, 114-5, 120, 126, 128, 151, 175, 178, 180-1, 192, 195, 209, 218, 233, 238, 245-6, 250-1, 257-9
Greenough, Tommy 132, 134-5, 152, 157
Griffith, Charlie 134, 237-9, 243, 246, 270
Griffith, SC (Billy) 173-4, 178-80, 182, 190, 195, 199, 201, 206, 219, 221, 226-7, 233, 236, 244, 251
Grout, Wally 125, 185
Guardian, The 38-9, 184, 200, 207, 215, 228, 252
Gul, Aftab 260
Gupte, SP 161, 165
Hall, Wesley 135, 138-9, 146, 150, 237-40, 243, 246
Harvey, Neil 61, 118, 120, 128
Hawke, Neil 225-6
Headley, George 22-3
Heine, Peter 99, 101
Higgs, Ken 220, 223, 233, 236
Hobart 78, 80-1
Hobbs, Robin 208, 233, 236, 254, 256
Holt, John 22, 25, 27
Howard, Geoffrey 44, 58, 75, 80, 196-7
Hughes, Margaret 39, 42, 49, 52-5, 57, 60, 65, 67, 77, 88, 111, 267
Hunte, Conrad 139
Hussain, Nasser 63
Hutton, Leonard 7-8, 10-16, 19, 21-32, 35-6, 38-41, 43-5, 52, 54-9, 62-4, 66-71, 75-80, 84-5, 87, 105, 112, 117, 123, 126, 214, 220, 230, 265, 267, 273
Hyderabad 163-4
Illingworth, Raymond 132, 152, 157, 176, 178, 264-5
Illness on tour 16, 91, 142, 149, 161, 194, 223, 232, 269, 272
India 10-1, 42, 73, 132, 140, 142, 154-5, 157, 159, 161-5, 167-9, 171-2, 175, 194-205, 211, 253, 272
Injuries on tour 26, 37, 88, 116, 125, 127-8, 147, 191, 254, 269
Insole, Doug 88, 92-3, 97, 106, 219, 233, 249-50, 252
Islamabad 158, 249
Jaisimha, ML 162, 167
Jamaica 5, 10, 19-20, 22, 25-6, 28-9, 35, 140, 144-6, 239
James, CLR 131, 140
Jardine, Douglas 40, 234
Johannesburg 95-8, 100, 105-7, 211, 214-6
Johnson, Ian 53, 62
Johnston, Brian 241, 251
Jones, Jeff 195, 220-1, 223, 225, 233, 239-240, 243-6, 250

Kahn, Roger 63-4
Kanhai, Rohan 148, 245
Kanpur 165, 199, 202-5, 214
Karachi 50, 59, 154, 170, 218, 255, 258, 261-3, 265, 270, 273
Keating, Frank 207, 228
Kennington Oval, London 9, 13, 28, 45, 80,86, 220, 234, 249-50, 252
Kenyon, Don 219, 249
Khan, Ayub 259
Kingston, Jamaica 20, 25-6, 146, 239
Knight, Barry 164-5, 167-8, 176, 185, 187-8, 192, 195, 197-8, 205, 223, 249, 267
Knott, Alan 233, 236, 243, 245-6, 250, 254-6, 262-3, 267
Lahore 86, 154, 156, 159, 259-60
Laker, Jim 13, 16, 21, 26, 28-9, 41, 45, 86-7, 107-9, 112, 121-3, 125, 127-8, 151, 182, 220, 274
Larkin, Philip 48, 274
Larter, David 176, 180, 185, 192, 195, 220-1, 223
Larwood, Harold 15, 67, 72, 266
Lawrence, DH 46-7, 54
Lawry, Bill 187, 191, 223, 228, 249
Lillee, Dennis 229
Lindwall, Ray 58, 70-1, 76, 124-5
Lloyd, Clive 243
Loader, Peter 41, 93, 101, 104, 114, 118, 125, 127-8
Lock, Tony 10, 13, 16, 24, 26-9, 39, 41, 45, 87-8, 92, 94, 101, 106-7, 112, 121, 123-4, 127, 156, 160, 162, 165, 168, 176, 180, 195, 242-3, 245-6
Lyallpur 156, 159, 259
Mackay, Ken 188
Madras 157, 168, 198-9
Manchester Evening Chronicle 76
Marylebone Cricket Club (MCC) 12, 14-5, 18-9, 27, 38-40, 44-5, 51, 56, 64, 66-7, 74, 77-8, 82, 85, 87-93, 100, 103-5, 107-9, 111, 115, 131-2, 137, 141, 144, 152-5, 157-8, 164, 166-7, 172-4, 178-84, 186, 189-90, 194-7, 200, 207, 218-9, 221-2, 232-3, 235, 244, 248, 251, 254-5, 258-9, 261, 263-6, 268, 270, 272-3, 275
Mankad, Vinoo 256
Manjrekar, Vijay 167
Martin-Jenkins, Christopher 274-5
May, Peter 9-10, 12, 16, 27, 32, 34, 41, 53, 56, 58-9, 62, 68, 70, 75-7, 79, 83-4, 88, 92-6, 101, 104-5, 113-121, 123-8, 131-2, 134-9, 141, 143-4, 148-152, 155, 180, 219, 249, 265, 273
McConnon, Jim 45, 56-7, 81, 87, 112
McGlew, Jackie 93, 95
McKenzie, Graham 226
McLean, Roy 106
McWatt, Clifford 32
Meckiff, Ian 116-8, 120-2, 125, 127-8
Melbourne 5, 51-5, 65-7, 72, 74-5, 78, 87, 109-10, 122, 125, 127, 176, 183-5, 188-90, 223-5, 227
Melford, Michael 198, 204, 206, 257, 259
Milburn, Colin 233, 236, 246, 261-2
Miller, Keith 56, 58, 62, 76, 274
Millman, Geoffrey 168
Milton, Arthur 109, 112, 116, 118, 120-2, 127
Monckton, Sir Walter 17, 108
Morris, Arthur 60-1, 68, 70
Mortimore, John 109-10, 115, 125, 176, 200-1, 204
Moss, Alan 16, 21, 27, 29, 35, 132, 135, 157
Murray, John 161, 179, 208, 216, 220, 250
Mushtaq Mohammad 158, 262
Nadkarni, RG 198, 200
New Zealand 36, 66, 82, 105, 109, 115, 127, 171, 173, 178, 192, 196, 228, 265
News Chronicle 38, 52
News of the World 113, 182
New South Wales 47, 55, 80, 122, 186, 226
Norfolk, Duke of 173, 177, 179, 181, 190-2
Nurse, Seymour 132, 244

Oakman, Alan 88, 91, 106, 108
Observer, The 7, 37-8, 40, 42, 49, 110, 114, 250
O'Neill, Norman 120, 186
Orsova, SS 7, 37-8, 41, 43, 45-6, 82, 88
Over rates 97, 151, 172, 216, 264
Oxford University 7, 48, 96, 131, 163, 200, 232, 267, 269
Packer, Frank 50
Packer, Kerry 50
Pakistan 10-1, 45, 85, 129, 154-7, 159-60, 163, 169, 170-2, 175, 196, 218, 248, 253-63, 265, 271-2
Palmer, Charles 16-7, 19-21, 26-9, 33
Palmer, Ken 195, 216
Parfitt, Peter 164,168, 170, 175-6, 184, 192, 200-1, 208, 213, 215, 220, 223
Parks, Jim 88, 91, 94, 132, 150, 176, 195, 198, 208, 210, 220-2, 229, 233, 236, 240, 243, 246
Pataudi, Mansoor 163-4, 167, 169, 203, 214
Peebles, Ian 37, 40, 42-3, 45-6, 50, 53, 55, 59, 62, 64, 68-9, 73-4, 76, 82, 88, 112-4, 116, 118, 133, 147, 267, 269, 275
Perth 43-5, 47, 49, 66-7, 112-3, 173, 177, 179-82, 184, 221
Pocock, Pat 233, 236, 243, 245, 250, 254
Pollock, Graham 216
Pollock, Peter 213
Port Elizabeth 105, 216-8
Port of Spain 32, 34, 137-8, 151
Price, John 195, 202, 204, 208, 212, 215-6
Prideaux, Roger 249-50
Pullar, Geoff 132, 135, 137-8, 141, 148, 151-2, 156, 161-2, 166, 168-9, 175, 191-2
Pretoria 90-2, 98, 108
Queensland 57, 62, 66, 186-7
Ramadhin, Sonny 15, 23-4, 31
Rawalpindi 156, 158, 239
Rhodesia 90, 208, 212, 218
Richardson, Peter 88, 91, 93-4, 96-8, 101, 104, 112, 114, 116, 118, 120-2, 124, 128, 156, 158, 160, 162-3, 168-9, 175, 195, 266
Rioting 10, 32-3, 89, 139, 141, 152, 154, 240-1, 245-6, 248, 254, 257, 259, 264, 270-1, 273
Roberts, Ron 62, 178
Robertson-Glasgow, RC 42, 55
Robins, Walter 14, 16, 132, 140, 149, 152-3, 172-3
Ross, Alan 7, 37-8, 40-3, 45-51, 53-6, 62, 66, 68, 71, 74, 77-9, 81, 83-5, 88-98, 100-3, 106, 110, 126, 132-3, 136, 144-8, 151, 154, 171, 175-6, 180, 185-6, 188-9, 191, 193, 234, 239, 250, 267-9, 273-4
Rostron, Frank 38, 133
Rowbotham, Denys 184
Russell, Eric 92, 158, 161, 164, 168, 175, 220-2
Sabina Park, Kingston 20, 25, 146-7, 152, 239
Salisbury, Rhodesia 90-1, 209
Selection issues 14-5, 17, 21, 23, 26-7, 29-30, 38-41, 55, 65, 88, 94, 108, 112-3, 116, 128, 135, 140, 176, 195, 201, 217-9, 236, 251, 253, 260, 269
Shackleton, Derek 195
Sharpe, Phil 195, 200
Sheppard, David 40, 171-2, 175, 177, 181, 189, 192, 253
Simpson, Bobby 186, 224, 226
Simpson, Reg 41, 53, 56-7, 59, 62, 87, 112
Singh, Charran 139-40
Smith, AC 176, 187
Smith, David 156, 164, 175
Smith, Leslie 178
Smith, MJK 10, 132, 137, 139, 156-7, 160, 163-4, 169, 178, 180, 195-6, 199, 205, 210-1, 213-5, 219-221, 223-7, 229, 234, 236,
Snow, John 233, 236-40, 242-4, 246, 250, 258, 260-1, 263, 265, 267
Sobers, Garry 35, 134, 136, 147, 150-2, 161, 183, 233, 235, 237-41, 243-5
South Africa 10, 64, 83-6, 88-90, 93, 95, 97, 99, 102-3, 105, 108-9,

143, 172, 192, 199, 207-8, 210, 212, 214, 216-7, 219-20, 249-51, 253, 258, 265-6, 273
South Australia 51-2, 183-4, 223
Spooner, Dick 21, 29, 34
Stackpole, Keith 226
Statham, Brian 10, 16, 22, 25-6, 28-9, 31-2, 34-5, 41, 45, 58, 69, 79, 83, 93, 98-9, 106, 109, 120, 124-5, 127-8, 132, 135, 137, 140, 144, 148-9, 152, 155, 175, 177, 180, 185, 189, 192, 195, 220, 264
Stewart, Micky 198, 200-1, 204
Stollmeyer, Jeff 21, 24, 26
Subba Row, Raman 29, 109, 112, 115, 131-2, 137, 148, 150, 153, 155
Suttle, Ken 21, 29, 264
Swanton, EW (Jim) 10, 13-4, 16-7, 20, 23-4, 26-7, 30, 36-40, 42, 46, 55, 59, 74, 80, 82, 85, 88, 90-2, 95-7, 99, 101-2, 104, 116-8, 120, 132-4, 138, 140, 143-4, 146, 173, 178-80, 184-5, 206, 219, 234, 244, 251, 266-8, 275
Swetman, Roy 109, 112, 121-2, 132, 150, 152
Tasmania 78, 189, 226
Tattersall, Roy 29
Tayfield, Hugh 91, 101-2, 104, 107
Taylor, Brian 87-8, 106
Tennekoon, Anura 258
Thomson, Ian 208, 212, 215-6
Titmus, Fred 176, 180, 183, 185, 192, 195, 198, 200, 204, 208, 210, 212-3, 215-7, 220, 225, 229, 233, 236, 239, 241-2
Tour management 64, 144, 152, 191, 194, 205, 226, 266, 273
Trinidad 14, 32, 34, 131, 137, 139, 141, 145-6, 151, 235-7, 244
Trueman, Fred 10, 16-7, 23, 25, 27, 29, 34-5, 37, 39, 41, 45, 87, 112, 115, 121-2, 125-6, 132, 134, 139-41, 144, 148, 150, 152, 155, 175, 178, 181, 183, 187, 189, 192, 195, 208, 211, 264, 266, 274
Tyson, Frank 38, 41, 43, 45, 51-2, 56, 58, 61, 67, 69-72, 77, 81-3, 85-6, 94, 98-9, 101, 104, 106-7, 114, 122, 124, 127, 220, 265, 267-8
Umpiring controversies 22, 34, 85, 92-3, 117, 120, 124, 160, 183, 202, 213, 255, 270
Underwood, Derek 250, 254, 261
Valentine, Alf 15, 23
Van Ryneveld, Clive 95-6, 99, 105
Victoria 67, 109-10, 122, 226
Vizianagram, Maharajkumar of 205-6
Walcott, Clyde 25, 34
Walters, Doug 222, 224
Wardle, Johnny 16, 21, 26-7, 29, 41, 54, 56, 68-9, 77, 80, 88, 94, 98-9, 101-2, 105-6, 112-3, 127, 132, 176
Warner, Pelham 14-5
Watson, Chester 138-9
Watson, Willie 23-4, 28, 33, 112, 114-5, 120, 122, 124, 128, 264
Weekes, Everton 25, 34
Wellings, EM (Lyn) 38, 65, 80, 112, 116, 119, 122-3, 174, 178, 182-4, 196, 198, 201, 206, 208, 267, 269, 275
West Indies 10-3, 15-20, 22-4, 27-8, 31, 33-4, 36-9, 49, 64, 85, 96, 103, 110, 131, 136-7, 139-42, 146, 148-50, 157, 176, 183, 195-6, 207, 211, 216, 229-35, 240, 242-5, 249-50, 265-7, 270, 273
Western Australia 43-5, 47, 113, 115, 173, 176, 180, 195, 221, 242, 261
White, Butch 156
White, Crawford 38, 52, 55, 178
Wilson, Vic 41, 56-7, 87, 112, 195
Woodcock, John 9, 38, 62, 80, 82, 88, 133, 178, 180-1, 184, 186, 199, 241
Wooldridge, Ian 174-5, 178, 181, 214, 217, 269
Worrell, Frank 28, 34, 131, 136, 140